MONOGRAPHS OF THE
SOCIETY FOR RESEARCH IN
CHILD DEVELOPMENT

Serial No. 252, Vol. 62, No. 4, 1997

PREFRONTAL CORTEX COGNITIVE DEFICITS IN CHILDREN TREATED EARLY AND CONTINUOUSLY FOR PKU

Adele Diamond
Meredith B. Prevor
Glenda Callender
Donald P. Druin

MONOGRAPHS OF THE SOCIETY FOR RESEARCH IN CHILD DEVELOPMENT
Serial No. 252, Vol. 62, No. 4, 1997

CONTENTS

ABSTRACT

DIAMOND, ADELE; PREVOR, MEREDITH B.; CALLENDER, GLENDA; and DRUIN, DONALD P. Prefrontal Cortex Cognitive Deficits in Children Treated Early and Continuously for PKU. *Monographs of the Society for Research in Child Development*, 1997, **62**(4, Serial No. 252).

To begin to study the importance of dopamine for executive function abilities dependent on prefrontal cortex during early childhood, the present investigation studied children in whom we predicted reduced dopamine in prefrontal cortex but otherwise normal brains. These are children treated early and continuously for the metabolic disorder phenylketonuria (PKU). Untreated PKU is the most common biochemical cause of mental retardation. The root problem is an inability to convert one amino acid, phenylalanine (Phe), into another, tyrosine (Tyr), the precursor of dopamine. Phe levels in the bloodstream soar; Tyr levels fall. Treatment with a diet low in Phe reduces the Phe:Tyr imbalance but cannot eliminate it. We hypothesized that the resultant modest elevation in the ratio of Phe to Tyr in the blood, which results in slightly less Tyr reaching the brain, uniquely affects the cognitive functions dependent on prefrontal cortex because of the special sensitivity of prefrontally projecting dopamine neurons to small decreases in Tyr.

In a 4-year longitudinal study, we found that PKU children whose plasma Phe levels were three to five times normal (6–10 mg/dl) performed worse than other PKU children with lower Phe levels, matched controls, their own siblings, and children from the general population on tasks that required the working memory and inhibitory control abilities dependent on dorsolateral prefrontal cortex. The impairment was as evident in our oldest age range (3½–7 years) as it was in the youngest (6–12 months). The higher a child's Phe level, the worse that child's performance. Girls were more adversely affected than boys. The deficit appears to be selective, affecting principally one neural system, since even PKU children with Phe levels three to five times normal performed well on the 13 control tasks. Clinical implications for the treatment of PKU and other neurodevelopmental disorders are discussed.

We report here the results of a 4-year longitudinal study designed to investigate cognitive neuropsychological functioning in children who we hypothesized would have a selective loss of dopamine in prefrontal cortex without other abnormalities in the brain. These children have a moderate increase in the ratio of one amino acid, phenylalanine (Phe), to another, tyrosine (Tyr), in their bloodstreams. (Tyrosine is the precursor of dopamine.) We predicted that, when the imbalance is moderate, it would selectively affect the dopamine projection to prefrontal cortex.

Children born with phenylketonuria (PKU) have a large imbalance between Phe and Tyr in their bloodstreams if they eat a normal diet. A diet low in Phe reduces that imbalance; however, if dietary treatment is started too late, or if the diet is not maintained, permanent, widespread brain damage can result. Our hypothesis pertains only to PKU children treated early and continuously. Moreover, the diet is able to control the Phe:Tyr imbalance better for some children than others, and some children adhere to the diet more strictly than others. When the diet succeeds and Phe levels do not rise above three times normal, the imbalance between Phe and Tyr is minimal. However, for many years it was considered acceptable for plasma Phe levels to rise as high as five times above normal. Our hypothesis pertains to PKU children whose plasma Phe levels remain primarily in the three to five times normal range, not to children who now have, or at any time after the first weeks of life had, plasma Phe levels above 10 mg/dl for any prolonged period of time or to children whose plasma Phe levels have generally been kept under 6 mg/dl.

Why should we worry about such a narrowly defined group of children who are following the medically prescribed treatment? PKU afflicts roughly 1 in every 10,000 children (Güttler, 1988), almost all of whom are now treated early and continuously. If our hypothesis is correct, we will have identified a problem that has gone largely unrecognized because most clinicians have assumed that PKU children do not suffer from cognitive impairments if their plasma Phe levels are maintained at five times normal or less. We will have identified what should correct the problem and improve the ability of these children to think and reason more clearly and creatively, to maintain their concentration and attentional focus more easily, to integrate and interrelate multiple facts and ideas more easily, and to act on the basis of what they choose to do rather than on the basis of prepotent action tendencies or strong environmental pulls.

Prefrontal cortex dysfunction has been implicated in a host of developmental disabilities, such as attention deficit hyperactivity disorder (ADHD). The behavioral measures and developmental norms reported here should help in evaluating such claims in general and especially in much younger children than was heretofore possible. Our work is an example of the contribution that research that combines cognitive development and neuroscience can make to the early detection of brain dysfunction and of the guidance that it can provide for isolating the particular neural system that may be involved. Developmental cognitive neuropsychology has progressed to the point where we now have precise measures of specific cognitive functions sensitive to the functions of particular neural subsystems and appropriate for use with young children.

We are not the first to notice cognitive deficits in PKU children despite treatment. However, we are the first to present a detailed hypothesis about the biological cause of these deficits. We have tested that hypothesis in three converging lines of research—an animal model of early treated PKU (Diamond, Ciaramitaro, Donner, Djali, & Robinson, 1994), an investigation of a visual deficit in contrast sensitivity in children treated early and continuously for PKU (Diamond & Herzberg, 1996), and an investigation of the pattern of cognitive deficits in children treated early and continuously for PKU (presented here). The results of all three lines of research provide support for the hypothesized mechanism.

The work presented here should provide a bridge between work on the basic neuroscience of the dopamine projection to prefrontal cortex in monkeys and rats and clinical findings of particular cognitive deficits in people treated for PKU. It has been demonstrated in rhesus macaques that deficits in the cognitive functions dependent on prefrontal cortex can result from depleting prefrontal cortex of dopamine (Brozoski, Brown, Rosvold, & Goldman, 1979; Sawaguchi & Goldman-Rakic, 1991). It has been demonstrated in rats that the dopamine projection to prefrontal cortex has unusual properties that render it especially sensitive to modest reductions in precursor availability (Bannon, Bunney, & Roth, 1981; Bradberry, Karasic, Deutch, & Roth, 1989; Thierry et al., 1977). We propose that children treated early and continuously for PKU, whose blood levels of Phe remain moderately elevated, provide an example, in human beings, of these two sets of findings previously demonstrated only in monkeys and rats.

The results reported here from tasks empirically linked to prefrontal cortex add to the growing body of evidence that, although prefrontal cortex is probably not fully mature until puberty, it is already subserving important cognitive functions during early infancy. The results also demonstrate that the ill effects on prefrontal cortex functions from a moderate Phe to Tyr imbalance in the bloodstream are already evident in early infancy.

BACKGROUND

PKU Defined

PKU is a genetic disorder that, if not controlled, results in widespread brain damage and severe mental retardation (e.g., Cowie, 1971; Hsia, 1970; Koch, Azen, Friedman, & Williamson, 1982; Tourian & Sidbury, 1978). Indeed, it is the most common biochemical cause of mental retardation. The core problem is a marked deficiency in the ability to convert (i.e., hydroxylate) one amino acid (Phe) into another (Tyr). Thus, PKU is one of a class of disorders called *inborn errors of metabolism.*

PKU—which was first described by Følling (1934)—is caused by any of a family of point mutations and microdeletions of the phenylalanine hydroxylase (PAH) gene on chromosome 12 (12q22–12q24.1; DiLella, Marvit, Lidsky, Güttler, & Woo, 1986; Lidsky, Law, Morse, Kao, & Woo, 1985; Woo, Lidsky, Güttler, Chandra, & Robson, 1983). That gene contains the instructions for the liver's production of the enzyme PAH. PAH is essential for hydroxylating Phe into Tyr. Phe and Tyr are both large neutral amino acids found in all dietary protein. In the roughly 1 in every 10,000 people born with PKU, PAH activity is either absent or markedly reduced.[1] Since Phe is hydroxylated minimally, if at all, it builds up in the bloodstream. When PKU is untreated, plasma Phe levels rise to well over 10 times normal (> 20 mg/dl, or $> 2,400$ μmol/l). Because little or no Tyr is being produced from Phe, the level of Tyr in the bloodstream is usually low (e.g., Nord, McCabe, & McCabe, 1988). (Tyr levels would be still lower were it not for the fact that we have some access to tyrosine directly through the foods we eat.) The result of these alterations in amino acid levels in the bloodstream is widespread brain damage, which in turn causes severe mental retardation.

---

[1] In the classic form of PKU, phenylalanine hydroxylase is absent or markedly less active. The phenylalanine hydroxylating system is complex, however. It consists of two enzymes, phenylalanine hydroxylase and dihydropteridine reductase (DHPR), and an essential coenzyme, tetrahydrobiopterin (BH4). In more recently discovered, less common variants of PKU, the defect appears to be in the regeneration of BH4 (caused by a lack of DHPR) or in the de novo biosynthesis of BH4 (Kaufman et al., 1978; Kaufman, Kapatos, McInnes, Schulman, & Rizzo, 1982).

3

Dietary Treatment: Restrict Phenylalanine Consumption

In 1954, Bickel, Gerrard, and Hickmans published the results of a bold experiment demonstrating that the mental retardation that results from PKU can be prevented if the child is kept on a diet low in Phe. In the early 1960s, Guthrie pioneered the development of a simple bacterial inhibition assay for measuring Phe levels in the bloodstream, which made newborn screening for PKU possible (Guthrie & Susi, 1963; see also Guthrie, 1996). Today, children born in any U.S. hospital are routinely tested for PKU at birth. Those with the disorder are soon placed on a special low-Phe diet that severely restricts their intake of all protein, including milk and milk products (such as ice cream, butter, and cheese), meat, and fish.

This diet succeeds in lowering plasma Phe levels so that they are closer to normal, which in turn succeeds in averting PKU's devastating effects on brain function and cognitive ability. Children who are started on the low-Phe diet shortly after birth and remain on the diet thereafter do not suffer major brain damage and do not become mentally retarded. They score within the normal range on generalized tests of intelligence (e.g., Bickel et al., 1973; Dobson, Williamson, Azen, & Koch, 1977; Holtzman, Kronmal, van Doorninck, Azen, & Koch, 1986; Hudson, Mordaunt, & Leahy, 1970; Koch, Azen, Friedman, & Williamson, 1984; Williamson, Koch, Azen, & Chang, 1981).

The focus of dietary treatment has been on reducing the drastic elevation in plasma Phe levels because conventional wisdom has attributed the ill effects of PKU on brain function to the detrimental effects of high Phe levels. However, as early as the 1970s, Bessman (1979) argued that low Tyr levels have detrimental effects as well.

Despite Dietary Treatment, a Modest Imbalance in the Plasma Phe:Tyr Ratio Remains

While a low-Phe diet reduces plasma Phe levels, it rarely results in normal Phe levels, and it does nothing to correct the plasma Tyr reduction. Phe levels remain moderately elevated as an inevitable consequence of consuming even a minimal amount of protein. The diet reflects the need to balance the requirement to restrict Phe intake with the requirement for protein. Phe occurs in food as one of the building blocks of protein; to eliminate all Phe from the diet, one would have to eliminate all dietary protein. Also, the body needs a small quantity of Phe to produce protein. In light of (*a*) the need for protein, (*b*) the difficulties complying with the restrictive low-Phe diet, and (*c*) the lack of mental retardation when plasma Phe levels are moderately elevated, Phe is not eliminated from the diet altogether. The U.S. National Collaborative Study of Treated PKU has advised parents of PKU children and their physicians that plasma Phe elevations up to five times normal are acceptable in PKU children: "Diet should be managed so that blood Phe levels neither exceed 10 mg/100 ml [five times normal] nor fall below 2 mg/100 ml" (Williamson et al., 1981, p. 165; see also Koch & Wenz, 1987). The consequence is that children treated early and continuously for PKU by following a dietary regimen of reduced Phe intake have a modest increase in Phe relative to Tyr in their bloodstreams.

Cognitive Deficits in Children Treated Early and Continuously for PKU

It stands to reason that, since the plasma level of neither Phe nor Tyr is fully normal even when PKU children follow the low-Phe diet, some problems might remain. Indeed, children treated early and continuously for PKU often have significantly lower IQs than their siblings (e.g., Berry, O'Grady, Perlmutter, & Bofinger, 1979; Dobson, Kushida, Williamson, & Friedman, 1976; Koch et al., 1984; Williamson et al., 1981) or other family members (e.g., Hudson et al., 1970; O'Flynn & Hsia, 1968). These PKU children often score in the 80s or 90s on IQ tests (e.g., Dobson et al., 1976; Smith & Beasley, 1989). That is, children treated early and continuously for PKU have IQs within the normal range, but often just barely.

Recent studies have also reported problems in attention control, concentration, problem solving, and "executive functions." For example, children treated early and continuously for PKU tend to be more easily distracted (Brunner, Jordan, & Berry, 1983), be more limited in the amount of information they can hold in mind at one time and manipulate (Faust, Libon, & Pueschel, 1986), and have more difficulty maintaining concentration until a problem is solved or a goal attained (Welsh, Pennington, Ozonoff, Rouse, & McCabe, 1990). (See also Brunner, Berch, & Berry, 1987; Krause et al., 1985; Pennington, van Doorninck, McCabe, & McCabe, 1985.) These difficulties are reminiscent of the deficits one sees after damage to prefrontal cortex, as others have noted (e.g., Welsh et al., 1990). Indeed, after prefrontal cortex is surgically removed, patients typically score in the 80s and 90s on IQ tests (e.g., Stuss & Benson, 1986, 1987)—the same low-normal range as PKU children who have been maintained on the low-Phe diet since shortly after birth.

Why Might a Modest Imbalance in the Levels of Phe and Tyr in the Bloodstream Produce Deficits in the Cognitive Abilities Dependent on Dorsolateral Prefrontal Cortex?

First, the moderate elevation in Phe relative to Tyr in the bloodstream results in moderately reduced levels of Tyr reaching the brain. All large neutral amino acids must bind to the same transporter proteins to cross the blood-brain barrier. Thus, Phe and Tyr compete for the same limited supply

5

of proteins for transport into the brain (e.g., Chirigos, Greengard, & Uden-friend, 1960; Miller, Braun, Pardridge, & Oldendorf, 1985; Oldendorf, 1973; Pardridge, 1977; Pardridge & Oldendorf, 1977). These protein carriers have a higher affinity for Phe than for Tyr. Thus, elevations in blood levels of Phe relative to Tyr place Tyr at a competitive disadvantage in finding transport into the brain. Because the ratio of Phe to Tyr in the bloodstream is only moderately increased in those on dietary treatment for PKU, the decrease in the amount of Tyr reaching the brain should be correspondingly modest. In this way, the moderate plasma Phe:Tyr imbalance should result in modestly reduced Tyr levels in the central nervous system (CNS).

Second, a modest decrease in cerebral levels of tyrosine is likely to dispro-portionately affect prefrontal cortex because of the unusual properties of the dopamine neurons that project to prefrontal cortex. (Tyr is hydroxylated to form dopa [3,4-dihydroxyphenylalanine], from which dopamine is then pro-duced. Tyr hydroxylation is the rate-limiting step in the production of dopa-mine.) A large decrease in Tyr availability would adversely affect all dopamin-ergic systems throughout the brain. However, most dopaminergic systems in the brain are insensitive to *moderate* changes in CNS Tyr levels. The prefrontal dopaminergic system is an exception to this; it is sensitive to even small Tyr fluctuations. The dopamine neurons in the ventral tegmental area (VTA) that project to prefrontal cortex have a higher baseline firing rate, and turn over dopamine faster, than do most other dopamine neurons in the brain (e.g., Bannon et al., 1981; Roth, 1984; Thierry et al., 1977). This makes prefrontal cortex acutely sensitive to even a modest change in Tyr availability (e.g., Tam, Elsworth, Bradberry, & Roth, 1990; Wurtman, Lorin, Mostafapour, & Fern-strom, 1974). Indeed, reductions in Tyr too small to affect dopamine synthe-sis in other neural regions (such as the striatum) profoundly reduce dopa-mine synthesis in prefrontal cortex (Bradberry et al., 1989).

Third, reducing dopamine in dorsolateral prefrontal cortex produces deficits in the cognitive abilities dependent on dorsolateral prefrontal cortex. Selectively depleting dorsolateral prefrontal cortex of dopamine can produce cognitive impairments as severe as those found when dorsolateral prefrontal cortex is removed altogether (Brozoski et al., 1979). Local injection of dopa-mine receptor antagonists into dorsolateral prefrontal cortex impairs perfor-mance on tasks dependent on prefrontal cortex in a precise, dose-dependent manner (Sawaguchi & Goldman-Rakic, 1991). Similarly, destruction of the dopamine neurons in the VTA that project to prefrontal cortex impairs per-formance on these tasks (Simon, Scatton, & LeMoal, 1980).

For these three reasons it seemed plausible that the moderate imbalance in the Phe:Tyr ratio in the plasma of children treated early and continuously for PKU might well result in deficits in the cognitive abilities dependent on prefrontal cortex without significantly affecting other brain regions or other cognitive abilities. This study was designed to test the prediction that children treated early and continuously for PKU have selective deficits in the cognitive functions dependent on prefrontal cortex.

Independent Evidence from Visual Psychophysics in Support of the Proposed Causal Mechanism

Another population of dopamine neurons shares all the same properties that make the prefrontally projecting dopamine neurons exquisitely sensitive to small changes in the level of Tyr. The dopamine neurons in the retina also fire rapidly, turn over dopamine rapidly, and have been shown empirically to be unusually sensitive to mild perturbations in the level of available Tyr (Fernstrom & Fernstrom, 1988; Fernstrom, Volk, & Fernstrom, 1986; Iuvone, Galli, Garrison-Gund, & Neff, 1978; Iuvone, Tigges, Fernandes, & Tigges, 1989). Moreover, the competition between Phe and Tyr at the blood-retinal barrier is comparable to that at the blood-brain barrier (Rapoport, 1976; Tornquist & Alm, 1986). Thus, if our hypothesis is correct about why a moderate Phe:Tyr imbalance in the bloodstream causes deficits in prefrontal cortex functions, then that same Phe:Tyr imbalance should also affect the retina.

The aspect of retinal function most firmly linked to the level of dopamine in the retina is contrast sensitivity. For example, patients with Parkinson's disease, who have greatly reduced levels of dopamine, show impaired sensitivity to contrast (Bodis-Wollner, 1990; Bodis-Wollner et al., 1987; Kupersmith, Shakin, Siegel, & Lieberman, 1982; Regan & Neima, 1984; Skrandies & Gottlob, 1986). It is thought that this occurs because dopamine is important for the center-surround organization of retinal receptive fields (Bodis-Wollner, 1988, 1990). (*Contrast sensitivity* refers to the threshold of how dark black lines [sinusoid gratings] or black letters, and how light the white background, must be for a person to be able to detect the black lines or letters.)

We measured contrast sensitivity over five spatial frequencies (1.5–18.0 cycles per degree)—that is, five different widths of alternating black-and-white bands. Diamond and Herzberg (1996) found that children treated early and continuously for PKU, whose plasma Phe levels were 6–10 mg/dl (three to five times normal), showed impaired contrast sensitivity across the entire range of spatial frequencies. That is, PKU children with moderately elevated Phe levels were significantly less sensitive to visual contrast than were their same-aged peers at each of the five spatial frequencies investigated, even though all children were tested under conditions of twenty-twenty acuity. These group differences remained robust even when the two PKU children whose IQs were below 90 were omitted from the analyses. At no spatial frequency was the contrast sensitivity of any PKU child better than that of his or her sibling.

No visual deficits had ever been previously reported in PKU children.

Indeed, visual acuity, which is normally measured under conditions of high contrast, was not worse in the PKU children tested by Diamond and Herzberg. Standard eye exams would not reveal an impairment in contrast sensitivity unless one specifically tested for it. We had predicted the contrast sensitivity deficit for the same reason we had predicted dorsolateral prefrontal cortex cognitive deficits—the special sensitivity of dopamine neurons that fire rapidly and turn over dopamine rapidly to moderate reductions in the level of available tyrosine. The dopamine neurons that project to prefrontal cortex and the dopamine neurons in the retina are the only known populations of dopamine neurons to have these characteristics.

The First Animal Model of Early and Continuously Treated PKU

To investigate the biological mechanism that we had proposed more directly, Diamond, Ciaramitaro, et al. (1994) developed and characterized the first animal model of early and continuously treated PKU. This enabled us to study the effect of moderate, chronic plasma Phe elevations on neurotransmitter and metabolite levels in different brain regions. We pharmacologically induced moderate plasma Phe elevations in rats by modifying a technique developed earlier to model untreated PKU (Brass & Greengard, 1982; Greengard, Yoss, & DelValle, 1976). We administered daily subcutaneous injections (24 mmol/10 g body weight) of α-methyl-phenylalanine, an inhibitor of phenylalanine hydroxylase (the enzyme that metabolizes Phe to Tyr), plus a small supplement of Phe (13 mmol/10 g body weight). The Phe supplement was needed because α-methyl-phenylalanine does not perfectly inhibit phenylalanine hydroxylase. There were two experimental groups: pups whose plasma Phe levels were elevated (a) postnatally and (b) pre- and postnatally. Control animals came from the same litters as those in the first experimental group and received daily subcutaneous injections of saline. Each group contained 12 animals (six male, six female).

All were tested on delayed alternation, a task sensitive to prefrontal cortex dysfunction (e.g., Bättig, Rosvold, & Mishkin, 1960; Bubser & Schmidt, 1990; Kubota & Niki, 1971; Larsen & Divac, 1978; Wikmark, Divac, & Weiss, 1973), as infants and again as juveniles. Different people tested and injected a given animal; testers were blind to the group assignment of their animals. Each of the three testers was assigned four animals in each group, and the order of testing was randomized across experimental condition. Blood samples were collected at three time points (the day before behavioral testing began, the day following the conclusion of infant testing, and the day following juvenile testing) to determine the animals' plasma Phe levels. High-performance liquid chromatographic (HPLC) analyses of the brain tissue assessed the distributions and concentrations of dopamine, serotonin, norepinephrine, and their metabolites in various brain regions.

As predicted, Diamond, Ciaramitaro, et al. (1994) found cognitive deficits (impaired performance on a behavioral task [delayed alternation] dependent on prefrontal cortex) and neurochemical changes (most notably, reduced dopamine and reduced homovanillic acid [HVA]—a dopamine metabolite—in frontal cortex) in both groups of early and continuously treated PKU–model animals. In contrast, the norepinephrine system was virtually unaffected in any of the neural regions investigated.

Both groups of PKU-model animals failed the delayed alternation task under the same conditions as do animals with lesions of prefrontal cortex. They were able to learn the task normally, and performed well when no delay was used, but were impaired when a delay was imposed. Thus, they were impaired when they had to hold in mind which arm of the maze they had just entered and inhibit repeating that response in order to alternate.

The most dramatic neurochemical effect was the reduction in both HVA and dopamine in prefrontal cortex in each of the experimental groups. There was almost no overlap between HVA levels in the prefrontal cortex of controls and HVA levels in either experimental group: all control animals but one had higher HVA levels in prefrontal cortex than any animal in either experimental group. Norepinephrine was not significantly affected in any of the four regions investigated (prefrontal cortex, anterior cingulate, caudate-putamen, and nucleus accumbens).

Moreover, the neurochemical variable most strongly and consistently related to performance on the delayed alternation task was the level of HVA in prefrontal cortex. This was significantly related to every dependent measure of performance on the task. This is consistent with previous work, which has demonstrated that, while delayed alternation performance is highly dependent on the level of dopamine in prefrontal cortex, it is uncorrelated with serotonin or norepinephrine levels (Brozoski et al., 1979; Sahakian et al., 1985; Simon et al., 1980) or with dopamine elsewhere in the brain (Sahakian et al., 1985; Simon et al., 1980). (There is some evidence linking the caudate, which receives a strong projection from prefrontal cortex, to delayed alternation performance [e.g., Goldman & Rosvold, 1972]. However, in our study, HVA levels in the caudate were not significantly lowered, and dopamine levels were only minimally affected, so it is unlikely that the observed impairment in delayed alternation performance was due to effects on the caudate dopaminergic system.)

Our predictions were not perfectly confirmed, however. We found some effects on the serotoninergic system in the early and continuously treated PKU–model animals and on dopamine metabolism in the anterior cingulate (although the latter may have been due to the inclusion of a portion of prefrontal cortex with the anterior cingulate samples). The lack of complete specificity may have been due to the fact that plasma Phe levels were raised a bit more than intended in the animals (to 6.5 times normal rather than 5 times or less) or to the fact that the neurochemical effects of moderately elevated plasma Phe levels are not as localized as we had hypothesized. Our lab is presently investigating this further with the genetic mouse model of PKU created by McDonald and his colleagues (McDonald, Bode, Dove, & Shedlovsky, 1990; Shedlovsky, McDonald, Symula, & Dove, 1993).

We had predicted that other neural regions receiving dopaminergic innervation would be less affected by a moderate elevation in plasma Phe than prefrontal cortex because that would reduce the amount of Tyr crossing into the brain only moderately and other neural regions are relatively unaffected by changes in CNS Tyr levels that are only moderate. We had predicted that the norepinephrine system would be unaffected even though norepinephrine is made from dopamine (and, hence, requires Tyr) because previous work has demonstrated that norepinephrine levels are relatively insensitive to alterations in precursor (Irie & Wurtman, 1987).

Tryptophan (Trp), another large neutral amino acid, is the precursor of serotonin. It, too, must compete with Phe and Tyr for transport from blood to brain. We had predicted that, in PKU children whose plasma Phe levels are elevated no higher than five times normal, CNS levels of Trp would not be lowered sufficiently to affect CNS serotonin levels significantly. We predicted that CNS Trp levels would be less affected than CNS Tyr levels for two reasons: (1) Trp competes more successfully for the protein carriers than does Tyr (Pardridge, 1988). (2) Plasma levels of Tyr, but not of Trp, are reduced in children with PKU; hence, the plasma Phe:Trp ratio is less out of balance than is the plasma Phe:Tyr ratio.

If the Phe:Tyr ratio in the bloodstream is elevated, increased quantities of Phe will enter the brain. If large amounts of Phe enter the brain, myelin formation is disrupted (e.g., Hommes & Moss, 1992; Huether, Kaus, & Neuhoff, 1982; Reynolds, Burri, Mahal, & Herschokowitz, 1992), as is catecholamine synthesis. At high concentrations, Phe inhibits the hydroxylation of both Tyr (into dopa, which in turn is used to produce dopamine) and Trp (into serotonin) (Fernstrom, Baker, & Fernstrom, 1989; Ikeda, Levitt, & Udenfriend, 1967; Katz, Lloyd, & Kaufman, 1976; Levitt, Spector, Sjoerdsma, & Udenfriend, 1965; Lovenberg, Jequier, & Sjoerdsma, 1968; McKean, 1972; Milner, Irie, & Wurtman, 1986).[2] We hypothesized that the primary effect on the brain when the plasma Phe levels of PKU children are only moderately elevated (less than five times normal) is not from the toxic effects of Phe but from the effect of a moderate Tyr reduction on the most chronically active dopamine neurons.

We have hypothesized this for two reasons: (1) A primary effect of ele-

---

[2] Phe is a competitive inhibitor of Tyr- and Trp-hydroxylase activity. This inhibition occurs because Phe competes with Tyr and Trp for the active binding site on their respective hydroxylating enzymes and because Phe disrupts the cyclic AMP-dependent phosphorylation of these hydroxylases (Roberts & Morelos, 1982).

vated CNS Phe levels would not be limited to the prefrontal dopaminergic system but would affect myelin and the hydroxylation of Tyr and Trp throughout the brain. This would be inconsistent with the selective effects on the cognitive functions dependent on dorsolateral prefrontal cortex that we and others seem to be finding. (2) In vivo (i.e., in living tissue, as opposed to in a test tube) Phe inhibits Trp and Tyr hydroxylation only at concentrations of Phe near, or higher than, the limit of the range of Phe levels in our children. For example, Fernstrom et al. (1989) found that, in vivo, the rate of Tyr hydroxylation was normal at all doses of Phe below five times normal (300 mg/kg) in rats pretreated with a phenylalanine hydroxylase inhibitor (*p*-chlorophenylalanine). Similarly, Milner et al. (1986) electrically stimulated superfused slices of the rat striatum to evoke the release of endogenous dopamine. When the concentration of Phe in the superfusing medium was raised, a dose-dependent inhibition of dopamine was observed, but only once the Phe concentration was raised above four times normal (> 200 µmol).

Finally, there is in vitro evidence that Phe can serve as a substrate for tyrosine hydroxylase. This might have meant that mild elevations in CNS levels of Phe might have yielded normal CNS levels of dopamine, even if Tyr levels in the CNS were below normal. However, there is no evidence that this happens in vivo; indeed, there is evidence that it does not. For example, Fernstrom et al. (1989) failed to find any evidence that Phe serves as a substrate for Tyr hydroxylase in vivo.

What we have said here about the selective effect on the dopamine system in dorsolateral prefrontal cortex applies only to the case in which there is a modest increase in the level of Phe in the bloodstream and a modest reduction in the level of Tyr in the bloodstream. If Phe levels climb above five times normal (e.g., if dietary compliance is lax), one would expect a negative effect on diverse neural systems throughout the brain.

What Is the Everyday Importance of the Cognitive Abilities Dependent on Dorsolateral Prefrontal Cortex?

The cognitive abilities dependent on dorsolateral prefrontal cortex are needed in daily living, especially when concentration is required. In part, dorsolateral prefrontal cortex enables one to keep information on the active "stage" of the mind—what is often referred to as *working memory* or *sustained attention*. Many activities, even simple ones, require holding information in mind. A simple working memory task, such as remembering a phone number you have just looked up, probably does not require dorsolateral prefrontal cortex. Dorsolateral prefrontal cortex is much more likely to be required if one needs to relate multiple pieces of information held in mind to each other or to inhibit an interfering response while at the same time keeping information in mind.

11

Suppose, for instance, that an old friend, whom you have called often, changes phone numbers. Now you must not only remember the new number but also inhibit your tendency to dial the old one. The situation could be made more difficult still by having both numbers begin with the same first few digits. If you do not concentrate while you are dialing, you may well slip into the routine of dialing the number you had dialed so many times in the past. With effort we can all dial the new number correctly, but it certainly requires less effort to remember and correctly dial other phone numbers (even if they are less well practiced) that do not require the inhibition of another number. Similarly, it requires less effort to dial your friend's new phone number if you are looking at the number written down as you dial it. It is when you must both hold information in mind and resist or override a strong countertendency that errors are most likely to occur and, we would contend, that dorsolateral prefrontal cortex is most clearly required.

Dorsolateral prefrontal cortex is particularly important when changed circumstances require some alteration of normal practice or when new goals demand the modification of existing routines (to paraphrase Reason & Mycielska, 1982, p. 40). This capacity to hold information in mind, so that it does not need to be perceptually present, and to use that information to guide your behavior, allowing you to resist taking the "well-trodden" path when another is more appropriate, is important not only for sophisticated endeavors such as creative problem solving but also for mundane activities such as writing the correct year after 1 January. It endows us with the flexibility to respond appropriately to changed circumstances.

The functions of dorsolateral prefrontal cortex are particularly critical when you are faced with a new problem or are trying to do something for the first time. For example, neuroimaging studies have shown that, the first time people try to solve Raven's matrices, dorsolateral prefrontal cortex is activated but that thereafter, when people work on Raven's matrices problems, activity in dorsolateral prefrontal cortex is not significantly above control levels (cited in Mesulam, 1995; for similar observations with different behavioral tests, see Jenkins, Brooks, Nixon, Frackowiak, & Passingham, 1994; Raichle et al., 1994). Similarly, the functions of dorsolateral prefrontal cortex are particularly critical when you are called on to be creative, as when you are asked to think of as many words as you can beginning with a particular letter (e.g., Benton & Hamsher, 1976; Borkowski, Benton, & Spreen, 1967; Phelps, Hyder, Blamire, Rothman, & Shulman, 1994; Spreen & Benton, 1969) or as many uses as you can think of for a particular object (e.g., Eslinger & Grattan, 1993). Dorsolateral prefrontal cortex is also required if (a) you must try to hold a lot of information in mind at the same time by being required not only to generate new answers but also to remember answers you have already given (e.g., Deiber et al., 1991; Petrides, Alivisatos, Meyer, & Evans, 1993) or (b) you must try to override the responses you would be inclined

12

to give, as, for example, when you are asked to complete sentences by giving inappropriate endings (Burgess & Shallice, 1996).

Why is dorsolateral prefrontal cortex required at such times? Perhaps the reason is that at such times the most mental effort and concentration are typically required. Or perhaps the reason has to do with the particular abilities required: the demands on working memory and inhibitory control may be especially high. One is able to be creative, in part, by recombining familiar things in new ways or by seeing relations among ideas or pieces of information that had never been considered together before. To do that, one must be able to hold multiple items in mind at the same time and manipulate them; that is, one needs the working memory ability that depends on dorsolateral prefrontal cortex.

To sustain the focused concentration required for a difficult task, one needs to be able to resist distraction, and, to act in new ways, one needs to resist falling back into one's usual way of acting or thinking; that is, one needs the inhibitory control ability dependent on dorsolateral prefrontal cortex. To relate several ideas and facts together, one must be able to resist focusing exclusively on just one idea or fact, and, to recombine ideas and facts in new, creative ways, one needs to be able to resist repeating old thought patterns. In addition, it is not enough to know something or remember it; one must get that knowledge into one's behavior. Young children, in whom dorsolateral prefrontal cortex is still immature, and adults in whom dorsolateral prefrontal cortex has been damaged or destroyed can sometimes get stuck in a behavioral rut from which they cannot easily extricate themselves despite their best intentions and despite knowing what correct performance demands. For example, consider a child who has just been sorting a set of cards by color, and who is then instructed to sort the cards by shape, but who continues sorting the cards by color—even though on each and every trial he or she correctly tells you what the new rule is (e.g., shape) and shows you where that means each card should be sorted (Zelazo, Frye, & Rapus, 1996).

It is easier to continue doing what you have been doing than to change, and it is easier to go on "automatic pilot" than to carefully consider what to do next. However, sometimes we need to change; sometimes we need to act differently than might be our first inclination. The ability to exercise inhibitory control frees us from being "unthinking" creatures of habit and permits us to act according to what we choose to do. The ability to hold information in mind enables us to consider alternatives or multiple factors, to bring conceptual knowledge and not just perceptual input to bear on our decisions, and to consider our remembered past and our future hopes when planning our present actions. These abilities not only enable us to be creative problem solvers but also enable us to exercise free will and self-determination. Such abilities are not needed all the time, but, when they are needed, we would all like to be able to exercise them, and we would like the same for our children.

II. PARTICIPANTS

To investigate our prediction that children treated early and continuously for PKU would have selective deficits in the cognitive functions dependent on dorsolateral prefrontal cortex, we tested 148 children longitudinally and 364 children cross-sectionally. The longitudinal sample consisted of (a) 37 children (20 male, 17 female) treated early and continuously for PKU, (b) 25 children (9 male, 16 female) with mild hyperphenylalaninemia (MHP), (c) 25 siblings (17 male, 8 female) of the PKU and MHP participants, (d) 36 control children (18 male, 18 female) matched to the children with PKU or MHP on a host of background and health variables, and (e) 25 infants (11 male, 14 female) from the general population. The cross-sectional sample consisted of children from the general population. In general, 20 such children (10 male, 10 female) were tested at each age on each of our tasks. On the $\overline{AB}$ and object retrieval tasks only, our normative data come from 25 infants tested longitudinally.

All the children with PKU had been placed on a low-Phe diet within 1 month after birth, and 80% had begun the special diet within 14 days after birth. All had been continuously maintained on the diet since, although some followed the diet more rigorously than others.

Non-PKU hyperphenylalaninemia is a milder form of the same disorder as PKU. It, too, is caused by mutations of the PAH gene on chromosome 12; however, the enzyme is minimally functional rather than altogether absent or nonfunctional (Ledley, Levy, & Woo, 1986; Levy et al., 1971). MHP children who eat a normal diet have plasma Phe levels comparable to those of PKU children on a low-Phe diet (i.e., between 4 and 10 mg/dl, or between 240 and 600 mmol/l). They provide a partial control for the effect of the diet.[3] MHP children differ from PKU children in two other respects as well:

---

[3] The children with MHP in our study had not been placed on a low-Phe diet because of the generally accepted rule of thumb that plasma Phe levels up to five times normal (up to 10 mg/dl) are acceptable. The MHP children all had plasma Phe levels five times normal or lower on a normal diet.

(1) They do not have grossly elevated plasma Phe levels during the first 2–4 weeks of life. (Until infants with PKU are placed on the Phe-restricted diet, their Phe levels are typically 10–20 times normal.) (2) Because MHP children have some PAH activity, their plasma levels of Tyr tend to be normal or only very slightly reduced.

All children born with PKU or MHP living in the eastern half of the state of Pennsylvania are referred to the PKU clinic in Philadelphia. All such children living in southern New Jersey are referred to the PKU clinic in Camden. Our participants came from these two clinics. Almost all had mean plasma Phe levels within the standard range of control: all participants but one had mean Phe levels between 3 and 10 mg/dl; one PKU toddler had a mean Phe level of 11.5 mg/dl. We tested two other children with PKU but excluded them from our analyses because we were concerned that they would inflate our group differences for spurious reasons. One child had a mean plasma Phe level of 18 mg/dl, which is outside the standard range of control. Her intellectual ability appeared to be much below that of our other participants; for example, even at 6 years she did not know the colors red, yellow, and green. The other child had marked language difficulties unrelated to his PKU, and we were concerned that he was not understanding the instructions for our tasks. Only three children (two with PKU, one sibling) dropped out of the study before the completion of testing, and all dropped out because their families moved away.

Our early results seemed to indicate that the critical variable was the plasma level of Phe, in particular whether a child's Phe levels were above or below 6 mg/dl (Diamond et al., 1992), even though Phe levels of 10–12 mg/dl have traditionally been accepted as adequate and levels of 10 mg/dl are still accepted in most PKU clinics in the United States (e.g., Brunner et al., 1987; Holtzman et al., 1986; Koch & Wenz, 1987). Other reports coming in at the time also seemed to indicate detrimental effects from Phe levels of 6 mg/dl or slightly higher (e.g., Costello, Beasley, Tillotson, & Smith, 1994; Levy et al., 1994; Medical Research Council Working Party on Phenylketonuria, 1993). Therefore, although for some of our analyses we have looked at plasma Phe levels as a continuous variable, for other analyses we have dichotomized the PKU and MHP groups, assigning children with Phe levels under 6 mg/dl (less than three times normal) to the *lower-Phe group* and children with Phe levels of 6 mg/dl or higher (three to five times normal) to the *higher-Phe group.*

Note that the children in the lower-Phe group still had levels of Phe in their bloodstreams above normal and that they still had the genetic disorder PKU or MHP; their group assignment simply reflects the fact that the elevation of their plasma Phe levels was lower than that of other PKU and MHP children. Note also that the children with higher Phe levels did not have plasma Phe levels considered clinically "high" or outside the range of accept-

TABLE 1

SOME OF THE CHARACTERISTICS OF TWO OF OUR PKU PARTICIPANTS AND THE CHILDREN WHO SERVED AS THEIR MATCHED CONTROLS

	James (PKU)	Richard (Control)	Gloria (PKU)	Valerie (Control)
Sex	Male	Male	Female	Female
Full-term	Yes	Yes	Yes	Yes
Birth weight	8 pounds, 9 ounces	8 pounds, 10 ounces	7 pounds, 7 ounces	7 pounds, 1 ounce
Mother:				
Age at birth of child	27 years	26 years	28 years	29 years
Education	High school grad. plus X-ray school	High school grad.	B.S.	B.A.
Occupation before child born	X-ray tech.	Bookkeeper	Sales-marketing	Asst. manager (real estate)
Occupation now	X-ray tech. (part-time)	Bookkeeper (part-time)	Same	Same
Religion	Catholic	Catholic	Catholic	Catholic
Father:				
Age at birth of child	28 years	28 years	29 years	32 years
Education	High school grad.	High school grad.	B.S.	B.A.
Occupation	Electrician	Self-employed (trucking business)	Financial planning	Chef
Religion	Catholic	Catholic	Methodist	Unitarian
Marital status	Married	Married	Married	Married
Child care	Preschool 3 half days	Preschool 2 half days	Parent care	Parent care
Siblings	Female, 8 years	Female, 18 months	None	None

NOTE.—The names used in this table are pseudonyms.

16

TABLE 2
DEMOGRAPHIC CHARACTERISTICS OF THE SUBJECT GROUPS

	Children Treated Early and Continuously for PKU		MHP Children		Siblings	Matched Controls	Normative Sample
	Higher Phe (≥ 6 mg/dl)	Lower Phe (< 6 mg/dl)	Higher Phe (≥ 6 mg/dl)	Lower Phe (< 6 mg/dl)			
Number of subjects[a]	19	18	10	15	25	36	389
Percentage born prematurely[a]	16	6	20	20	8	11	0
	(3)	(1)	(2)	(3)	(2)	(4)	0
Mean gestational age at birth (in weeks)	38.1	38.8	37.9	38.0	38.9	38.1	39.0
Mean birth weight (pounds, ounces)	7, 9	7, 10	6, 15	7, 8	7, 15	7, 9	7, 14
Mean plasma Phe level (mg/dl)[b]	7.3	4.4	8.1	4.5	2.4[c]	...	...
Range in mean plasma Phe levels (mg/dl)[b]	6.0–10.2	2.0–5.8	6.0–11.5	3.5–5.7	1.0–4.0[c]	...	...
Range in plasma Phe levels (mg/dl)[b]	1.0–20.0	.6–17.0	1.4–22.0	1.6–15.3	1.0–4.0[c]	...	...
Mean plasma Phe:Tyr ratio[d]	8.9	3.6	5.2	2.9	1.3[c]	...	...
Percentage Euro-Caucasian	100	88.8	90.0	93.3	92.0	94.0	94.8
Percentage Hispanic	0	11.1	10.0	6.6	8.0	6.0	1.4
Mean IQ[e]	90.4	104.2	96.7	106.3	...	109.7	...
Range in IQ scores	80–100	86–132	89–107	97–103	...	98–129	...
Mean number of siblings	1.1	.9	.9	1.2	1.0	1.7	...
Mean age of mother at child's birth (in years)	27.2	29.0	27.1	28.6	27.5	29.2	...
Mean number of years of education of mother	12.9	13.7	13.3	14.1	13.6	13.9	...
Percentage of mothers working since child's birth	68.4	77.8	90.0	80.0	76.2	76.7	...
Mean age of father at child's birth (in years)	28.9	31.5	32.0	29.7	30.3	30.59	...
Mean number of years of education of father	12.9	13.8	13.4	14.5	13.9	13.9	...
Percentage of families intact	89.5	77.8	80.0	93.3	88.0	88.0	...

[a] Children born prematurely were excluded from the normative sample. Number of subjects is given in parentheses.
[b] Blood samples were not taken from matched controls or children from the general population; however, the mean Phe level in the general population is approximately 1.5 mg/dl.
[c] Based on only a small subset of siblings.
[d] Based on the subjects referred to us from Cooper Hospital, Camden; subjects from the PKU clinic in Philadelphia not included.
[e] Based on scores on the Stanford-Binet Test at 4 years of age.

TABLE 3

Number of Participants in Each Group Tested in the Three Age Ranges

	Mean Plasma Phe Level (and Range)	Total Number	Number of Males	Number of Females	Number Who Had PKU	Number Who Had MHP
Infants:[a]						
Infants with higher Phe levels	7.01 (6.0–8.5)	8	4	4	5	3
Infants with lower Phe levels	4.74 (3.5–5.7)	7	3	4	3	4
Matched controls		9	5	4		
Siblings		6	4	2		
Normative sample[b]		25	11	14		
Normative sample[c]		12[d]	6	6		
Toddlers:[e]						
Subjects with higher Phe levels	8.29 (6.0–11.5)	10	5	5	5	5
Subjects with lower Phe levels	4.98 (2.8–5.5)	8	3	5	4	4

18

Group	Phe level					
Matched controls		12	5	7		
Siblings		7	4	3		
Normative sample		20[d]	10	10		
Young children:[f]						
Subjects with higher Phe levels	7.98 (6.0–10.1)	15	7	8	12	3
Subjects with lower Phe levels	4.83 (2.0–6.0)	14	7	7	8	6
Matched controls		15	8	7		
Siblings		12	9	3		
Normative sample		20[d]	10	10		

[a] Tested at 1-month intervals from 6 to 12 months of age.

[b] 25 infants from the general population were tested longitudinally on the AB̄ and object retrieval tasks.

[c] 12 infants from the general population were tested at each age on spatial discrimination and visual paired comparison. Anyone can have a particularly good or bad day. By following participants longitudinally, we were able to obtain a more accurate and reliable indication of each child's ability and developmental trajectory than would have been possible had we tested each child only once. These repeated observations over time provided our statistical analysis with enough power to detect group differences despite the fact that the number of subjects in our groups was not large.

[d] At each age.

[e] Tested at 6-month intervals from 15 to 30 months of age.

[f] Tested at 6-month intervals from 3½ to 7 years of age.

able control; rather, their group assignment simply reflects the fact that their plasma Phe levels were toward the higher end of the acceptable range.

Because no control group is ever perfect, we have included more than one kind of control group. Siblings provide a partial control for family background and genetic makeup. We were lucky to have two sets of twins in the study; one pair was discordant for PKU and the other discordant for MHP. Siblings are an imperfect control group because, except for twins, they are not matched for age or birth order and are often not matched for gender or health status. Therefore, we also studied children unrelated to our PKU and MHP participants but matched to them on a host of background and health variables such as gender, gestational age at birth, birth weight, ethnic background, religion, age at beginning of testing, community of residence, child-care arrangements, number of siblings, birth order, and the age, level of education, and occupational status of each parent. To find each matched control child, we made close to 100 phone calls.[4] Table 1 lists some of the characteristics of two of our PKU participants and the children who served as their matched controls.

Selecting control subjects by matching on a list of variables is imperfect as well, however, because the children thus selected may not match on other critical variables that we had not considered. Therefore, we complemented our use of siblings and matched controls with a normative sample of children from the general population. With this last group, we attempted to get an estimate of the normal developmental progression on each of our tasks, although we did not have a representative, random sample of the entire population, and although we generally tested 20 children on each task at each age rather than hundreds of children. Our participants from the general population were obtained by soliciting parents who had a child in one of the local schools, who had announced their child's birth in one of the local newspapers, or whose name had made its way onto a marketing list targeting parents of young children.

The characteristics of the children in each group of participants are summarized in Table 2. Almost all participants were full-term (100% of the children tested cross-sectionally; 96% of the children tested longitudinally). Because PKU is found primarily among Caucasians, almost all our participants were Caucasian (95% of the children tested cross-sectionally; 93% of the children tested longitudinally). All participants for whom the data are available had IQs between 80 and 132. Participants from lower-, middle-, and upper-middle-class backgrounds are represented in all subject groups.

---

[4] Because of our strict criteria for matching controls to our PKU and MHP participants, we were unable to obtain a matched control for every PKU and MHP child. We have concentrated on finding controls for our PKU and MHP participants with higher Phe levels; most control subjects are matched to these children.

Because of the large age range studied (from 6 months to 7 years), three different batteries of cognitive neuropsychological measures were used—one for infants (6–12 months of age), one for toddlers (15–30 months of age), and one for young children ($3\frac{1}{2}$–7 years old). The relevant sample sizes to keep in mind when considering these results are those within the relevant age groups, as only children within one of these three age ranges received any given measure. Information on sample sizes is provided in Table 3.

III. PROCEDURES

MEASURES OF PLASMA LEVELS OF PHE AND TYR

Plasma Phe levels were monitored in all PKU and MHP children from birth by the two referring PKU clinics. In PKU children, these levels were generally checked every 2 weeks during the first year of life and every 1–2 months thereafter. In those MHP children whose Phe levels were low and stable, blood samples were taken less often, as there seemed to be no medically justifiable reason for more frequent sampling. The New Jersey metabolic disorders laboratory analyzes the plasma levels of both Phe and Tyr; however, the Pennsylvania lab analyzes only the plasma levels of Phe. Hence, for the children from the Camden PKU clinic, we have both Phe and Tyr levels from each blood sample, but, for the children from the Philadelphia PKU clinic, we have only Phe levels. The staff responsible for drawing the blood and for maintaining the records of plasma amino acid levels was separate from the staff responsible for the cognitive neuropsychological testing.

The New Jersey blood samples were subjected to HPLC analyses. The Pennsylvania blood samples were assessed using the Guthrie test when Phe levels were well below 10 mg/dl; whenever Phe levels approached 10 mg/dl, an HPLC assay or the McCaman-Robins fluorometric procedure was used. HPLC and fluorometric assays are quantitative, precise measures. The Guthrie technique (Guthrie & Susi, 1963) is less precise but is acceptable when Phe levels are low.

The measures that we derived from the individual Phe and Tyr readings were the following:

1. *The mean plasma Phe level for the 6-week period prior to a cognitive testing session (see Table 4).*

Thus, one value for the *concurrent Phe level* was generated for each testing session for each PKU and MHP child.

2. *The plasma Phe reading closest to the day of cognitive testing and within the range of not more than 4 weeks before the testing session.*

TABLE 4

PLASMA PHE AND TYR LEVELS (in Mg/Dl) OF THE PKU AND MHP PARTICIPANTS

	CHILDREN WHOSE CONCURRENT PLASMA PHE LEVELS WERE ≥ 6 MG/DL		CHILDREN WHOSE CONCURRENT PLASMA PHE LEVELS WERE < 6 MG/DL	
	PKU	MHP	PKU	MHP
Infants:				
Mean concurrent Phe levels[a]	6.47	7.13	4.47	4.70
Mean Phe levels during the first month of life	12.97	14.98	. . .[b]	4.37
Mean concurrent Tyr levels[c]	1.33	1.86	1.94	1.87
	(N = 2)	(N = 2)	(N = 2)	(N = 1)
Mean concurrent Phe:Tyr ratio	7.42	6.68	2.28	2.97
	(N = 2)	(N = 2)	(N = 2)	(N = 1)
Toddlers:				
Mean concurrent Phe levels	7.95	8.27	4.33	4.51
Mean Phe levels during the first month of life	18.35	11.95	. . .[b]	4.89
Mean concurrent Tyr levels[c]	1.36	1.79	1.89	2.20
	(N = 2)	(N = 2)	(N = 2)	(N = 2)
Mean concurrent Phe:Tyr ratio	6.16	7.17	2.46	2.32
	(N = 2)	(N = 2)	(N = 2)	(N = 2)
Young children:				
Mean concurrent Phe levels	7.41	8.83	4.30	4.35
Mean Phe levels during the first month of life	19.17	7.45	. . .[b]	4.64
Mean concurrent Tyr levels[c]	1.44	N.A.	1.86	2.26
	(N = 5)		(N = 4)	(N = 2)
Mean concurrent Phe:Tyr ratio	10.65	N.A.	2.52	2.03
	(N = 5)		(N = 4)	(N = 2)

NOTE.—N.A. = not available.

[a] *Concurrent* refers to the 6-week period preceding each cognitive testing session.

[b] No PKU child in our sample had a mean plasma Phe level under 6 mg/dl during the first month of life.

[c] Tyr values are available only for children from New Jersey.

Again, one value for the *most recent Phe level* was generated for each testing session, except where no Phe measurement had been taken during the 4-week period preceding a testing session.

3. *The mean plasma Phe level during the child's first month of life (see Table 4).*

4. *The grand mean of the mean of every 2-week period during the child's first year of life.*

The mean of the semimonthly means was used to avoid counting one month more heavily than another just because more Phe measurements might have been taken during a given month.

5. *The grand mean of the mean of every 2-week period during the child's first year of life excluding the first month.*

The mean plasma Phe level for the 11 months from 1 to 12 months of age excluded the period prior to when PKU children began their low-

23

Phe diet. The extremely high Phe levels prior to diet initiation sometimes markedly affected the mean for the period from birth to 12 months of age.

    6. The mean plasma Phe level during the period of cognitive testing (6–12 months, 15–30 months, or 3¹/₂–7 years of age).

For infants and toddlers, the grand mean of the mean of every 2-week period during the relevant age span was used. For young children, whose plasma Phe levels were assessed less often, the mean for every 1-month period throughout the relevant age span was used.

    7. The percentage of a child's plasma Phe levels that were between 2 and 6 mg/dl during the period of cognitive testing.

Some reports have suggested that Phe levels that are too low (< 2 mg/dl) are as detrimental as higher Phe levels (> 6 mg/dl) and that PKU children whose plasma Phe levels remain stably between 2 and 6 mg/dl look much better than PKU children who may have the same mean plasma Phe level but whose Phe levels fluctuate between being excessively high or low (e.g., van der Schot, Doesburg, & Sengers, 1994).

    8. The percentage of a child's plasma Phe levels that were between 2 and 6 mg/dl during the child's first year of life.

    9. The plasma Phe:Tyr ratio closest to the day of cognitive testing and within the range of not more than 4 weeks before the testing session.

    10. The mean plasma Phe:Tyr ratio for the 6-week period prior to a cognitive testing session (see Table 4).

The procedure was similar to that used to calculate measure 1 above: one value for the concurrent Phe:Tyr ratio was generated for each testing session for each PKU and MHP child.

    11. The grand mean of the mean Phe:Tyr ratios for every 2-week period during the child's first year of life excluding the first month.

    12. The mean plasma Phe:Tyr ratio during the period of cognitive testing (6–12 months, 15–30 months, or 3¹/₂–7 years of age).

The same procedure as used for measure 6 above was used here.

We were most interested in the relation between plasma amino acid levels around the time of cognitive testing and performance during that testing session (concurrent Phe level). We feel that a child's mean plasma Phe levels during the 6 weeks prior to a cognitive testing session best reflect this for two reasons. First, amino acid levels in the bloodstream vary by what one has eaten and how long ago one last ate. A single reading is thus a less reliable measure than is the average of a few measurements. Second, we had close to complete data for the 6-week measure, whereas for the Phe level closest to the test date within the preceding 4 weeks we had more missing data.

Since our hypothesis concerns the amount of Phe relative to Tyr in the bloodstream, the mean plasma Phe:Tyr ratio would have been an even better measure. Unfortunately, we had information on plasma Tyr levels only for our PKU and MHP participants from New Jersey. The sample sizes in the analyses were therefore simply too small when we included only those PKU and MHP children for whom we could calculate Phe:Tyr ratios. However, as can be seen in Table 4, most of our PKU participants (for whom Tyr data were available) whose plasma Phe levels were three to five times normal (6–10 mg/dl) had elevated Phe:Tyr ratios, whereas most PKU and MHP participants with lower plasma Phe levels had much lower, closer-to-normal Phe:Tyr ratios. Thus, Phe levels seemed to be a fairly accurate indicator of the Phe:Tyr ratio and allowed us to include more children in our analyses.

All our results are presented first using the concurrent Phe level measure, that is, the mean of each child's plasma Phe level during the 6-week period preceding each testing session. When we do not specify the Phe measure to which we are referring, we always mean this current Phe level measure. All analyses were then repeated substituting measures 2–8. When we do not report the results for a measure and performance on a given cognitive task, it is because none of the analyses using that measure yielded any significant relation with performance on that task.

We used measures 1–8 as continuous variables when analyzing the results of the PKU and MHP participants. Blood samples were taken to assess plasma amino acids only in the PKU and MHP children. There was no medically justifiable reason for drawing blood from the other children as all children whose PAH gene is normal have plasma Phe levels of 1–3 mg/dl and plasma Phe:Tyr ratios close to 1. Thus, all analyses of plasma Phe level as a continuous variable had to exclude the sibling, matched control, and normative sample groups.

However, all subject groups could be included in all analyses where the PKU and MHP children were dichotomized according to high and low plasma Phe levels on any of our nine measures. In these analyses, plasma Phe level was not entered as a separate independent variable. Rather, the subject groups consisted of PKU children with plasma Phe levels three times normal or higher (i.e., PKU children with higher Phe levels), MHP children with higher Phe levels, PKU children with plasma Phe levels above normal but less than three times normal (i.e., PKU children with lower Phe levels), MHP children with lower Phe levels, siblings, matched controls, and children from the general population. When the percentage of plasma Phe levels between 2 and 6 mg/dl was used to assign PKU and MHP children to higher and lower groups, the higher group was defined as children whose plasma Phe levels were outside the 2–6 mg/dl range more than 20% of the time; conversely, the lower group consisted of PKU and MHP children whose plasma Phe levels remained within the 2–6 mg/dl range 80% or more of the time. When the Phe:Tyr ratio was used to assign PKU and MHP children to higher and lower groups, the higher group was defined as children with Phe:Tyr ratios of 4 or greater; children in the lower group had Phe:Tyr ratios under 4.

STATISTICAL ANALYSES

Except where otherwise specified, the data were analyzed using the PROC MIXED procedure developed by the SAS Institute. This allows one to analyze, within the same multiple regression framework, data based on longitudinal, repeated measures as well as cross-sectional data—hence the name *mixed*. This allowed us to include the cross-sectional data from children from the general population tested only once in the same analyses with all the other children, who were tested longitudinally.

Orthogonal contrasts were used for pairwise comparisons between each subject group and every other subject group.[5] If one performs multiple comparisons, one would expect some comparisons to yield a difference just by chance. Therefore, one wants a more stringent criterion for "significance" if many pairwise comparisons are made. Since we made 10 pairwise comparisons for each task—comparing the high-Phe group, the low-Phe group, their matched controls, their siblings, and children from the general population (the normative sample)—we multiplied the normally accepted level of significance ($p \leq .05$) by 10 and used $p \leq .005$ as the level at which pairwise comparisons would be considered significant. This achieves an effect comparable to that achieved by using the Bonferroni correction. For analyses not involving pairwise comparison, such as the regression of performance on age, IQ, gender, or Phe level, the normally accepted significance level of $p \leq .05$ was used.

All analyses—(*a*) group comparisons among PKU and MHP children with higher plasma Phe levels, PKU and MHP children with lower plasma Phe levels, the normative sample, matched controls, and siblings; (*b*) similar group comparisons omitting the MHP children or omitting the PKU children; and (*c*) plasma Phe level entered as a continuous variable—were performed for each dependent measure of each of the 19 behavioral tests. In all analyses, sex and age were also entered as independent measures. The analyses outlined above were repeated for each plasma Phe variable. Analyses were repeated with IQ, demographic variables, and health variables entered into the equation. To examine whether performance covaried with plasma Phe level within the same child over time, we calculated the Pearson correlation between plasma Phe level and performance on a given task for each PKU and MHP participant within the age range tested on the task. We report the average of these Pearson product moment values, although as far as we know

---

[5] We predicted that PKU and MHP children with higher plasma Phe levels, or PKU children alone with higher plasma Phe levels, would perform significantly worse than all other groups. When testing whether our results were consistent with these directional hypotheses, we used one-tailed tests. We had not predicted any differences in performance among any other groups of subjects; when testing whether any differences that emerged among those groups were statistically significant, we used two-tailed distributions.

it is not clear how to test the statistical significance of such averaged correlation coefficients.

MEASURES OF COGNITIVE PERFORMANCE

The general intelligence (IQ) of our PKU, MHP, and matched control children was assessed when the children were 4 years old using the Stanford-Binet test. Nineteen cognitive neuropsychological measures were also administered: nine measures required cognitive functions dependent on dorsolateral prefrontal cortex; 10 required other neural systems. Of the nine measures linked to dorsolateral prefrontal cortex, six required working memory and inhibitory control (see Table 5).

Three tasks required working memory, but not inhibitory control, and are sensitive to the functions of a more medial region of dorsolateral prefrontal cortex. Three tasks required recognition memory and depend on the functions of the medial temporal lobe; one of these tasks (delayed nonmatching to sample) requires the medial temporal lobe when recognition memory is taxed at longer delays but appears to require the symbolic and relational abilities made possible by ventrolateral prefrontal cortex in order to learn the basic principle of the task. Three tasks required spatial analyses dependent on parietal cortex. In addition, four tasks were closely matched to the tasks dependent on dorsolateral prefrontal cortex but differed in a critical dimension that made dorsolateral prefrontal cortex unnecessary for their successful performance.

Infants were tested on four tasks (two working memory and inhibition tasks and two other tasks). Toddlers were tested on five tasks (one working memory and inhibition task and four other tasks). Young children were tested on 10 tasks (three working memory and inhibition tasks and seven other tasks).

For longitudinal testing, infants were tested every month from 6 to 12 months of age (with sessions scheduled every 28 days, ± 4 days, beginning at 6 months, 0 days), toddlers every 3 months from 15 to 30 months (± 7 days), and young children every 6 months from 3½ to 7 years (within 10 days of their birthday and half birthday). Children from the general population were tested cross-sectionally at each of these ages. The range in their ages was, however, larger: ± 7 days for infants, ± 14 days for toddlers, and ± 2½ months for young children.

Almost all children tested longitudinally were tested in their homes. Children in the cross-sectional sample were tested either in the Infant and Early Child Development Laboratory at the University of Pennsylvania or in their day-care center or school. For all cognitive neuropsychological testing, both a tester and an assistant were present. The assistant recorded the child's per-

TABLE 5

Tasks Used with Infants (Ages 6–12 Months)

Tests of Working Memory and Inhibitory Control,
Dependent on Dorsolateral Prefrontal Cortex

A̅B̅.—A hiding task requiring working memory and inhibition of a previously
rewarded response. Subject sees reward hidden to left or right (two identical hiding
wells); after a delay, subject is allowed to search one well. Linked to dorsolateral
prefrontal cortex by work with rhesus monkeys (e.g., Diamond & Goldman-Rakic, 1989).

Object retrieval.—A transparent barrier detour task. Subject can see the reward
through all sides of a transparent box but can reach through only the one open side
(Diamond, 1981, 1990a). Linked to dorsolateral prefrontal cortex by work with rhesus
monkeys (e.g., Diamond & Goldman-Rakic, 1985).

Tests That Do Not Require Working Memory and Inhibitory Control

Spatial discrimination.—An associative rule-learning and memory task. Hiding done
unseen; subject must learn and remember that reward is always hidden to left or right
(two identical hiding places); after delay between trials, subject is allowed to reach. Not
impaired by lesions to prefrontal cortex (e.g., Goldman & Rosvold, 1970).

Visual paired comparison.—A recognition memory task where a sample is presented, a
delay is imposed, and then subject is given a choice of that stimulus or something new.
Linked to the medial temporal lobe (Bachevalier, Brickson, & Haggar, 1993; McKee &
Squire, 1993).

Tasks Used with Toddlers (Ages 15–30 months)

Tests of Working Memory and Inhibitory Control,
Dependent on Dorsolateral Prefrontal Cortex

A̅B̅ *with invisible displacement.*—A hiding task requiring memory of where the
container with the reward was last moved and inhibition of a previously rewarded
response. Similar to A̅B̅ for infants, but not independently, directly linked to prefrontal
cortex.

Tests That Do Not Require Working Memory and Inhibitory Control

Three boxes (boxes scrambled after each reach).—A memory task where subjects are to try
to open all boxes without repeating a choice; a delay is imposed between reaches. Subject
must remember color/shape of the boxes; spatial location is irrelevant. Linked to
dorsolateral prefrontal cortex by work with rhesus monkeys (Petrides, 1995).

Three boxes (stationary).—Here, uncovering the boxes in spatial order will suffice.
Similar to a condition not impaired by damage to dorsolateral prefrontal cortex (M.
Petrides, personal communication, 1990).

Delayed nonmatching to sample.—A recognition memory task where one is rewarded for
reaching to the stimulus not matching the sample that was presented shortly before.
Linked to the medial temporal lobe by work with rhesus monkeys and amnesic patients
(e.g., Murray et al., 1989; Squire, Zola-Morgan, & Chen, 1988; Zola-Morgan, Squire, &
Amaral, 1989).

Global-local (preferential looking procedure).—A visuospatial attention task. Assesses
attention to the global and the local features of composite stimuli (e.g., an *H* made up of
S's). Similar to a task linked to parietal cortex by work with brain-damaged patients (e.g.,
Lamb, Robertson, & Knight, 1989; Robertson, Lamb, & Knight, 1988) and to a task linked
to parietal cortex through functional magnetic imaging (fMRI) of neural activity in
normal adults (Shedden, Christoforou, Nahmias, Hahn, & Noll, 1997).

TABLE 5 (*Continued*)

TASKS USED WITH YOUNG CHILDREN (Ages 3½–7 Years)

Tests of Working Memory and Inhibitory Control,
Dependent on Dorsolateral Prefrontal Cortex

Day-night Stroop-like test.—Requires holding two rules in mind and exercising inhibitory control. Subject must say "night" when shown a white-sun card and say "day" when shown a black-moon card. Hypothesized to require the functions of dorsolateral prefrontal cortex but not yet studied in relation to brain function.

Tapping.—A conflict test requiring memory of two rules and inhibitory control. When experimenter taps once, subject must tap two times; when experimenter taps twice, subject must tap once. Linked to prefrontal cortex by work with brain-damaged patients (Luria, 1980).

Three pegs.—Subject is shown a board containing three colored pegs arranged in the order red, yellow, green. Subject is instructed to tap the pegs in the order red, green, yellow. This requires remembering the instructed sequence and inhibiting the tendency to tap the pegs in their spatial order. It has yet to be studied in relation to brain function.

Tests That Do Not Require Working Memory and Inhibitory Control

Corsi-Milner test of temporal order memory.—Subject is shown a series of stimuli one at a time and is periodically shown two previously presented stimuli and asked, "Which of these two pictures did you see last?" Linked to prefrontal cortex by work with brain-damaged patients (Milner, Corsi, & Leonard, 1991).

Six boxes (boxes scrambled after each reach).—A memory task where subject must try to open all boxes without repeating a choice; a delay is imposed between reaches. Similar to tasks linked to prefrontal cortex in rhesus monkeys (Petrides, 1995) and in brain-damaged human adults (Petrides & Milner, 1982).

Stroop control condition.—Requires learning and remembering two rules (as does Stroop above) but requires no inhibition (unlike Stroop above)—two arbitrary patterns used; to one must say "day," to the other "night."

Corsi-Milner test of recognition memory.—Shown a series of pictures; periodically asked, "Among the pictures I've shown you, which of these two have you already seen?" Linked to medial temporal lobe by work with brain-damaged patients (Milner, 1982; Milner et al., 1991).

Six boxes (stationary).—Here, uncovering the boxes in spatial order will suffice. Similar to a condition not impaired by damage to dorsolateral prefrontal cortex (M. Petrides, personal communiction, 1990).

Global-local (forced choice procedure).—A visuospatial attention task. Assesses attention to the global and the local features of composite stimuli (e.g., an *H* made up of *S*'s). Linked to parietal cortex by work with brain-damaged patients (e.g., Lamb et al., 1989; Robertson et al., 1988) and by functional magnetic imaging (fMRI) of neural activity in normal adults (Shedden et al., 1997).

Line bisection.—A spatial perception task. Subject is asked to indicate the middle of each line. Linked to parietal cortex by work with brain-damaged patients (e.g., Benton, 1969).

formance, entertained the child during delay periods, and helped get materials ready for the tester. All sessions were recorded on videotape for detailed analyses. Infant and toddler testing took about 45 min, and sessions with young children took about 1 hour, 15 min. In all sessions, breaks were provided between tasks whenever needed. Descriptions of the procedures for the 19 cognitive neuropsychological tests used in this study follow.

The order of testing was as follows: Infants were administered the spatial discrimination task first, then object retrieval, A̅B̅, and finally visual paired comparison. The toddler tests were administered in the order A̅B̅-invisible, three boxes task (boxes remain stationary), three boxes task (boxes scrambled after each reach), global-local spatial processing (preferential looking procedure), and finally delayed nonmatching to sample. Preschoolers were administered the day-night Stroop-like task (or its control version) first, followed by the six boxes task (boxes remain stationary), the six boxes task (boxes scrambled after each reach), the Corsi-Milner tests of short-term temporal order memory and short-term recognition memory, the tapping test, global-local spatial processing (forced choice reaction time procedure), the three pegs task, line bisection, and the Corsi-Milner test of recognition memory after a half hour delay.

Stimulus presentation times, delay durations, fixation times, and response latencies were verified or determined from the videotape records of each session. On-line coding of the participant's and experimenter's actions, such as response accuracy or change of reward, was always rechecked by subsequent coding of the videotape. Intercoder reliability was greater than .90 (alpha coefficient) for all measures for all tasks, except for reaction time measures on the day-night Stroop-like task and the tapping task, where the reliabilities were greater than .85, and except for object retrieval. Because coding of the object retrieval task was so difficult, we had one highly skilled person code all the object retrieval sessions; her intracoder reliability was greater than .90. The videotape coders were generally blind as to the group membership of the children, although they did know which children were being longitudinally tested and which were from the general population and hence tested only once.

PROCEDURES FOR THE COGNITIVE NEUROPSYCHOLOGICAL TESTS ADMINISTERED TO INFANTS (6–12 MONTHS OF AGE)

For all tests, all infants were tested while seated on the caregiver's lap, facing the experimenter across the testing table. The testing tables were specially constructed to be portable, and the same tables were used for sessions in infants' homes.

The A̅B̅ Task

The A̅B̅ task requires working memory and inhibition of a previously rewarded response (Diamond, 1985, 1991a, 1991b). The participant watches as a reward is hidden and then a few seconds later must retrieve it. Devised by Piaget (1937/1954), this task has been used in labs throughout the world.

Each infant sat at a rectangular testing table (90 × 30 × 70 cm [length × width × height]) with two embedded wells (9.4 cm in diameter, 5 cm deep, and 30 cm apart center to center). The infant was kept centered between the two wells. The wells were identical except that one was to the left and the other to the right. A session always began with a few different kinds of toys on top of the table, freely accessible to the infant, to determine which toy the infant preferred and to give the infant time to get used to the experimenter, the assistant, and the testing table. At least one of the two blue cloths (22 × 22 cm) that would be used to cover the hiding wells during testing was also on the tabletop, to give the infant time to explore the cloth and grow bored with it.

Pretesting began with the experimenter placing the preferred toy in the center of the table and partially covering it with a blue cloth. The infant was allowed to retrieve the toy immediately. This procedure was then repeated, except this time the toy was covered completely. Anytime it was unclear whether the infant had really been reaching for the hidden toy (e.g., if he or she showed interest in the cloth or waited several seconds before reaching to uncover the toy), this second pretest trial was repeated. Only infants who could retrieve a hidden object were tested on the AB task.

A trial began with the experimenter holding up a toy in which the infant had demonstrated keen interest; then the caregiver restrained the infant's arms. (*Interest* was always judged empirically, by the infant smiling on seeing the toy, reaching for it, choosing it over other proffered toys, playing with it throughout the allotted playtime, or protesting or resisting when the toy was taken away.) As the infant watched, the experimenter placed the toy in one of the hiding wells and then covered the two wells simultaneously with identical blue cloth covers. Care was taken to ensure that the infant had seen where the toy was placed, and the hiding was repeated if there was any doubt about whether the infant had observed this. If no delay was imposed (i.e., if the delay was 0 sec), as soon as the covers were in place, the infant was allowed to reach to find the toy. For delays of 1 sec or longer, the experimenter called to the infant to break the infant's visual fixation on the correct well, and the caregiver held the infant's arms and torso firmly to prevent moving or straining toward the correct well. Then the infant was allowed to reach.

Once the infant moved a cover, he or she was scored as having reached to that well. Thus, if an infant started to reach toward a well, or even touched the well's cover, but did not begin to remove that cover, he or she was not scored as having chosen that well. On the other hand, even if the infant did not look where he or she was reaching or did not look in the well after uncovering it and immediately tried to reach to the other well, as long as the cover was at least partially removed the infant was scored as having chosen that

31

well. If the infant did not reach to either well, he or she was scored as being incorrect on that trial. When an infant reached incorrectly, uncovering the empty well, or did not reach at all, the experimenter showed the infant where the toy had been but did not allow the infant to have the toy. The infant was allowed to play with the toy only when he or she chose the correct well.

When infants chose correctly, not only were they allowed to play with the toy, but they received enthusiastic cheers and praise from the experimenter and assistant. When infants uncovered the empty well, the experimenter and assistant sounded very disappointed and sad but encouraged them to try again. Infants were discouraged from trying to uncover both wells simultaneously. If an infant did this once, the experimenter placed her hands on both covers and would not release either cover until the infant pulled on only one.

The same well served as the hiding place on all trials until the infant was correct on two trials in a row; then the toy was hidden in the other well and the procedure repeated. For half the participants, the toy was hidden in the well to the right on the first trial. For all participants, the initial side of hiding alternated over testing sessions. We tried to balance administering the same total number of trials to all with administering the same number of reversal trials to all. Reversals are the critical trials because that is where errors are most likely to occur. However, participants who make more errors will receive fewer reversal trials if the total number of trials is kept constant because reversals are administered only after two consecutively correct reaches. Therefore, we used the following rules:

1. Always administer at least three reversals.
2. If, by the time an infant reaches correctly on two trials in a row following the third reversal, fewer than 12 trials have been administered, continue testing.
3. If, by the time an infant reaches correctly on two trials in a row following the fourth reversal, fewer than 15 trials have been administered, continue testing.
4. Never administer more than five reversals.

We tried to end all sessions with the infant being correct on two trials in a row. If an infant was incorrect on five consecutive trials anytime during a session, we tried to break that perseverative string by covering only the correct well on the next trial. Performance on that single-well trial was not included when tabulating performance during the session. We tried to keep interest in the toy constant throughout the testing session, rather than keeping the toy itself constant throughout the session. Therefore, we changed toys during AB testing when an infant's interest in the toy we had been using appeared to wane. As at the outset of the session, we looked for overt, observable signs of interest in another toy before using that on a trial. We tried not to switch toys on reversal trials.

Once an infant could uncover a completely hidden object, we began $\overline{AB}$ testing with a 0-sec delay. If the infant was correct at the initial hiding place on trials 1 and 2 and on the first reversal trial, the delay was incremented 2–3 sec, and testing began again with two trials at the well last used at the shorter delay. If the infant again reached correctly over the next three trials (the two at the same well and the reversal trial), the delay was again incremented 2–3 sec, and testing began again. On the other hand, if an infant was distressed at the initial delay and made more than one error at the initial hiding place (*before* any reversal), the delay was decreased 2–3 sec, and testing began again using this same hiding well. If the infant again erred on more than one trial prior to the first reversal, the delay was decreased a further 2–3 sec, and testing began again. The delay was never changed more than two times in a single session, and it was never changed after the beginning of a session. It could be increased twice, decreased twice, increased and then decreased, or the reverse, but two changes was the limit. Performance was scored only over the trials at the final delay used; trials at earlier delays were considered pretest trials.

We adjusted the delay length in order to find the delay at which the infant would make the "$\overline{AB}$ error," where errors are confined primarily to reversal trials and the trials immediately following reversals. When infants are performing flawlessly, we do not know how much longer a delay they might have been able to tolerate. Similarly, when they are failing miserably, we do not know how much shorter we would have needed to make the delay before they would have been able to perform reasonably well. Once we have the $\overline{AB}$ error, however, we know that at delays 2–3 sec shorter the infant will perform flawlessly and that at delays 2–3 sec longer the infant will perform miserably (Diamond, 1985). The delays used in this study were 0, 3, 5, 8, 10, 12, and 15 sec. Over our longitudinal testing, if an infant had been correct on 90% or more of the trials in the preceding session, the present session started at a delay 2 sec longer than had been used in the previous session. A delay 2 sec longer was also used if an infant had committed the $\overline{AB}$ error on both of the preceding two testing sessions. Otherwise, testing started at the same delay as had been used for the last testing session. We allowed ourselves two opportunities to correct the choice of delay, as noted above, if this initial estimate was incorrect.

Evidence Identifying the Neural Basis for Successful Performance

Ablation of dorsolateral prefrontal cortex disrupts performance on $\overline{AB}$ in adult monkeys (Diamond & Goldman-Rakic, 1989) and infant monkeys

(Diamond & Goldman-Rakic, 1986). Ablation of other brain regions—medial temporal lobe (Diamond, Zola-Morgan, & Squire, 1989) or posterior parietal cortex (Diamond & Goldman-Rakic, 1989)—does not affect $\overline{AB}$ performance. Moreover, $\overline{AB}$ and delayed response are essentially the same task (Diamond, 1990b; Diamond & Doar, 1989; Diamond & Goldman-Rakic, 1989), and there is no behavioral task more firmly linked to dorsolateral prefrontal cortex than delayed response. Successful delayed response performance has been shown to depend on dorsolateral prefrontal cortex by such diverse techniques as ablation studies (Butters, Pandya, Sanders, & Dye, 1969; Goldman & Rosvold, 1970; Jacobsen, 1936), reversible cooling (e.g., Bauer & Fuster, 1976; Fuster & Alexander, 1970), single-unit recording (e.g., Fuster, 1973; Fuster & Alexander, 1971; Niki, 1974), pharmacological manipulation (Brozoski et al., 1979), and 2-deoxyglucose metabolic labeling (Bugbee & Goldman-Rakic, 1981). MPTP[6] injections, which disrupt the fronto-striatal dopamine system, also impair performance on this task (Schneider & Kovelowski, 1990).

The Object Retrieval Task

In the object retrieval task, infants must detour around a small transparent box open on one side to retrieve the toy within, inhibiting the pull to reach straight to the visible reward. As infants get older, the memory of having looked through the opening is enough; they can look through the opening, sit up, and reach in while looking through a closed side. Still older infants do not need to look along the line of reach at all. Retrieval times decrease with age as participants remember which sides of the box they have already tried and found closed. This task thus requires working memory and inhibitory control.

The following variables were manipulated: (a) which side of the box was open (front, top, left, or right), (b) distance of the toy from the box opening (partially out, just inside the opening, or deep inside the box), (c) position of the box on the testing surface (e.g., near the front edge of the table or far from it), (d) box size ($4.5 \times 4.5 \times 2$ inches or $6 \times 6 \times 2$ inches in size), and (e) box transparency (transparent or opaque). The toy was always visible when the box was transparent, but the experimental variables jointly determined whether the infant saw the toy through a closed side of the box or through the opening. All boxes were constructed in such a way that they had four closed sides and two sides missing. With a box placed so that the front, left, or right was open, the box had no bottom. With a box placed so that the top was open, the box had no back.

---

[6] 1-methyl-4-phenyl-1,2,3,6-tetrahydropyridine.

The infant was seated on the caregiver's lap, and the height of the caregiver's chair was adjusted until the infant's shoulders were 6 inches above the tabletop. Before testing began, the infant was allowed to play with a variety of toys to determine a toy preference. The two clear boxes were also left out on the testing table so that the child could explore them and grow bored with them. Each trial began with the experimenter holding up a desired toy to attract the infant's attention and the caregiver restraining the infant's hands just long enough for the experimenter to put the toy and box in place. For trials where the opening was at the front, left, or right, the experimenter placed the toy on the table and then placed the box directly over the toy, without giving any cue as to which side was open. The experimenter held the box in place on all trials by holding the upper back corners, left and right. The toy was changed as often from one trial to the next as necessary to maintain a high level of interest.

Trials were presented in blocks; within a block the orientation of the box remained constant. For all sessions, testing began with the top-open orientation, followed by trials at the front-open orientation, and ending with trials at the two side-open orientations (order of the right- and left-open orientations was alternated over sessions). Within each orientation, testing always began with the transparent boxes, and trials always proceeded according to a standard protocol from easier to more difficult (toy partially out of the box, just inside the opening, deep inside the box where the infant could see the opening but could not see the toy through the opening, and deep inside the box with the infant unable to see the opening). Then a similar sequence of trials at the same orientation was administered using the opaque box, followed by any transparent box trials that the infant had earlier failed.

If the infant became distracted or seemed to be giving up, the experimenter tapped the box or jostled it, rattling the toy, to regain the infant's attention. This usually succeeded in eliciting renewed retrieval attempts, although sometimes these attempts were short-lived. If, despite verbal encouragement and the experimenter's tapping or jostling the box, an infant still could not succeed on a given trial and refused to try any longer, the experimenter intervened by providing clues or aids.

The first kind of aid the experimenter provided was temporary and is classified as *show and change*. Here the experimenter moved the box or toy, showing the infant the toy through the box opening, but then returning the box or toy to its original position as the infant began to reach. The experimenter waited until the infant started to reach before returning the box to its original position, making sure that the box was back in place before the infant had touched the toy. For front-open trials, temporary experimenter aids consisted of (*a*) sliding the box off the toy and then back over it as the infant began to reach and (*b*) tilting the box up (using the back of the box as a fulcrum) and then lowering it back down as the infant began to reach. When the box was thus tilted, the front opening of the bottomless box became quite large, and the infant could then see the toy through this opening. For left- and right-open trials, the *show and change* aids consisted of (*a*) turning the box about 45° so that the opening faced more toward the front and the infant could see the toy through the opening and then turning the box back as the infant began to reach, (*b*) sliding the box off the toy and then back over it as the infant began to reach, and (*c*) trailing the toy out of the box and then back into it as the infant followed with his or her hand, in hot pursuit of the toy.

If an infant did not succeed after one of these aids, the same or another aid was presented again. If, after receiving four of these temporary aids, the infant still could not retrieve the toy, the experimenter provided a permanent aid. That is, the experimenter tilted or turned the box, or slid it partially off the toy, and maintained the box in that position until after the infant had retrieved the toy. Note that, with the box in one of these permanent positions, the task no longer presented a detour problem, and the box could be largely ignored.

Whenever an infant required either temporary or permanent assistance on a trial, the trial was immediately administered again to see whether the infant could then succeed without any help or with less help. When an infant first succeeded with permanent assistance and then succeeded with temporary assistance, the trial was administered a third time to see whether the infant could then succeed without any help at all. These sets of two or three trials were scored together as one unit when judging the level at which an infant could perform on that particular kind of trial.

On the rare occasions when infants could not succeed even with the box permanently held out of the way, they received a score of 0 for that trial set. When they succeeded only when the box position was permanently changed, they received a score of 1. When they succeeded on the first trial with permanent assistance and on the second trial with temporary assistance but could do no better than that, they received a score of 2. When they succeeded only when the box position was temporarily changed, they received a score of 3. When they succeeded on the first trial with temporary help and then were able to succeed without any help on the second trial, they received a score of 4. When they succeeded on their own without any experimenter assistance, they received a score of 4.5. (Tapping or jostling was not considered a clue as this did not provide information about where the opening was or how to get the toy; these actions by the experimenter were ignored when scoring the difficulty level at which infants succeeded.)

There were, of course, several intermediate scores. For example, when infants needed permanent help on the first trial, temporary help on the next,

TABLE 6

0 = failed
1 = succeeded only with box permanently moved out of the way
2 = on trial 1 of set, succeeded only with box permanently moved out of the way; on re-presentation of the trial, succeeded with temporary help (i.e., a "show and change" cue)
3 = succeeded only with temporary help (i.e., a "show and change" cue)
4 = on trial 1 of set, succeeded with temporary help (i.e., a "show and change" cue); on re-presentation of the trial, could succeed on own, without any help whatsoever
4.5 = succeeded without any help whatsoever

Examples of Intermediate Levels

3.5 = on trial 1 of set, succeeded only with box permanently moved out of the way; on re-presentation of the trial, succeeded with temporary help (i.e., a "show and change" cue); on third presentation of the trial, could succeed on own, without any help whatsoever
3.75 = on trial 1 of set, succeeded only with box permanently moved out of the way; on re-presentation of the trial, could succeed on own, without any help whatsoever

If an infant required any assistance on a trial, that trial was always re-presented to see if the infant could now succeed without any help or without as much help. If the infant succeeded with less help on the re-presentation of a trial, that trial was presented a third time, to see if the infant could now succeed without any help at all. A trial and its re-presentation(s) are referred to as a *trial set*.

Where it is noted that a subject succeeded only with permanent or temporary help, that means that this was true on the initial trial of the set and its re-presentation. Where it is noted that, on trial 1 of set, subject succeeded with box permanently moved out of the way and that, on re-presentation of the trial, subject succeeded with temporary help, that means that on the third presentation of the trial the infant still needed temporary help.

and no help on the third, a score of 3.5 was assigned. When infants needed permanent assistance on the first trial but then were able to succeed without any help at all on the second trial, a score of 3.75 was assigned. The scoring system is outlined in Table 6.

When an infant scored 3 or below on a given trial set, the next more difficult trial at that orientation was not administered during that testing session. For example, if an infant could never retrieve the toy when it was just inside the opening despite having had permanent and/or temporary help from the experimenter, then that infant was not tested with the toy deep inside the box with that side of the box open during this testing session.

Evidence Identifying the Neural Basis for Successful Performance

Lesions of dorsolateral prefrontal cortex in macaques disrupt performance on the object retrieval task (Diamond & Goldman-Rakic, 1985), while lesions of the medial temporal lobe (Diamond et al., 1989) or of posterior parietal cortex (Diamond & Goldman-Rakic, 1989) do not. Disruption of the prefrontal-striatal dopamine system by MPTP injection also produces deficits on the task (e.g., Saint-Cyr, Wan, Doudet, & Aigner, 1988; Taylor, Roth, Sladek, & Redmond, 1990). 6-hydroxy-dopamine (6-OHDA) lesions of dorsolateral prefrontal cortex also impair performance on the object retrieval task (Roberts et al., 1991).

The Spatial Discrimination Task

Spatial discrimination is an associative rule-learning or conditioning task where the infant must learn that the toy is always hidden in the box on the left or right. The boxes are identical except for their left-right location. A screen is lowered while the toy is hidden so that the infant cannot observe the hiding.

Only infants who could retrieve a hidden object were tested on this task. Before testing began, the infant was allowed to play with a variety of toys to determine a toy preference. Two identical felt-covered boxes (12 × 9 × 15 cm [length × width × depth]) were fastened to the tabletop, one to the right and one to left, 12 inches apart. The boxes were open on one side and were placed so that the open side faced the infant. A felt cloth was attached to the top of the open side of each box; when the cloth was drawn down, it was not possible to see inside the box. The infant was seated midway between the boxes.

Before testing began, the assistant placed a white poster-board screen between the infant and the boxes, and the experimenter placed a desired toy partially inside one of the boxes. The screen was then removed, and the infant was encouraged to retrieve the toy. If the infant did not reach or did not reach correctly, the trial was presented again. This procedure was then repeated with the box on the other side. These trials constituted the pretesting period.

For testing proper, the white screen was put in place before each trial. The experimenter silently hid the toy in one of the boxes and drew the front covers down on both boxes. Then the screen was removed, and the experimenter tapped both boxes. Once it was clear that the infant had seen both boxes, the infant was allowed to reach. When infants reached correctly, they were allowed to play with the toy, and the experimenter and assistant cheered and praised the infant. During the play period, the experimenter lifted the cover on the empty well so that both wells would be ready to be covered again on the next trial. When infants reached incorrectly, the experimenter showed them where the toy had been, but they were not allowed to play with the toy, and the experimenter and assistant sounded sad and disappointed. The toy was hidden in the same box on all 16 trials of the testing session. The toy was changed whenever there was any indication of flagging interest.

For the first testing session and every odd-numbered session thereafter, two identical blue felt-covered boxes were used, and the toy was always hidden in the box to the infant's right. For the second testing session and every even-numbered session thereafter, two identical red boxes were used, and the toy was hidden to the infant's left on all trials.

Evidence Identifying the Neural Basis for Successful Performance

Spatial discrimination is an excellent control task for $\overline{AB}$ because the tasks are similar in a number of ways (e.g., the participant's task is to retrieve a reward located in one of two hiding places that differ only in left-right location), yet spatial discrimination has been shown repeatedly to be normal in monkeys with lesions of prefrontal cortex (e.g., Brody, Ungerleider, & Pribram, 1977; Goldman & Rosvold, 1970). Lesions of inferotemporal cortex disrupt performance on spatial discrimination (e.g., Bachevalier, 1990).

The Visual Paired Comparison Task

The visual paired comparison task tests recognition memory. Participants examine a stimulus briefly; then, after a delay, they are given the choice of exploring that stimulus further or exploring a new one. Since infants prefer novelty, if they remember the initial stimulus, they tend to choose the novel stimulus; hence, this task has long been used to assess recognition memory. It was devised by Fagan (1970) and has been used in dozens of infant labs since. We use a version of the task that allows participants to reach for the stimulus they want, rather than only looking at it. We have demonstrated that this reaching version—which has several advantages over looking-time procedures—yields results comparable to those obtained with the looking version (Diamond, 1990c, 1995).

Before testing began, the infant was given the two large objects (a yellow ball and wooden box) that would be used during the delays so that he or she could become familiar with them. Each trial consisted of a familiarization or presentation phase (during which a novel object—the sample—was presented alone at the midline), a delay, and a test phase (during which a new object and the sample were presented together).

In sessions administered at 6 and 9 months of age, infants were allowed

39

to explore and manipulate the sample during familiarization until they had habituated to it. Infants could indicate boredom with the sample by looking away from it or by discarding it. The sample was removed after the infant reached the habituation criterion, which was any combination of four instances of either looking away from the sample for 3 sec or more or discarding the sample (e.g., looking away from the sample twice and discarding it twice, looking away from it once and discarding it three times, etc.). When the infant discarded the sample, the experimenter returned it, and, when the infant had looked away for 3 sec, the experimenter directed the infant's attention back to the sample, continuing this process until the habituation criterion had been met. When the infant looked away for less than 3 sec, the experimenter did nothing, and this did not count toward the habituation criterion.

We wanted the infants to have visual as well as tactile exposure to the sample since during the test phase they would have to choose an object on the basis of its visual appearance. Infants were therefore discouraged from putting the sample object in their mouths during familiarization.

For sessions administered at 7 and 10 months of age, rather than continuing testing until a habituation criterion was reached, infants were given the sample for set periods of time during familiarization. The presentation times were 15, 30, and 45 sec at 7 months and 5, 15, and 30 sec at 10 months. If an infant looked away from the sample before the allotted presentation time had expired, his or her attention was immediately brought back to the sample. Similarly, if an infant discarded the sample before the presentation time had expired, the sample was immediately returned to him or her.

As soon as the habituation criterion had been reached or the set presentation time was over, the sample was removed, and the delay period began. During all delays, the caregiver and experimenter interacted with the infant. For delays of 1 min or more, the infant could also play with the two large toys introduced before testing started or move around the room. For delays of 3 min or more, the infant could also eat or drink.

At 6 and 9 months of age, the delays were presented in the following order: 15 sec, 3 min, 10 min, 10 sec, and 1 min. Infants of 7 months were tested on two trials at each of the three presentation times; on one trial a delay of 15 sec was used for each presentation time, and on the other trial the delay was 1 min for each presentation time. Infants of 10 months were also tested at two delays for each presentation time—1 min and 3 min. At 7 and 10 months, trials at a given delay or presentation time were randomly intermixed; all infants of the same age were tested with the same order of trials and the same stimuli.

No stimuli were reused over trials within the same session or over sessions; all stimuli were novel. Because of the constraint that no stimuli were to be reused, we did not have enough stimuli to administer the task at every age; therefore, visual paired comparison was tested at 6, 7, 9, and 10 months only.

For the test phase, the two large toys and any food or drink were removed. The experimenter asked the caregiver to center the infant at the testing table and to close her eyes (so that she would not influence the infant's choice). The experimenter then presented the sample and a novel object side by side at the midline on the far side of the table. The two objects were moved apart and back together to ensure that the infant had seen both of them. After the infant had clearly seen both, the two objects were moved forward at a uniform rate and placed at the boundary of the infant's reach and 8 inches to the left or right of the midline. The infant was allowed to reach for one of the objects. The objects were placed just barely within reach to force the infant to stretch to reach either object, hence discouraging reaching for both objects simultaneously. Once the infant touched an object, the other object was removed, and the caregiver was told to open her eyes. Infants were allowed to play with the object they selected for 15–20 sec.

Evidence Identifying the Neural Basis for Successful Performance

Lesions of the medial temporal lobe impair the visual paired comparison performance of adult monkeys (Saunders, 1989) and infant monkeys (Bachevalier, 1990; Bachevalier, Brickson, & Hagger, 1993). Human adults who are amnesic because of medial temporal lobe damage are also impaired on the task (McKee & Squire, 1993).

PROCEDURES FOR THE COGNITIVE NEUROPSYCHOLOGICAL TESTS ADMINISTERED TO TODDLERS (15–30 MONTHS OLD)

Toddlers were seated on a parent's lap for all testing except the delayed nonmatching to sample task, where the toddler sat at a toddler-size table and the parent sat in the background. For all trials on all tasks, correct performance was greeted by cheering and applause from the experimenter and parent and rewarded by the receipt of a small object or toy. When a response was incorrect, the experimenter sounded quite sad and disappointed, and the child received no toy or small object.

The $A\overline{B}$ Task with Invisible Displacement

The $A\overline{B}$ task with invisible displacement was devised by Piaget (1937/1954) as the next step in his object permanence testing series after the $A\overline{B}$ task administered to infants. In many respects, the procedure used here is

41

identical to that used for the $A\overline{B}$ task with infants. The main difference is that here the participant watched the toy being placed in a container at the center of the table and then watched that container being moved to the right or left side of the table. That is, in $A\overline{B}$ with invisible displacement, the participants did not actually see the toy itself being placed at the right or the left (as on $A\overline{B}$); rather, they saw the box containing the toy being placed at the right or left. Because of this one difference in procedure, $A\overline{B}$ with invisible displacement required a bit of pretraining not necessary for $A\overline{B}$. Otherwise, the tasks were the same.

As on $A\overline{B}$, a session always began with a few different kinds of toys on top of the table, freely accessible, to determine which toy the toddler preferred and to give the toddler time to get used to the experimenter, the assistant, and the testing situation. The participant was also encouraged to explore the two light blue containers ($12 \times 9 \times 15$ cm [length $\times$ width $\times$ depth]) that would be used during testing so that he or she would become bored with them and comfortable with reaching inside them. The experimenter made sure the toddler was centered before the start of each trial.

For the preliminary training, only one container was used. First, the toddler watched as the experimenter hid the toy in the container. The container was always oriented so that the opening was on the front side of the box, facing toward the toddler. It was not moved to the right or the left but remained at the midline. As soon as the cover was drawn over the container's opening, the experimenter encouraged the toddler to find the toy. Next, as the toddler watched, the experimenter again hid the toy in the container. Then, as the caregiver restrained the toddler's hands, the experimenter moved the container to one side. The assistant then placed a white posterboard screen momentarily in front of the toddler. After the screen was removed, the toddler was allowed to reach and retrieve the toy. This procedure was repeated with the box moved to the opposite side.

For testing, the toddler watched as before, and the box was moved to the same side it had been moved to on the last training trial. Care was taken to ensure that the toddler had seen the toy going in the box, the box moving to the side, and where the box ended up. Once the box reached the side, to give the toddler time to get a fix on where the box with the toy was now located, a full second elapsed before the screen was interposed. If there was any doubt about whether the toddler had observed the entire hiding sequence, the sequence was repeated. A 5-sec delay was used on all trials. During the delay, the other, empty container was silently positioned on the other side. The caregiver continued to restrain the toddler's arms and torso throughout the delay. After 5 sec, the screen was removed, and the experimenter tapped both boxes. Once the toddler had looked to both containers, the caregiver released the toddler's hands, and the toddler was encouraged to find the toy.

As on the $\overline{AB}$ task for infants, once testing began, the box containing the toy was always moved to the same side until the toddler was correct twice in a row: then the box was moved to the other side and the procedure repeated. If a toddler was wrong on five trials in a row, only the box containing the toy was used on the next trial to help break the error string; this single-container trial was not included in analyses of performance during the session. On trials where toddlers reached to the wrong side or did not reach at all, the experimenter showed them where the toy had been but did not allow them to play with it. To try to maintain a constant level of interest in the toy, the toy was changed whenever the toddler seemed to be losing interest in it, although we tried not to change toys on reversal trials. The rules for the number of trials and number of reversals were identical to those for the infant $\overline{AB}$ task.

Toddlers from the general population were tested only once. For half these children the box containing the toy was moved to the right initially; for the other half it was moved to the left initially. For toddlers tested longitudinally, the box containing the toy was always moved to the left initially in session 1; in subsequent sessions the first side to which the box was moved alternated over sessions.

Whereas delay was incremented on the $\overline{AB}$ task as the infants got older to provide information on age-related improvements in the ability to withstand longer and longer delays, delay was held constant on the $\overline{AB}$ task with invisible displacement administered to toddlers to allow us to look at whether the ability to override the prepotent tendency to repeat the previously rewarded response improved over age.

Evidence Identifying the Neural Basis for Successful Performance

This task is similar to the $\overline{AB}$ task administered to infants, which has been demonstrated empirically to require the functions of dorsolateral prefrontal cortex. The neural basis for this version of the task, however, has yet to be empirically established.

The Three Boxes Task (Boxes Scrambled after Each Reach)

The three boxes task (boxes scrambled after each reach) is a working memory task requiring participants to keep track of which boxes they have already opened. All three boxes are baited; the participant's task is to find all three rewards in the least number of reaches. A brief delay is imposed after each reach. The boxes differ in color and shape. Since they are scrambled after each reach, memory of which boxes have already been searched must be based on the appearance of the boxes; spatial location is irrelevant.

43

Two sets of boxes were used. Each box was approximately 6 cm in length, 6 cm in width, and 5 cm in depth and was mounted on its own wooden base, measuring 14 cm in length, 14 cm in width, and 2 cm in depth. These bases enabled us to keep the boxes a constant 8 cm distance apart despite moving them after each reach. Each box was covered by a lid attached to the box by a string. From the toddler's vantage point, the most salient feature of each box was its lid. The boxes used for trial 1 were square and made of plastic. One was covered by a red wooden diamond, another by a yellow plastic circle, and the third by a blue rubber pentagon. All boxes were the same color as their lids. The boxes used for trials 2 and 3 were egg shaped and made of plastic; their lids were three-dimensional. One box was purple; its purple lid was molded into the shape of a rooster. Another box was yellow; its yellow lid was sculpted into the shape of a duck. The third box was pink; its pink lid had the shape of a rabbit. Each lid was approximately 5 cm high.

At the outset of each trial, the line of three boxes was positioned toward the rear of the testing table, out of reach of the toddler. The trial began with the toddler watching the experimenter open the lids of all three boxes and place a reward in each box. The rewards included small plastic animals, balls, dolls, or marbles. On any given trial, all rewards were the same—all balls, for example, or all animals. The experimenter then closed the three lids, pushed the boxes within reach of the toddler, and encouraged the toddler to choose a box.

As soon as the toddler retrieved the reward from the box, the experimenter re-covered the box and moved the line of boxes back to the rear of the table, and the assistant positioned a white opaque screen between the toddler and the boxes. A 5-sec delay was imposed, during which time the toddler and assistant played with the reward and the experimenter scrambled the boxes. The delay was timed from the moment there was no visible cue indicating which box the toddler had just opened (i.e., from the moment the experimenter replaced the box's lid). After 5 sec, the screen was removed, the experimenter moved the line of boxes to within reach, and the procedure described above was repeated. Each time, the experimenter encouraged the toddler to open another box and find another reward.

When a participant reached back to a box that had already been opened, the experimenter tilted the open box toward the toddler so that he or she could see that the box was truly empty. Since it was empty, the toddler had no reward to play with during the 5-sec delay. When necessary, the experimenter held the lids down so that the toddler could not open two boxes simultaneously or open a second immediately after the first. A trial ended when the child had retrieved all the rewards (opened all boxes) or after five errors in a row. An error consisted of reaching back to a previously opened box.

Evidence Identifying the Neural Basis for Successful Performance

This task was devised by Petrides, who has demonstrated that rhesus macaques with lesions of dorsolateral prefrontal cortex are impaired in its performance (Petrides, 1995). The prefrontally lesioned monkeys were impaired when three boxes were used but not when only two boxes were used. The impairment with three boxes was present whether the order in which the boxes were opened was externally imposed by the experimenter or chosen by the animal. Petrides designed this task for macaques to be similar to tasks linked to prefrontal cortex function in humans (Petrides, Alivisatos, Evans, & Meyer, 1993; Petrides & Milner, 1982). However, Owen, Morris, Sahakian, Polkey, and Robbins (1996) found that, when they presented adult participants with "boxes" on a computer screen, each of which looked different, and scrambled their position on the screen after each reach, patients with frontal lobe damage required no more reaches to "open" all the boxes than did control participants. All participants found this a very difficult memory test, not easily amenable to the use of a strategy or plan.

The Three Boxes Task (Boxes Remain Stationary)

The three boxes task (boxes remain stationary) is a working memory task requiring participants to keep track of what boxes or positions they have already chosen. All three boxes are baited; the participant's task is to find all three rewards in the least number of reaches. A brief delay is imposed after each reach. The boxes differ in color and shape. Since the boxes remain stationary here, memory of which boxes have already been searched can be based on the appearance of the boxes and/or their spatial locations. This task is very similar to the other version of the three boxes task described above. It differs only in that the boxes are not scrambled during the delay period; instead they remain stationary.

The boxes used here were round and made of plastic. The leftmost box was black with a triangular lid. The box at the center had an orange base and a tan-and-white checkered circular lid. The rightmost box had a white base and a square white-rimmed mirror for its lid. As above, the dimensions of each box were roughly $6 \times 6 \times 5$ cm, and each box was mounted on its own wooden base, which measured $14 \times 14 \times 2$ cm. The stationary trial was administered before the trials where the boxes were scrambled.

Evidence Identifying the Neural Basis for Successful Performance

The neural system required for successful performance on this condition of the task is unknown. However, when Petrides and Milner (M. Petrides,

45

personal communication, 1990) administered the task on which Petrides based the three boxes task to human adults, they found that, when the stimuli remained stationary, participants could solve the task using a simple spatial strategy and that participants with prefrontal cortex damage performed as well as control participants. On the basis of that finding, we reasoned that the stationary version of the three boxes task should not require prefrontal cortex involvement.

The Delayed Nonmatching to Sample Task

The delayed nonmatching to sample task is a test of recognition memory. As in the visual paired comparison task, each trial consists of a familiarization phase (where a single sample object is presented at the midline), a delay, and test phase (where the sample and a new object are presented to the right and left of midline). Unlike the visual paired comparison task, however, participants' responses are rewarded here, and participants thereby receive feedback about whether a response is correct.

The rewards were food (e.g., a Cheerio or raisin), marbles (which could be collected and rattled in a cup or rolled down a ramp), pennies (which could be placed in a windup bank), or tiny plastic animals (which could be collected or given a ride in a truck). The stimuli were novel junk objects; no object was ever used on more than one trial. The stimuli were arranged in fixed pairs, and all participants received the same object pairs in the same order. The left-right positions of the sample and novel object were varied pseudorandomly over trials according to the Gellerman series. Each stimulus was presented on a small wooden base (7.3 × 7.3 × 3.5 cm). Embedded in each base was a well (4 cm in diameter, 1.6 cm in depth), and the reward was hidden in the appropriate well. Each participant was seated in a toddler chair by a toddler-size testing table (70 × 65 × 50 cm [length × width × height]).

The testing procedure closely resembled that used with amnesic patients (Squire, Zola-Morgan, & Chan, 1988) and monkeys (e.g., Zola-Morgan, Squire, & Amaral, 1989). Like amnesic patients and monkeys, the toddlers were not told the principle determining which response would be correct. They were told only that we would hide a reward each time and that we wanted to see if they could find it.

Preceding each trial, out of view of the toddler behind an opaque screen, the experimenter hid a reward in both wells. The sample, with the well underneath it, was then positioned at the midline at the rear of the testing table. At the outset of each trial, the opaque screen was removed, and the experimenter pushed the sample object atop its well forward toward the child, encouraging the child to reach and retrieve the reward. After the child displaced the sample and retrieved the reward, the sample object and well were removed, the opaque screen lowered, and a delay imposed.

During the delay, out of sight of the child, a new object and the familiar sample, atop their wells, were positioned at the rear of the testing table, out of reach of the toddler. After the delay, the opaque screen was removed, and the experimenter presented the sample and novel objects atop their wells side by side at the midline on the far side of the table. Once it was clear that the toddler had seen both stimuli, the stimuli and their wells were pushed forward diagonally, one to the left and one to the right (7.5 cm from midline), so that they were equidistant from the toddler and just barely within reach. The stimuli were kept at this distance to discourage the toddler from reaching simultaneously for both objects. When the toddler displaced the new object (the one that did not match the sample), a reward was revealed underneath it that he or she could have. When the object matching the sample was displaced, the toddler found nothing hidden underneath. On such occasions, the experimenter showed the toddler where the reward had been, but he or she was not allowed to have the reward. Participants were not told the rule (reach to the novel, nonmatching object); they had to deduce it.

In each session, the participant was first trained on the basic task using a 5-sec delay, as is done with amnesic patients. These trials continued until the participant was correct on five in a row. The delay was then incremented to 30 sec for the remainder of the 25 trials per session. The intertrial interval was approximately 10 sec. Two new stimuli were used on every trial. Therefore, 50 novel, junk objects were needed per testing session. We were able to come up with 100 such objects and so had to limit the number of sessions in which delayed nonmatching to sample could be administered. We began delayed nonmatching to sample testing at 21 months because both we (Diamond, Towle, & Boyer, 1994) and Overman, Bachevalier, Turner, and Peuster (1992) had found that most children do not begin to perform well on the task until about 21 months of age. At 21 and 24 months of age, the task was administered with test stimuli the children had never seen before; at 27 months, the stimulus set that had been used at 21 months was readministered. We analyzed the data both including and excluding the data at 27 months.

The reason for using a nonmatching rather than a matching to sample rule is that infants and young children (e.g., Cohen & Gelber, 1975; Fagan 1970, 1973; Fantz, 1964), like monkeys (Brush, Mishkin, & Rosvold, 1961; Gaffan, Gaffan, & Harrison, 1984; Harlow, 1950; Mishkin, Prockop, & Rosvold, 1962), have a natural preference for novelty, and this version of the task is therefore much easier for them to learn than delayed matching to sample (Brush et al., 1961; Gaffan et al., 1984; Harlow, 1950; Mishkin et al., 1962). The task was conceived as a straightforward measure of recognition

47

memory for objects. The rationale was that, given this demonstrated preference for novelty, if participants remember the sample, they will want to reach
for the new object rather than the familiar sample.

Evidence Identifying the Neural Basis for Successful Performance

Ablation of the medial temporal lobe (especially perirhinal and entorhinal cortex) impairs delayed nonmatching to sample performance in adult
monkeys (e.g., Meunier, Bachevalier, Mishkin, & Murray, 1993; Mishkin,
1978; Suzuki, Zola-Morgan, Squire, & Amaral, 1993; Zola-Morgan et al.,
1989), infant monkeys (Bachevalier & Mishkin, 1984), and human adults amnesic because of medial temporal lobe damage (Squire et al., 1988). Indeed,
delayed nonmatching to sample is one of the classic tests used to study medial
temporal lobe function in macaques. Ablation of dorsolateral prefrontal cortex does not impair performance on this task (Bachevalier & Mishkin, 1986).

Lesions of the medial temporal lobe do not disrupt performance at delays under 15–30 sec. The medial temporal lobe is not required to hold information in mind very briefly. Participants with lesions of the medial temporal
lobe perform progressively worse as the delay between the sample presentation and the test portions of a trial is increased; hence, it is the memory
aspects of the task that appear to require the medial temporal lobe structures.
Although these participants appear to understand and remember the rule
for correct performance on the task, they appear to have difficulty remembering what the sample stimulus had been, especially with delays of 60 sec or
longer.

The developmental progression that has been charted in children on
the delayed nonmatching to sample task pertains primarily to coming to act
consistently in accord with the nonmatching rule at the 5- or 10-sec training
delay. It is unlikely that recognition memory is the limiting factor here (*a*)
because toddlers can remember all manner of things for far longer than 5
or 10 sec well before 21 months of age and (*b*) because, once toddlers succeed on delayed nonmatching to sample at the 5-sec delay, they usually perform comparably at the longer 30-sec delay within the very same session (e.g.,
Diamond, Towle, & Boyer, 1994).

This pattern of behavior (extraordinary difficulty in mastering the task
even with extremely brief delays and the absence of any effect of increasing
delays once participants succeed at the brief, training delay) is seen in monkeys after lesions of ventrolateral prefrontal cortex (the inferior convexity)
(Kowalska, Bachevalier, & Mishkin, 1991). Even with extensive preoperative
training, so that all the animals had to do was remind themselves of the rules
underlying the task, monkeys with lesions of the inferior convexity succeeded
at the brief training delay only after over 700 retraining trials. Normal con-

trols, with the same amount of previous training, needed no retraining to succeed. However, once the monkeys with ventrolateral prefrontal cortex lesions passed criterion at the training delay, they performed as well as the normal control animals at all the longer delays.

Churchland and Diamond (1996) have proposed that the critical late-maturing competence, which may depend on ventrolateral prefrontal cortex, is the ability to grasp the relation between stimulus and reward, to understand the role of the stimulus as a marker or symbol for the reward's location. When the stimulus itself is the reward (Diamond, 1990c, 1995), when the reward is physically attached to the stimulus (Churchland & Diamond, 1996), or when the stimulus and the reward are separate but the act of moving the stimulus produces the reward directly and immediately (Diamond & Lee, in preparation), infants in the first year of life can learn the delayed nonmatching to sample rule.

The Global-Local Spatial Processing Task
(Using the Preferential Looking Technique)

The global-local spatial processing task (using the preferential looking technique) assesses visual attention to the global outline of a stimulus and to the smaller items of which the stimulus is composed. Each trial consisted of four parts: (1) a composite stimulus (e.g., an *H* made up of *S*'s or an arrow made up of stars) presented for 2–3 sec; (2) the global or local component of that stimulus paired with something else (e.g., an *H* and a *V*), with their right-left position reversed after 3 sec; (3) the composite stimulus presented again momentarily to remind the child what it looked like; and (4) the other component of the composite stimulus paired with something new (e.g., an *S* and a *G*), with right-left position again reversed after 3 sec. The dependent measure was the percentage of time the child fixated each member of the stimulus pairs in parts 2 and 4. This is a control task; it requires little working memory or inhibitory control.

At the start of each trial, the toddler was shown a familiarization card, 60 cm away, for 2–3 sec. The familiarization stimulus, or model, consisted of a hierarchical, composite figure (Martin, 1979; Navon, 1977; Robertson, Lamb, & Knight, 1991). The global stimuli ranged in size from 12 × 10 cm to 8 × 14 cm. The local stimuli were one-tenth that size.

The test phase followed immediately. There were two tests per trial (one for the local feature, one for the global feature), conducted by presenting a feature from the model to the right or left and a new stimulus on the other side. For the first test, the experimenter held up two cards, 60 cm from the toddler, about 30 cm apart, and lightly tapped the cards on the table to ensure that the toddler saw both. After 3 sec, the sides on which the two cards were held were switched, and the cards were presented for another 3 sec. The model was shown again briefly ($\leq$ 1 sec) and then removed. Then the second test was presented with another pair of test cards. After 3 sec, the sides on which the cards were presented were reversed. Five trials were presented within a session. The intertrial interval was 4 sec.

Trials were grouped into sets of 10; different sets were administered at different ages. Since there were two tests per trial, that meant 20 tests per set. The matching stimulus was on the right for 10 of these tests (five local, five global). Pictures were used on eight trials and letters on two. For the two letter trials, the global feature was tested first on one trial and the local feature first on the other. On both, the test stimuli were of medium size, and the correct choice was on the left for the first test and on the right for the second (counterbalancing global/local with side of correct choice). For the eight picture trials, the global feature was tested first on half the trials. The matching global stimulus appeared equally often on the right and left sides, as did the matching local stimulus. Of the four picture trials where the global feature was tested first, two trials used small test stimuli (opposite in size to the global feature in the model), and two used test stimuli of the same size as those in the model. The same counterbalancing was used for testing the local feature. (For an example of the first six trials in one of our trial sets, see Figure 1.)

Evidence Identifying the Neural Basis for Successful Performance

Damage to parietal cortex in human adults (e.g., Lamb, Robertson, & Knight, 1989; Robertson, Lamb, & Knight, 1988) impairs performance on the global-local task when a forced choice reaction time procedure is used (as we used with young children; see below). Patients with right hemisphere damage are impaired in global feature detection, whereas patients whose damage is in the left hemisphere of the brain are impaired in local feature detection (e.g., Lamb, Robertson, & Knight, 1990; Robertson & Delis, 1986). Similarly, in the intact brain, the same regions of parietal cortex (the superior parietal lobule and the temporal-parietal juncture) identified by work with brain-damaged patients have been found to increase their activity during processing of the global and local elements of hierarchical objects, and the same hemispheric differences in the processing of the global-local elements have emerged as well (Shedden, Christoforou, Nahmias, Hahn, & Noll, 1997). Damage restricted to dorsolateral prefrontal cortex does not impair performance on the task (Robertson et al., 1991). The neural system involved in performance on the modified preferential looking version of the task administered to toddlers has yet to be empirically determined.

Model   Test 1   Test 2

FIGURE 1.—Examples of the stimuli used for the global-local spatial processing task

The Delayed Alternation Task

In the first year of the study, we administered an additional test, delayed alternation, to all participants 15–30 months of age, for a total of 20 tests in all. On this task, the testing table contained two embedded wells, which differed only in left-right location, as on the A$\overline{B}$ task. The participant had to learn to reach alternately to the two wells and had to remember to which well he or she had last reached over the delay between trials. The reward was always hidden in the well the participant had not reached to on the previous trial. We administered six practice trials, where the child saw the experimenter hide the toy and could then immediately retrieve it. After that, the hiding was done silently and out of view by an assistant positioned underneath the table. This enabled us to use intertrial intervals as brief as 2 sec.

Successful performance on this task has been linked to the integrity of prefrontal cortex by numerous ablation studies in macaques (e.g., Bättig et al., 1960; Jacobsen & Nissen, 1937; Kubota & Niki, 1971) and rats (Bubser & Schmidt, 1990; Larsen & Divac, 1978; Wikmark et al., 1973). Research using unit recordings has complemented this with demonstrations that, on trials where neurons within prefrontal cortex fire during the delay and sustain their firing throughout the delay, participants reach to the correct well on the task (Fuster, 1973; Fuster & Alexander, 1971; Kubota & Niki, 1971; Niki, 1974). Moreover, we used this task with our animal model of early and continuously treated PKU (Diamond, Ciaramitaro, et al., 1994), and we very much wanted to have evidence of the performance of PKU children, and of our rodent model, on the same task. Our initial results indicated that PKU children whose Phe levels were moderately elevated were performing significantly worse than the other groups of children, just as we had predicted.

We dropped this task, however, for two reasons. First, the hallmark of what one finds following ablation of prefrontal cortex on the delayed alternation task, or on A$\overline{B}$ or other similar tasks, is that prefrontally lesioned participants are able to learn the task normally when no delay is imposed but fail when a delay is introduced. What we found was that PKU children whose Phe levels were moderately elevated were impaired at learning the task, at figuring out that they were supposed to alternate reaching to the right and left wells. To report that these children were impaired on this task, known to require the functions of prefrontal cortex, might have led people mistakenly to conclude that the children failed because of problems in the prefrontal neural circuit.

Second, there was an important difference in how we had to administer this task to children and how the task is always administered to animals, a difference that we felt made it impossible to compare performance across species and that made us concerned about how well any of the toddlers understood what was required on the task. When monkeys, rats, or other animals are tested, they are tested every day. Gradually, over days and sometimes weeks, they figure out the alternation rule. We tested our participants only once at each age; for toddlers, testing sessions were 3 months apart. Animals do not learn the task in a single session, and neither did most of our toddlers. In addition, the toy mysteriously appearing first in one well and then in the other understandably struck the toddlers as strange, and it was often difficult to coax them to complete the delayed alternation testing.

PROCEDURES FOR THE COGNITIVE NEUROPSYCHOLOGICAL TESTS ADMINISTERED TO YOUNG CHILDREN (3¹/₂–7 YEARS OF AGE)

The Day-Night Stroop-like Task

The day-night Stroop-like task (Gerstadt, Hong, & Diamond, 1994) requires participants to hold two rules in mind and to inhibit saying what the stimuli really represent; instead, they must say the opposite. When they see a picture of the sun, they are to say "night," and, when they see a picture of the moon and stars, they are to say "day."

Two training cards and 16 testing cards were used. All measured 13.5 × 10 cm. The front of half the cards was black with a moon and stars. The front of the other cards was white with a bright yellow sun (see Figure 2*a*). The experimenter instructed the participant to say "day" when shown the black moon card and to say "night" when shown the white sun card. A brief pretest followed.

On the pretest, the experimenter turned over a white sun card and waited for the child to respond with the proper word. If the participant hesitated, the experimenter prompted the child by saying, "What do you say for this one?" If the participant responded correctly, the experimenter praised the child and proceeded to a practice trial with the black moon card. If the participant responded correctly again, the experimenter praised the child, and these first two trials were then counted as trials 1 and 2 of testing. If the participant responded incorrectly or did not respond at all on either of these trials, these two trials were counted as practice, and the experimenter reminded the participant of both rules, beginning with the card the child had identified incorrectly. Then the pretest began again. If the participant was wrong on either of these two pretest trials, the instruction and pretest procedure was repeated one last time. Then testing began.

A participant needed to have answered each rule correctly at least once during practice or during trials 1 and 2 for the session to be counted as usable. That is, we needed to see some evidence early on that the child understood what we were asking. The reason we counted early practice trials, if answered correctly, as part of testing was that children who readily grasped

53

a

 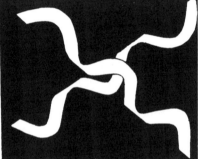

b

FIGURE 2.—The stimuli used for the day-night Stroop-like task. *a*, Cards used in the standard condition. Subjects were instructed to say "night" when shown the sun card and to say "day" when shown the moon and stars card. *b*, Cards used for the control condition. Half the subjects were instructed to say "night" when shown the checkerboard card and half to say "day." Likewise, half the subjects were instructed to say "day" when shown the squiggle card and half to say "night."

what we were asking became very bored if we tried to give them much practice.

Sixteen trials were administered in which eight "day" cards and eight "night" cards were presented according to a pseudorandom sequence, with no more than three "day" or "night" cards in a row. During these trials, no feedback was given to the participant. The dependent variables were response accuracy and latency. Response latency was measured from the time the child first saw the "day" or "night" card until he or she gave a verbal response.

It was coded from the videotape, and intercoder reliability was .88. For those children tested longitudinally, this test was administered at every age except 4 years, when the control version was administered instead. (A description of the control version is given below.) For participants from the general population, who were tested only once, we were able to administer this version even at 4 years; 20 4-year-olds from the general population were tested on this condition, and another 20 4-year-olds from the general population were tested on the control condition.

Evidence Identifying the Neural Basis for Successful Performance

In the standard Stroop test, the names of colors are printed in ink of another color (e.g., the word *blue* is printed in red ink), and participants are instructed to report the color of the ink. This requires that participants keep that instruction in mind and inhibit their customary tendency when reading, which is to ignore the ink in which a word is printed and instead attend to the word's meaning. Perret (1974) reported that adults with damage to dorsolateral prefrontal cortex fail the Stroop test. Frontal patients tend to revert to reciting the words rather than naming the color of the ink or take much longer to make the correct response. Others have replicated this finding in patients with large frontal lobe removals (e.g., Richer, Decary, Lapierre, Rouleau, & Bouvier, 1993). Neuroimaging studies have consistently found higher regional cerebral blood flow in the anterior cingulate during Stroop test performance (Bench et al., 1993; Casey, Cohen, Noll, Forman, & Rapoport, 1993; Pardo, Pardo, Janer, & Raichle, 1990), although Bench et al. (1993) also found activation in orbitofrontal cortex and the frontal pole, which led them to conclude that there is widespread activation of frontal regions during performance of the task. Note, however, that neither the anterior cingulate nor orbitofrontal cortex is part of dorsolateral prefrontal cortex.

We did not administer the standard Stroop test. There is no empirical evidence yet of the neural basis for success on our task. We have hypothesized that our task would be more likely to require the functions of dorsolateral prefrontal cortex than the standard Stroop test. The latter places a heavy demand on inhibitory control, but its demand on working memory is minimal; all participants remember that they are supposed to report the color of the ink. While our day-night task still places a heavy demand on inhibitory control, it requires that participants keep two rules in mind. We hoped in this way to tax seriously both working memory and inhibitory control in young children. Patients with damage to "nonmedial" frontal cortex are impaired when asked to remember two rules that require that they act contrary to their natural inclination—press a blue key when a red light appears, and press a red key when a blue light appears (Drewe, 1975). Continuous performance tasks, such as the "two-back" test, which require memory of a rule plus inhibition of a prepotent response, consistently elicit activation of dorsolateral prefrontal cortex in neuroimaging studies (e.g., Cohen et al., 1994). On the two-back test, participants must remember a rule such as, "Respond when, and only when, you see an *x* that follows two items after an *a*," and they must resist the temptation to respond when they see an *x* under all other circumstances.

The Control Version of the Day-Night Stroop-like Task

The control version of the day-night Stroop-like task (Gerstadt et al., 1994) requires participants to hold two rules in mind, but it does not also require inhibition of the tendency to say what the stimuli really represent because the stimuli are abstract designs. Other than the stimuli on the cards, the procedure here was the same as for the regular version of the day-night task described above. Here, the front of half the cards had a red-and-blue checkerboard pattern. The front of the other cards had a blue background with two red squiggles that formed an *x* (see Figure 2*b*). This control version of the task was administered only at 4 years of age. Half the participants in the normative sample were told to say "day" when shown the squiggle card and half to say "night." For all children tested longitudinally, the instructions were to say "day" to the squiggle card and "night" to the checkerboard card.

Evidence Identifying the Neural Basis for Successful Performance

This has yet to be investigated.

The Tapping Task

The tapping task (Diamond & Taylor, 1996) requires the ability to hold two rules in mind and to inhibit the tendency to mimic the experimenter's actions, instead of doing the opposite. The rules for the task were as follows: Immediately after the experimenter tapped once with a wooden dowel (22.5 cm long, 2.5 cm in diameter), the child was to tap twice with the dowel. Immediately after the experimenter tapped twice, the child was to tap once.

The experimenter instructed the child in these rules, allowing the child to practice each rule immediately after the instruction. Then the experimenter administered a very brief pretest. She tapped once and handed the dowel to the child for a response. If the child was correct, the experimenter praised him or her. Then the experimenter tapped twice and handed the dowel to the child. If the child was correct again, he or she was praised, and these two trials counted as the first two trials of testing. If the child responded incorrectly on either of these trials, the experimenter reminded the child of both rules again after the two trials were over, explaining first the rule the child had executed incorrectly. Then testing began.

As it turns out, only the fastest learners succeeded in passing the pre-testing, although many of the other children went on to perform well above chance during testing. Because eliminating all the children who did not per-form well during the brief pretesting eliminated much of the variation among children, and because the testing performance of many of those who did not perform well during pretesting indicated that they understood the task instructions, we report the results here once with all the children included (even those who failed the pretest) and once for only the children who passed the pretest.

Each session consisted of a pseudorandom series of 16 trials, with no more than three of one kind in a row. On each trial, the experimenter tapped, then handed the dowel to the child for a response, after which the child returned the dowel to the experimenter. We used only one dowel for both the experimenter and the child so that neither the child nor the experi-menter would begin tapping before the other had finished. No feedback was given during testing.

Evidence Identifying the Neural Basis for Successful Performance

Adults with large frontal lobe lesions fail the tapping test (Luria, 1980). They have similar problems when instructed to raise their finger in response to the experimenter making a fist and to make a fist in response to the experi-menter raising a finger (Luria, 1980). Patients with large frontal lobe lesions also display related problems with inhibitory control and with holding two rules in mind (see the discussion of the neural basis for success on the day-night Stroop-like task).

Examples of problems with inhibitory control can be seen in the occa-sional automatic reaching of frontally damaged patients for a presented ob-ject, even if instructed not to do so, and even if they do not want the object: "Taking a pack of cigarettes, he hesitated a moment, then opened it and drew out a cigarette. He looked puzzled at it, being a nonsmoker" (L'Her-mitte, 1983, p. 246). Patients with damage to the frontal eye fields or the supplementary motor area have unusual difficulty inhibiting the normal ten-dency to look toward a cue on the antisaccade task (Guitton, Buchtel, & Douglas, 1985; O'Driscoll et al., 1995).

Difficulty in holding two things in mind can be seen when a person with frontal lobe damage is given two instructions (e.g., clean the windshield and change the oil) or asked to solve a two-step math problem (e.g., Barbizet, 1970; Luria, 1980).

The Three Pegs Task

The three pegs task (Balamore & Wozniak, 1984) requires participants to remember a three-item sequence and to inhibit a natural response tendency. The child is shown a pegboard containing three pegs arranged in the order red, yellow, green. However, the child is asked to tap the pegs in the order red, green, yellow. This requires inhibiting the tendency to tap the pegs in their spatial order.

The children were pretested to make sure that they knew the color of each peg; any child who could not point to the correct peg when the experimenter said its color was not tested on the task in that session. Testing began with the "verbal instruction" condition. The experimenter said slowly and deliberately, "With the hammer, I want you to tap each peg one time, the red peg first, then the green peg, and then the yellow peg." The hammer was then given to the child. If the child tapped the pegs in the correct order, the child was praised and asked to do that again. The experimenter reminded the child of the instructions ("tap the red peg, then the green, then the yellow"). If the child was correct on this confirmation trial, testing ended.

If the child was wrong on the first trial or its confirmation, the "demonstration plus verbal instruction" condition was administered. The experimenter said, "Watch me. I would like you to tap the red peg, then the green peg, and then the yellow peg, like this, . . ." and demonstrated the order in which the pegs should be tapped as she spoke. Then she handed the hammer back to the child. If the child tapped the pegs in the correct order, the experimenter asked the child if he or she could do that again and repeated the instructions (without demonstration). If the child was correct on this confirmation trial, testing ended.

If the child was wrong after the experimenter's demonstration or on the confirmation trial, he or she was again given verbal instructions, shown what to do, and also asked to name each peg by color as he or she tapped it. The experimenter gave the instructions, "With the hammer, tap the red peg first, then the green peg, and then the yellow peg. But this time, I want you to *say* the colors at the same time you tap the pegs, like this, . . ." and then demonstrated. Then the experimenter returned the hammer to the child. If the child did not say "red" when tapping the first peg, the experimenter held the hammer briefly and reminded the child to say the color as he or she tapped. If the child tapped the pegs in the wrong order, testing ended here. If the child was correct, a confirmation trial was administered.

The children were allowed to correct themselves at almost any point during this task. For example, if a child started to tap the pegs in their spatial order but then changed and tapped the pegs in the order instructed, we proceeded to the confirmation trial. If the child was correct on the confirmation trial, the child was given credit for having succeeded at that level. If a child started to err on a confirmation trial and then corrected his or her mistake, the confirmation trial was administered again. A child needed to perform correctly, without self-correction, on this second confirmation trial to be given credit for having succeeded at that level.

Evidence Identifying the Neural Basis for Successful Performance

The neural basis for successful performance on this task has yet to be empirically determined.

Corsi-Milner Test of Temporal Order Memory

For the Corsi-Milner test of temporal order memory, participants are shown a series of pictures sequentially, each on its own card. Periodically, participants are shown a question card containing two pictures and are asked which of the two pictures they saw last. Thus, to answer correctly, participants must keep track of the order in which the stimuli were presented.

Before testing began, the child had to demonstrate understanding of the words *seen last*. During the pretesting period, the experimenter showed the child first one picture card, then another, and then a question card containing both pictures. The child was asked, "Which of these two pictures did you see last?" If the child pointed incorrectly, the experimenter explained the error. If the child pointed correctly, the experimenter cheered enthusiastically and put both picture cards back on the table anyway, saying, "That's right. I showed you this one first, and then I showed you this one last, so this is the one I showed you last, just like you said. That was right!" Whether the child was right or wrong, a second practice trial was administered. If the child responded incorrectly on either the first or the second practice trial, a third was administered. Children needed to be correct on two of these practice trials for their data in that session to be considered valid.

During testing, the child was shown a series of stimuli one at a time. At $3\frac{1}{2}$ years, and at yearly intervals thereafter, simple black-and-white line drawings of common objects served as the stimuli. Beginning at 4 years of age, and at every testing session near a child's birthday thereafter, colorful, complex abstract images (reproductions of museum artwork) served as the stimuli. Stimulus presentation time was approximately 1.5 sec for the simple line drawings and approximately 3 sec for the complex images. Through trial 30, a question card with two of the previously presented stimuli on it was shown to the child after every 10 trials, and he or she was asked, "Which of these pictures did you see last?" In addition, a question card was presented after trials 34 and 38. No feedback was given during testing.

Evidence Identifying the Neural Basis for Successful Performance

Researchers have found the performance of patients with frontal cortex excisions to be impaired on this task, despite performing well when tested on their recognition memory of other stimuli in the set (Corsi, 1972, cited in Milner, 1972; Milner, Corsi, & Leonard, 1991). Similarly, patients with frontal cortex damage are impaired in reproducing the order in which words are presented, although the patients performed within the normal range on recognition and recall of those words (Shimamura, Janowsky, & Squire, 1990). Shimamura et al. also found that frontal patients were impaired at reconstructing the chronological order of public events that occurred between 1941 and 1985. Finally, McAndrews and Milner (1991) found that adults with frontal cortex excisions were impaired at remembering the order in which objects had been shown to them unless they were instructed to act on each object—told, for example, to "squeeze the sponge"—in which case they performed normally.

On the other hand, Mangels (1997) reports that frontal patients in her study performed no worse than control participants at remembering the order in which a series of unrelated words had been presented but were impaired at remembering the order in which a series of related words had been presented. Control participants appeared to use strategies to remember the order of presentation of the related words, while frontal patients did not.

The Corsi-Milner Test of Recognition Memory

For the Corsi-Milner test of recognition memory, participants are shown a series of pictures, each on its own card. Periodically, participants are shown a question card containing two pictures, one of which was previously presented, and asked if they recognize which one they have already seen.

Before testing began, the child had to demonstrate understanding of the words *already seen*. The experimenter showed the child one picture card, then another, and then a question card containing two pictures, one of which the child had just seen and one he or she had not seen. The child was asked, "Out of these two pictures, which one have I already shown you?" The child was corrected if wrong and received enthusiastic praise if correct. If the child was correct, the experimenter put both of the picture cards the child had been shown back on the table anyway, saying, "That's right. I showed you these two cards, and this one matches that one, so this is the one you already saw, just like you said. That was right!" Whether the child was right or wrong, a second practice trial was administered. For the second practice trial, and for the rest of the testing session, the experimenter used the phrasing, "Out of all the pictures I've shown you, which one have you already seen?" If the child responded incorrectly on either the first or the second practice trial, a third was administered. Children needed to be correct on two of these practice trials for their data in that session to be considered valid.

The recognition memory condition of the Corsi-Milner test was administered at the same time as the temporal order condition. The stimuli and presentation times were exactly the same as described above for the temporal order condition. Short-term recognition memory was tested after trials 15, 25, 32, 36, and 40.

Because of concern that ceiling effects might obscure potential group differences, beginning in the second year of the study we introduced another set of 10 recognition memory questions that were administered after a 25-min delay filled by the administration of other tests.

Evidence Identifying the Neural Basis for Successful Performance

Patients who have had portions of their medial temporal lobes removed are impaired on this task (Corsi, 1972, cited in Milner, 1972; Milner et al., 1991). They have difficulty recognizing the previously seen stimulus on the question card. It is a well-replicated finding that patients who are amnesic owing to medial temporal lobe damage have great difficulty recognizing stimuli they have seen previously (e.g., Shimamura et al., 1990; Squire & Shimamura, 1986).

The Six Boxes Task (Boxes Scrambled after Each Reach)

The six boxes task (boxes scrambled after each reach) is a working memory task requiring participants to keep track of which boxes they have already opened. It is very much like the three boxes task administered to toddlers (described above), except that twice as many boxes are used. On both tasks, the boxes differed in appearance; the child saw that all boxes were baited; the child was allowed to reach to any box in any order but was permitted to open only one at a time; a delay was imposed between reaches, during which time the boxes were scrambled; and the child was penalized—by finding no reward—for reaching back to a previously opened box. Perfect performance consisted of opening all the boxes in the least number of reaches (i.e., without repeating a choice).

Plastic soap boxes (10.0 × 6.0 × 3.0 cm) were individually attached to wooden bases (14.9 × 11.5 × 1.9 cm) to preserve a constant distance of 5.5 cm between adjacent boxes in each row. The boxes were aligned in two horizontal rows of three boxes each. The size of the entire array was 45.7 × 23.1 cm. Different colored stickers arranged in diverse spatial patterns decorated the lids of the boxes. The boxes for trial 1 were yellow, those for trial 2 white, and different stickers in different patterns were used to decorate the lids of the boxes on the two trials.

At the start of each trial, the child chose six stickers and watched as the experimenter placed a sticker in each box and then closed all six lids. The boxes were then pushed forward toward the child, and the child was encouraged to find a sticker. As soon as the child retrieved a sticker from a box, the experimenter re-covered the box and slid all the boxes back to the rear of the table. If a child reached to a previously opened box, the experimenter tipped the open box forward to show the child that it was empty, saying things like, "That's too bad," or, "There's nothing in there," in a sad, disappointed tone; the box was then re-covered and all boxes slid back. The delay period of 10 sec began from the moment the opened box was re-covered (i.e., from when there was no visible cue indicating which box had been opened).

During all delay periods, unseen by the child, the experimenter scrambled the boxes according to a set protocol. During the first delay period, the assistant handed the child a piece of paper to make a picture with the retrieved sticker and, during that and subsequent delay periods, talked with the child about the picture as he or she added the newly retrieved sticker to the emerging picture. Whenever the child chose incorrectly, the assistant counted to 10 with the child to fill the delay period or talked with him or her about the stickers that had already been found and fastened to the page. At the end of the 10-sec delay period, the experimenter moved the boxes back within reach and encouraged the child to open another box and find another sticker. A trial ended when a child found all the rewards (opened all boxes) or reached incorrectly five times in a row. An error consisted of reaching back to a previously opened box. This was a particularly popular task because the children loved making pictures with the stickers.

Evidence Identifying the Neural Basis for Successful Performance

This task is similar to the three boxes task (Petrides, 1995), which has been linked to prefrontal cortex function in rhesus macaques, and to the self-ordered pointing task, which has been linked to prefrontal cortex function in human adults (Petrides, 1993; Petrides & Milner, 1982), but the neural system underlying successful performance on this particular version of the task has yet to be investigated. See the discussion presented above of the neural system required for the three boxes task (boxes scrambled after each reach).

The Six Boxes Task (Boxes Remain Stationary)

The six boxes task (boxes remain stationary) is a working memory task requiring participants to keep track of which boxes or positions they have already chosen. All boxes are baited; the participant's task is to find all the rewards in the least number of reaches. A brief delay is imposed after each reach. Each box has different stickers arranged in distinctive patterns on the box lid. Since the boxes remain stationary here, memory of which boxes have already been searched can be based on the appearance of the boxes and/ or their spatial locations.

This task is very similar to the comparable three boxes task administered to toddlers and to the six boxes task (boxes scrambled after each reach) that was also administered to children 3½–7 years old. The only differences between this version of the six boxes task and that described above were that, on this version, (a) the boxes were not scrambled during the delay period but remained stationary and (b) a different set of boxes was used, red soap boxes with a third set of stickers arranged in new and different patterns on the lids. The stationary trial was administered before the trials where the boxes were scrambled.

Evidence Identifying the Neural Basis for Successful Performance

The neural system required for successful performance on this condition of the task is unknown. However, when Petrides and Milner (1982) administered a similar task to human adults, they found that, when the stimuli remained stationary, participants could solve the task using a simple spatial strategy and that participants with prefrontal cortex damage performed as well as control participants (M. Petrides, personal communication, 1990). On the basis of that finding, we reasoned that the stationary version of the six boxes task should not require prefrontal cortex involvement.

The Global-Local Spatial Processing Task (Forced Choice Procedure)

The global-local spatial processing task (forced choice procedure) requires attention to the global outline of a stimulus and to the smaller items of which the stimulus is composed, just as in the global-local task administered to toddlers. Children are shown the composite stimulus (e.g., an *H* made up of *S*'s) for 2 sec. Then they are shown the global or local component of that stimulus paired with something else (e.g., an *H* and a *V*) and are asked

63

to point, as fast as they can, to the choice that looks like that first picture or that looks like things that were in that first picture. Then the children are shown the other component of the model paired with something else (e.g., an *S* and a *G*) and are again asked to point. This is a control task; it requires neither memory nor self-control.

The same stimuli and order of presentation used for the first two sessions administered to toddlers (see above) were used here within a single session and on all sessions, supplemented by two additional trials to make a total of 12 trials per session. The added test pairs were opposite in size from the corresponding feature in the model, with the result that there were four trials each where the test stimuli were the same size as, medium in size in relation to, and opposite in size from the corresponding feature in the model. Pictures served as the stimuli on nine trials and letters on only two because many of the children were first learning to read and were distracted by letter stimuli.

Participants were instructed to keep their hands in a constant starting position on all trials, marked by the outline of two hands cut out of red paper and placed in front of the testing apparatus. A computerized board with two buttons was used to present the cards. The board was portable (being battery powered) and contained three light-emitting-diode (LED) six-digit counter modules that were driven by a 1-msec crystal-controlled time base. This apparatus permitted standard presentation time and stimulus placement and yielded an accurate millisecond record of stimulus presentation time and participant reaction time.

When the experimenter placed the model card on the display board, an infrared photobeam was broken, starting a timer. When the card was removed, the photobeam was restored, stopping the timer. The internal logic then automatically switched to the test 1 counter and illuminated the LED next to that display. When the experimenter inserted the card displaying the two stimuli for test 1 for that trial, the photobeam was again broken, starting the timer and simultaneously activating the participant's right and left response buttons. When the participant pressed one of these buttons, an LED indicator to the right or left was illuminated, and the timer stopped. When the experimenter removed the card, the unit automatically switched to the test 2 counter. Again, when the experimenter inserted the test card, the photobeam was broken, starting the timer and activating the response buttons. When the participant responded, an indicator to the right or left was illuminated, and the timer stopped. On removal of the card for the second and last test for a trial, the apparatus automatically reset itself. If during either of the tests the participant did not respond within 20 sec, the card containing the two stimuli was removed, thereby stopping the timer.

Participants received two training trials with correction in each session before testing began. The model (a hierarchical stimulus, such as a triangle made up of circles) was presented for 2 sec (timed automatically in milliseconds by the breaking of the photobeam). One practice trial was administered with this composite stimulus visible throughout, the other with the model removed from view after 2 sec, the procedure followed during testing. Before each test, participants were reminded to look at both stimuli and to have their hands in the starting position (on the red hands in front of the choice buttons). For each test, participants were asked to press the button in front of the choice that looked like the picture they saw (for global feature tests), or that was in the picture they saw (for local feature tests), as fast as they could. The apparatus automatically recorded presentation time of the choice stimulus card, response latency, and response choice.

For the two letter trials, the global feature was tested first on one trial, the local on the other. On both, choice stimuli were of medium size, and the correct choice was on the left for the first test and the right for the second (counterbalancing global/local with side of correct choice). For the 10 picture trials, half tested the global (or local) feature first. The correct global (and local) answer appeared equally often on the right and left sides. Size of choice stimuli was counterbalanced.

No feedback was given during testing. The intertrial interval was 5 sec. Accuracy and response latency were the dependent measures. Response times and choices were recorded by the computer and verified by coding from the videotape.

Evidence Identifying the Neural Basis for Successful Performance

Damage to parietal cortex in human adults (e.g., Lamb et al., 1989; Robertson et al., 1988) impairs performance on this task, and parietal cortex is activated during performance of this task in normal adults (Shedden et al., 1997). (See the discussion of the neural basis for success on the toddler version of the global-local task.) Damage restricted to dorsolateral prefrontal cortex does not appear to impair performance on the task (Robertson et al., 1991).

The Line Bisection Task

Line bisection is a spatial perception task. Our procedure for administering this task followed the general form of that used by other researchers. Participants were given twelve sheets of paper (each $8\frac{1}{2} \times 14$ inches, oriented horizontally) with lines drawn on them and asked to find the midpoints of the lines. The pages were presented one at a time, one line per page. The lines varied in length and position on the page. The child was asked to put a mark at the middle of each line as the sheets were presented. The experimenter demonstrated the procedure once before testing, and no feedback was given. This is a control task; it requires neither memory nor self-control.

Evidence Identifying the Neural Basis for Successful Performance

This is a classic test for the assessment of parietal cortex function in adult patients (e.g., Kolb & Whishaw, 1985, pp. 388–394; Warrington, James, & Kinsbourne, 1966). Adults with parietal cortex damage have unusual difficulty finding the centers of the lines.

IV. RESULTS: PHENYLALANINE LEVELS AND IQ

PLASMA LEVELS OF PHENYLALANINE

While some PKU children on diet and some MHP children had Phe levels between 6 and 10 mg/dl, one possibility might have been for the MHP children's Phe levels to be closer to 6 mg/dl and for the PKU children's Phe levels to be closer to 10 mg/dl. However, the results show almost the opposite. At all ages (except the first month of life), whether Phe levels were calculated during the period immediately preceding testing, during the entire year, or any other way, the mean Phe levels of the MHP children with Phe levels between 6 and 10 mg/dl were always higher than the mean Phe levels of the PKU children with Phe levels in the same range, although this difference was never significant. For example, the mean concurrent Phe levels were 7.13 and 6.47 mg/dl for the infant MHP and PKU participants, 8.27 and 7.95 for the toddlers, and 8.83 and 7.41 for the $3^{1}/_{2}$–7-year-olds, respectively (see Table 4 above). The comparable means of the MHP and PKU children with Phe levels under 6 mg/dl were 4.70 and 4.47 mg/dl for the infants, 4.51 and 4.33 mg/dl for the toddlers, and 4.35 and 4.30 mg/dl for the $3^{1}/_{2}$–7-year-olds, respectively; here, too, there were no significant differences.

IQ TEST PERFORMANCE

All children had IQs of 80 or more. Even so, IQ was inversely related to the mean level of Phe in a child's bloodstream during the years that IQ was tested. The Pearson correlation between IQ and mean Phe level was significant among children with PKU and also among children with MHP ($r = -.54$, $p < .05$, and $r = -.56$, $p < .05$, respectively). PKU children whose plasma Phe levels were toward the high end of the range that has been considered safe (6–10 mg/dl) had significantly lower IQs than their matched controls ($\overline{X} = 90.4$, SD = 7.8, and $\overline{X} = 110.0$, SD = 11.5, respectively; $F[4, 45] = 5.57$, $p = .001$; orthogonal contrast: high PKU vs. controls = 21.09, $p <$

.0001). They also tended to have lower IQs than other PKU children whose plasma Phe levels were closer to normal ($\bar{X}$ = 104.2, SD = 12.8, orthogonal contrast: high PKU vs. low PKU = 7.47, p < .01), although the latter difference did not reach our cutoff of p < .005. PKU children whose Phe levels were under 6 mg/dl generally obtained IQ scores that were intermediate between those of other PKU children with Phe levels of 6–10 mg/dl and those of matched controls.

There was no significant difference in IQ between the children with PKU and the children with MHP controlling for plasma Phe level. The average IQ score of MHP children whose plasma Phe levels were 6–10 mg/dl was 100.5 (SD = 9.2), intermediate between those of PKU children with comparable Phe levels and the other groups of children. The average IQ score of MHP children with lower plasma Phe levels was 109.3 (SD = 3.8).

Girls had significantly higher IQs than boys ($F[1, 45]$ = 4.12, p < .05). There was no significant gender × group interaction. The sex difference was smallest, however, among children with PKU.

OVERVIEW OF THE STRUCTURE OF THE RESULTS CHAPTERS THAT FOLLOW

The results for each behavioral task are organized so that the performance of children with higher Phe levels (PKU and MHP children combined), children with lower Phe levels (PKU and MHP combined), children from the general population, matched controls, and siblings of the higher-Phe PKU and MHP children are compared first. Age-related changes in performance are also discussed in this initial section. For each task, this section is titled "Group Differences: PKU and MHP Groups Combined."

The next section under each dependent measure for each task is titled "Group Differences: PKU and MHP Groups Analyzed Separately." Here, results for PKU children are compared to those for the MHP children, and the analyses reported in the first section for the PKU and MHP groups combined are reported now for the two groups separately (e.g., just among PKU participants, did those children with higher Phe levels perform worse than other PKU children with lower Phe levels, MHP children with higher Phe levels, children from the general population, matched controls, and siblings?). Analyses for Phe level as a continuous variable are also reported here, both within the PKU and MHP groups individually and combined. In the final section for each dependent measure for each task, any differences in the performance of boys and girls are reported.

V. RESULTS: INFANTS

THE AB̄ TASK

Group Differences: PKU and MHP Groups Combined

There was a clear improvement in performance on the AB̄ task as infants grew older ($F[1, 340] = 435.64$, $p < .0001$; see Figure 3). PKU and MHP infants with higher plasma Phe concentrations (i.e., with Phe levels in the 6–10 mg/dl range) could not withstand delays as long as could infants in the normative sample ($F[4, 339] = 12.68$, $p < .0001$; orthogonal contrast: higher Phe vs. norms = 15.50, $p = .0001$; see Figure 3 and Table 7). These higher-Phe infants also tended to perform worse than matched controls and their own siblings, although these differences were not significant at $p < .005$ (see Table 7). Data are plotted in Figure 3 beginning at 9 months because almost none of the infants with higher Phe levels could uncover a hidden object until that age and hence could not be tested on the AB̄ task until then. There was no significant difference between the performance of PKU and MHP infants with Phe levels of 6–10 mg/dl and that of PKU and MHP infants with Phe levels under 6 mg/dl. As a group, even the PKU and MHP infants who had low plasma Phe levels performed significantly worse than the normative sample (orthogonal contrast: lower Phe vs. norms = 35.05, $p < .0001$).

Among PKU and MHP infants with plasma Phe levels under 6 mg/dl, there was a significant difference in AB̄ performance by whether the infants' Phe levels remained stably down or whether their Phe levels showed wide swings from high to low levels ($F[5, 338] = 13.70$, $p < .0001$; orthogonal contrast: low stable vs. low jump = 18.32, $p < .0001$; see Figure 4). Infants whose Phe concentrations remained stably under 6 mg/dl performed comparably to the normative sample, matched controls, and siblings. However, infants whose mean Phe levels were also under 6 mg/dl, but who had a number of individual Phe readings of 6 mg/dl or more, performed comparably to the infants whose Phe levels remained at 6 mg/dl or higher and significantly worse than the normative sample (orthogonal contrast = 48.30, $p < .0001$),

69

The AB̄ Task

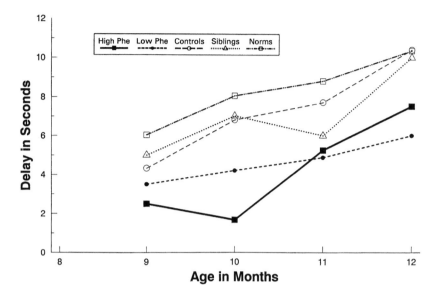

FIGURE 3.—Performance on the AB̄ task of infants in the five subject groups

matched controls (orthogonal contrast = 15.82, p = .0001), and siblings (orthogonal contrast = 17.25, p < .0001; see Figure 5). By 10 months of age, when all other groups of infants had reached delays of roughly 6 sec, infants with higher Phe levels, and infants with low mean Phe levels that masked erratic swings, had reached delays of only 2–3 sec. Thus, performance on the AB̄ task was depressed in those infants (N = 3) whose plasma Phe levels showed pronounced peaks and valleys, even if their plasma Phe levels were kept low on average. On the other hand, those infants (N = 4) whose Phe levels were kept stably between 2 and 6 mg/dl performed well on the AB̄ task. Stability, as well as the mean, of plasma Phe level appeared to be important here.

This effect is also reflected in analyses based on the area outside the 2–6 mg/dl range under the curve of each child's Phe levels. PKU and MHP infants with more than 20% of the area under their Phe curve outside the 2–6 mg/dl range performed significantly worse on the AB̄ task than other PKU and MHP infants whose Phe concentrations remained stably within the 2–6 mg/dl range and significantly worse than the normative sample, matched controls, and siblings ($F[4, 340]$ = 14.20, p < .0001; orthogonal contrasts: outside range vs. inside range = 11.49, p < .001; outside range vs. norms = 51.41, p < .0001; outside range vs. controls = 11.46, p < .001; outside range vs. siblings = 12.66, p < .0005).

The delay that infants could tolerate on the $\overline{AB}$ task between 8 and 12 months of age was also related to their mean plasma Phe levels during the first month of life. PKU and MHP infants whose mean Phe levels were 6 mg/dl or higher during this month performed significantly worse than the normative sample, matched controls, and siblings ($F[4, 339] = 13.46$, $p < .0001$; orthogonal contrasts: higher PKU vs. norms = 48.21, $p < .0001$; higher PKU vs. controls = 10.48, $p = .001$; higher PKU vs. siblings = 11.50, $p < .001$).

There were no significant differences among the $\overline{AB}$ performance of infants matched to the PKU and MHP participants, infants drawn from the general population, and the infant siblings of PKU and MHP participants.

Group Differences: PKU and MHP Groups Analyzed Separately

There were no significant differences in the $\overline{AB}$ performance of PKU and MHP infants, controlling for plasma Phe levels during the period immediately before each testing session. PKU infants whose mean plasma Phe levels during the period immediately preceding each testing session were 6–10 mg/dl performed significantly worse than the normative sample ($F[6, 337] = 8.75$, $p < .0001$; orthogonal contrast: higher PKU vs. norms = 13.53, $p < .0005$). (Values for the other orthogonal contrasts were as follows: higher PKU vs. controls = 4.38, $p < .02$; higher PKU vs. siblings = 4.20, $p = .02$; higher PKU vs. lower PKU = 3.62, $p = .06$.) MHP infants whose Phe levels were 6–10 mg/dl during the same period performed at levels between those of PKU infants with Phe levels 6–10 mg/dl and the control groups. The $\overline{AB}$ performance of these MHP infants with higher Phe levels did not differ significantly from that of any other group.

Similar results were obtained looking at the area under the curve. MHP infants whose Phe levels were outside the range of 2–6 mg/dl more than 20% of the time did not perform differently than PKU infants with comparable Phe profiles or any of the control groups.

The $\overline{AB}$ performance of PKU infants was inversely related to their mean Phe level during the period immediately before each testing session ($F[1, 6] = 6.28$, $p < .05$), their mean Phe level throughout the first year of life ($F[1, 6] = 6.29$, $p < .05$), the percentage of the area under their Phe curve outside the 2–6 mg/dl range ($F[1, 6] = 12.34$, $p < .03$), and their mean Phe level during the first month of life ($F[1, 6] = 19.33$, $p < .001$). Among MHP infants, $\overline{AB}$ performance was inversely related to mean Phe level throughout the first year of life ($F[1, 6] = 9.81$, $p < .03$), the percentage of the area under the Phe curve outside the 2–6 mg/dl range ($F[1, 6] = 9.21$, $p < .03$), and mean Phe level during the first month of life ($F[1, 6] = 9.79$, $p < .03$), but not to mean Phe level during the period immediately before each testing session. Within the same infant over time, the Pearson correlation of concur-

TABLE 7

SUMMARY OF THE RESULTS ON THE FOUR COGNITIVE NEUROPSYCHOLOGICAL TESTS ADMINISTERED TO INFANTS

	$A\overline{B}$ [Delay for $A\overline{B}$ Error]	
	{Concurrent Phe Level}	{% of Phe Levels w/in 2–6 Mg/Dl}
High Phe vs. low Phe	N.S.[a]	**, H < L
High Phe vs. norms	****, H < N	****, H < N
High Phe vs. controls	.025, H < C	**, H < C
High Phe vs. siblings	.03, H < S	***, H < S
Low Phe vs. norms	****, L < N[a]	N.S.
Low Phe vs. controls	.01, L < C[a]	N.S.
Low Phe vs. siblings	.01, L < S[a]	N.S.
Controls vs. norms	N.S.	N.S.
Controls vs. siblings	N.S.	N.S.
Siblings vs. norms	.01, S < N	.01, S < N
High PKU vs. low PKU	N.S.	***, H < L
High PKU vs. norms	***, H < N	****, H < N
High PKU vs. controls	.02, H < C	***, H < C
High PKU vs. siblings	.02, H < S	***, H < S
Low PKU vs. N, C, S	N.S.	N.S.

MHP vs. PKU	N.S.	N.S.
High MHP vs. high PKU	N.S.	N.S.
Low MHP vs. low PKU	N.S.	N.S.
High MHP vs. low MHP	N.S.	N.S.
High MHP vs. norms	N.S.	N.S.
High MHP vs. controls	N.S.	N.S.
High MHP vs. siblings	N.S.	N.S.
Low MHP vs. N, C, S	N.S.	N.S.
Other Phe measures showing a group difference	Mean Phe level during first month; % of levels w/in 2–6 mg/dl	Concurrent Phe level; mean Phe level during first month
Phe measures directly, inversely related to performance for PKU subjects	Concurrent Phe level; mean level during first month; mean level during first year; % of levels w/in 2–6 mg/dl	Concurrent Phe level; mean level during first month; mean level during first year; % of levels w/in 2–6 mg/dl
Phe measures directly, inversely related to performance for MHP subjects	Mean level during first month; mean level during first year; % of levels w/in 2–6 mg/dl	Mean level during first month; mean level during first year; % of levels w/in 2–6 mg/dl
Sex differences:		
PKU	.05, F < M	.05, F < M
MHP	.01, M < F	.01, M < F
Norms	****, M < F	****, M < F
Controls	***, M < F	***, M < F

TABLE 7 (*Continued*)

OBJECT RETRIEVAL.
[Highest Level at Which Child Succeeded]
[Concurrent Phe Level]

	Front of Box Open		Left or Right Side Open	
	Small Box	Large Box	Small Box	Large Box
High Phe vs. low Phe	****, H < L	.015, H < L	****, H < L	****, H < L
High Phe vs. norms	.015, H < N	****, H < N	****, H < N	.01, H < N
High Phe vs. controls	.01, H < C	N.S.	****, H < C	****, H < C
High Phe vs. siblings	***, H < S	*, H < S	****, H < S	****, H < S
Low Phe vs. norms	*, N < L	N.S.	N.S.	.02, N < L
Low Phe vs. controls	N.S.	N.S.	N.S.	N.S.
Low Phe vs. siblings	N.S.	N.S.	N.S.	N.S.
Controls vs. norms	N.S.	N.S.	N.S.	.04, N < C
Controls vs. siblings	N.S.	N.S.	N.S.	N.S.
Siblings vs. norms	.02, N < S	N.S.	N.S.	****, N < S
High PKU vs. low PKU	**, H < L	**, H < L	****, H < L	****, H < L
High PKU vs. norms	.035, H < N	N.S.	****, H < N	*, H < N
High PKU vs. controls	.015, H < C	N.S.	****, H < C	****, H < C
High PKU vs. siblings	*, H < S	*, H < S	****, H < S	****, H < S
Low PKU vs. N, C, S	N.S.	N.S.	N.S.	N.S.

Measure				
MHP vs. PKU	N.S.	N.S.	N.S.	N.S.
High MHP vs. high PKU	N.S.	N.S.	N.S.	****, M > P
Low MHP vs. low PKU	N.S.	N.S.	N.S.	N.S.
High MHP vs. low MHP	*, H < L	****, H < L	N.S.	*, H < L
High MHP vs. norms	N.S.	*, H < N	*, H < N	N.S.
High MHP vs. controls	.025, H < C	*, H < C	*, H < C	*, H < C
High MHP vs. siblings	*, H < S	**, H < S	****, H < S	****, H < S
Low MHP vs. N, C, S	N.S.	N.S.	N.S.	N.S.
Other Phe measures showing a group difference	Mean level throughout testing period	Mean level throughout testing period	Mean level throughout testing period; mean level during first month and first year omitting first month; % of levels w/in 2–6 mg/dl	Mean level throughout testing period; % of levels w/in 2–6 mg/dl
Phe measures directly, inversely related to performance for PKU subjects	Concurrent Phe level	Mean level throughout testing period	Mean level during first month; mean level during first year omitting first month; % of levels w/in 2–6 mg/dl	Concurrent Phe level; mean level throughout testing period
Phe measures directly, inversely related to performance for MHP subjects	Mean level during first month	Mean level during first month	Mean level during first month; mean level during first year omitting first month; % of levels w/in 2–6 mg/dl	Mean level during first month; mean level during first year omitting first month
Sex differences				
Among PKU	None	None		.03, F < M
Among siblings				
Among low Phe	**, F < M			*, F < M

TABLE 7 (*Continued*)

| | VISUAL PAIRED COMPARISON [% of Trials Where Novel Stimulus Was Chosen] | | |
SPATIAL DISCRIMINATION [% Correct] {Concurrent Phe Level}	At Briefest Presentation {Mean Phe Level during First Year of Life}	At Longest Delay {Concurrent Phe Level}	At Other Delays and Presentations {Concurrent Phe Level}
High Phe vs. low Phe	N.S.	N.S.	.02, H < L	N.S.
High Phe vs. norms	N.S.	N.S.	*, H < N	N.S.
High Phe vs. controls	N.S.	N.S.	N.S.	N.S.
High Phe vs. siblings	N.S.	N.S.	N.S.	N.S.
Low Phe vs. norms	N.S.	N.S.	N.S.	N.S.
Low Phe vs. controls	N.S.	N.S.	N.S.	N.S.
Low Phe vs. siblings	N.S.	N.S.	N.S.	N.S.
Controls vs. norms	N.S.	N.S.	N.S.	N.S.
Controls vs. siblings	N.S.	N.S.	N.S.	N.S.
Siblings vs. norms	.05, N < S	N.S.	.05, S < N	N.S.
High PKU vs. low PKU	N.S.	N.S.	.05, H < L	N.S.
High PKU vs. norms	N.S.	N.S.	.05, H < N	N.S.
High PKU vs. controls	N.S.	N.S.	N.S.	N.S.
High PKU vs. siblings	N.S.	N.S.	N.S.	N.S.
Low PKU vs. N, C, S	N.S.	N.S.	N.S.	N.S.

MHP vs. PKU	N.S.	N.S.	N.S.
High MHP vs. high PKU	N.S.	.05, M < P	N.S.
Low MHP vs. low PKU	N.S.	N.S.	N.S.
High MHP vs. low MHP	N.S.	.06, H < L	.01, H < L
High MHP vs. norms	N.S.	.05, H < N	.01, H < N
High MHP vs. controls	N.S.	.01, H < C	.04, H < C
High MHP vs. siblings	N.S.	.05, H < S	N.S.
Low MHP vs. N, C, S	N.S.	N.S.	N.S.
Other Phe measures showing a group difference		% of levels w/in 2–6 mg/dl: high MHP < C, N	Concurrent Phe level
Phe measures directly, inversely related to performance for PKU subjects		Mean level throughout testing period; % of levels w/in 2–6 mg/dl	
Phe measures directly, inversely related to performance for MHP subjects		Mean level during first year; mean level during first month; % of levels w/in 2–6 mg/dl	
Sex differences	None	None	None

NOTE.—Dependent measures are given in square brackets, plasma Phe measures in curly braces. H = high Phe (plasma Phe levels 6–10 mg/dl); N = norms (children from the general population); C = controls (matched controls for the PKU and MHP participants with higher plasma Phe levels); L = low Phe (plasma Phe levels 3–6 mg/dl); S = siblings (siblings of the PKU and MHP participants); M = high/low MHP; P = high/low PKU. For sex differences only: M = male; F = female. N.S. = not significant. Concurrent Phe level = the mean plasma Phe level during the 6-week period preceding testing.

a Although the low-Phe group looks as bad or worse than the high-Phe group on AB, the low group contains several infants whose levels were often high (i.e., ≥ 6 mg/dl), but, because their levels were also sometimes extremely low, their mean Phe levels were < 6 mg/dl. When those infants whose Phe levels were < 6 mg/dl were omitted from the low-Phe group, the performance of the low-Phe group was indistinguishable from that of the three comparison groups on the AB task. When the infants whose levels were often high were combined with those whose levels were high on average, the performance of this group on AB was markedly different from that of all comparison groups. See Figure 6.

* p < .005.
** p < .001.
*** p < .0005.
**** p < .0001.

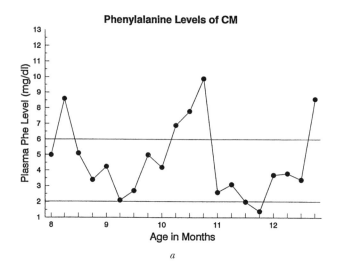

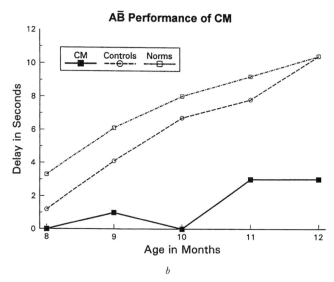

FIGURE 4.—A͞B performance in two infants whose plasma Phe levels were between 2 and 6 mg/dl on average but who differed in how stably their Phe levels were kept within this range. *a,* Phe levels of infant CM. *b,* A͞B performance of CM. *c,* Phe levels of infant GR. *d,* A͞B performance of GR.

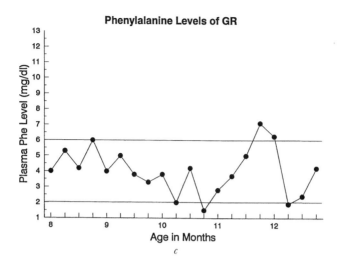

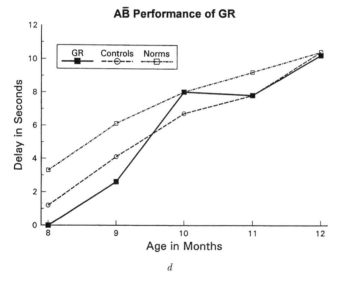

FIGURE 4 *(Continued)*

rent plasma Phe level with $\overline{AB}$ performance varied from $-.98$ to $.32$. The mean was $-.56$. As an infant's Phe level varied, so too, inversely, did $\overline{AB}$ performance.

Sex Differences

There were sex differences in performance and sex $\times$ group interactions. In the regression of $\overline{AB}$ performance on sex, age, and subject group,

79

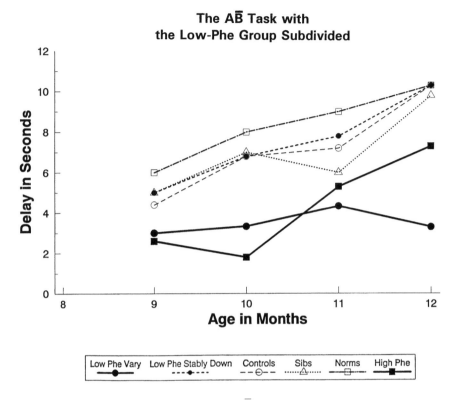

FIGURE 5.—Performance of infants on the A̅B̅ task by subject group with the low-Phe group subdivided: those with Phe levels that generally remained within the range of 2–6 mg/dl and those with mean Phe levels that were also low but with at least 20% of their Phe levels outside the 2–6 mg/dl range. Note that, even though their mean level was low, the infants whose Phe levels varied greatly performed as poorly as the infants whose mean Phe levels were high (6–10 mg/dl). All other subject groups performed significantly better.

the sex difference was significant ($F[1, 339] = 19.76$, $p < .0001$). When the interaction term (sex × group) was added, sex itself was no longer significant, but the interaction was ($F[4, 335] = 4.21$, $p < .005$). Among infants drawn from the general population, and among matched controls, girls could withstand significantly longer delays on the A̅B̅ task than could boys of the same age (orthogonal contrasts: norms = 35.60, $p < .0001$; controls = 12.63, $p < .0005$). However, among infants with PKU, regardless of whether their Phe levels were high or low, boys performed better on the A̅B̅ task than girls (orthogonal contrasts: higher PKU = 3.97, $p < .05$; lower PKU = 5.55, $p < .02$). Among siblings of the PKU and MHP participants, there was no sex difference in A̅B̅ performance. For a summary of the results on the A̅B̅ task, see Table 7.

THE OBJECT RETRIEVAL TASK

Results are reported here only for those conditions of the task that were challenging. Results for trials where the toy was partially out of the box or easily visible through the box opening and for trials where the opaque box was used are not reported here because, as predicted, all infants performed well on these easy conditions. When the box is opaque, there is no need to inhibit the tendency to reach straight to the visible goal because the toy is not visible through any of the closed sides of the box. When the toy is partially out of the box, the task does not present a detour problem as part of the toy is freely accessible. When the toy can be seen through the box opening, the infant's tendency to reach along the line of sight happens to coincide with the correct solution.

Results are reported here for the trials where the toy was deep inside the transparent box and the box was positioned at the midline, that is, those trials where at the outset the infant saw the toy through a closed side of the box. Results for trials where the left or right side of the box was open are combined here and designated *side-open* trials. There was no significant difference between performance when the right or left side of the box was open, and pooling these results yielded a more robust indicator of performance level.

Front of the Box Open, Small Box

Group Differences: PKU and MHP Groups Combined

Infants with higher plasma Phe concentrations were generally unable to retrieve the toy from the small box open at the front, even when momentarily shown the toy through the box opening, until they were 9–10 months old. By the age of 8 months, most infants in all other subject groups could retrieve the toy under those conditions when momentarily shown the toy through the box opening, and, by 9 months, over half were retrieving the toy under those conditions without any help at all (main effect for age, $F[1, 337] = 378.81$, $p < .0001$). Infants with higher Phe concentrations were about $1\frac{1}{2}$ months behind other infants in their performance (see Figure 6*a*).

The poor performance of infants with higher Phe levels was not due to lack of motivation or lack of effort. These infants persisted at length at the side of the box through which they saw the toy. Each trial lasted until the participant succeeded or refused to try any longer, and the trials of infants with higher Phe levels were at least as long as those of other participants. This is true for all types of trials for which results are reported below.

In short, infants with higher plasma Phe levels performed significantly

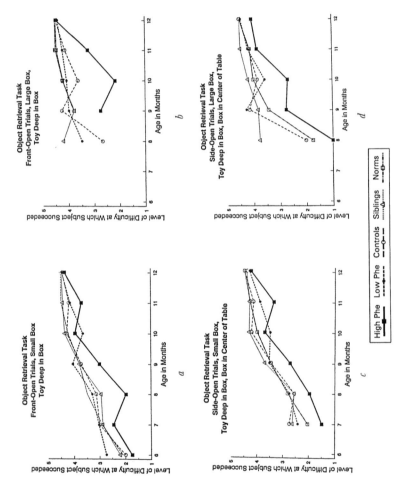

FIGURE 6.—The performance level on the object retrieval task with the toy deep inside the box for infants in the five subject groups. (*Side open* refers to when the left or right side of the box was open.) *a*, Front-open trials, small box. *b*, Front-open trials, large box. *c*, Side-open trials, small box, box in center of table. *d*, Side-open trials, large box, box in center of table.

worse on front-open trials, even when the smaller box was used, than other infants with PKU or MHP with lower plasma Phe levels and than infant siblings ($F[4, 336] = 5.49$, $p < .0003$; orthogonal contrasts: higher Phe vs. lower Phe $= 16.10$, $p < .0001$; higher Phe vs. siblings $= 12.99$, $p < .0002$). They also tended to perform worse than the other comparison groups (norms and matched controls), although the latter differences were not significant at $p \leq .005$ (see Table 7). After 9 months, ceiling effects became prominent on trials with the small box open at the front; hence, the difference in performance between infants with higher Phe levels and all other infants is more pronounced if one looks only at the ages of 6–9 months ($F[4, 160] = 7.71$, $p < .0001$; orthogonal contrasts: higher Phe vs. lower Phe $= 25.27$, $p < .0001$; higher Phe vs. siblings $= 15.02$, $p < .0001$; higher Phe vs. norms $= 7.24$, $p < .005$; higher Phe vs. controls $= 5.58$, $p < .01$).

Infants whose plasma Phe concentrations were only slightly elevated (less than three times normal) performed normally (i.e., there were no significant differences between their performance and those of the matched control, sibling, or normative groups). Moreover, the matched control, sibling, and normative groups performed similarly to one another.

Dividing the PKU and MHP infants into higher- and lower-Phe groups on the basis of their mean plasma Phe level during the period of 6–12 months of age yielded results comparable to those reported above, which are based on the Phe levels during the 6-week period immediately preceding each behavioral testing session. The differences between the performance of infants with higher Phe levels and the performance of the comparison groups were generally not as large, however, when mean Phe levels between 6 and 12 months were used to assign participants to groups.

Group Differences: PKU and MHP Groups Analyzed Separately

Regardless of whether an infant had PKU or MHP, those infants whose plasma Phe levels were greater than three times normal performed significantly worse on front-open trials with the small box than other PKU or MHP infants with lower Phe levels and worse than the sibling group ($F[6, 336] = 3.69$, $p < .002$; orthogonal contrasts: higher PKU vs. lower PKU $= 9.10$, $p = .001$; higher PKU vs. siblings $= 8.50$, $p < .002$; higher MHP vs. lower MHP $= 6.54$, $p = .005$; higher MHP vs. siblings $= 6.96$, $p < .005$).

Infants with MHP whose Phe levels were three times normal or higher were as impaired on this task as PKU infants with similar Phe levels. Indeed, among infants whose Phe levels were 6 mg/dl or higher, or among infants whose Phe levels were under 6 mg/dl, there were no significant differences in performance in this condition between those participants with PKU and those with MHP.

Concurrent Phe level (the Phe level during the 6 weeks immediately before testing) was inversely and linearly related to performance for the PKU and MHP infants combined ($F[1, 14] = 6.39$, $p < .03$), and for the PKU participants considered alone ($F[1, 7] = 10.57$, $p < .03$), but not for the MHP infants. The mean level of Phe in an infant's bloodstream from 6 to 12 months of age or from birth to 12 months of age was not significantly related to performance on the object retrieval task in the front-open, small-box condition.

Sex Differences

There was no significant sex difference for the small box, front-open condition when all the subject groups were combined, but there was a significant sex × condition interaction for the PKU and MHP participants ($F[1, 73] = 5.23$, $p < .03$) and a significant sex difference among the PKU participants ($F[1, 41] = 8.68$, $p < .001$). Infant boys with PKU outperformed infant girls with PKU. Among other subject groups, the sex difference was not significant and, if anything, tended to be in the opposite direction.

Front of the Box Open, Large Box

Group Differences: PKU and MHP Groups Combined

Results when the front of the large box was open were similar to those for the small box. Infants with higher Phe levels could not even be tested with the large box until they were 9 months old, so difficult did they find the task. Thus, comparisons are made here only over the 9–12-month age range. Infants with higher Phe levels performed significantly worse than the normative sample and siblings ($F[4, 279] = 4.21$, $p < .003$; orthogonal contrasts: higher Phe vs. norms = 14.69, $p < .0001$; higher Phe vs. siblings = 6.60, $p = .005$; see Figure 6b). They also tended to perform worse than the other comparison groups (other PKU and MHP children with less elevated Phe levels and matched controls); however, the latter differences were not significant at $p \leq .005$ (see Table 7). None of the control groups differed significantly from one another. There was a strong main effect for age ($F[1, 279] = 42.73$, $p < .0001$).

Group Differences: PKU and MHP Groups Analyzed Separately

Regardless of whether an infant had PKU or MHP, those infants whose plasma Phe levels were three times normal or higher during the 6-week period preceding testing performed poorly on front-open trials with the large box. PKU infants with plasma Phe levels three times normal or higher performed significantly worse than other PKU infants with Phe levels closer to normal and than the sibling group ($F[6, 232] = 5.37$, $p < .0001$; orthogonal contrasts: higher PKU vs. lower PKU $= 10.83$, $p < .001$; higher PKU vs. siblings $= 6.62$, $p < .005$). They also tended to perform worse than the normative and matched control groups. MHP infants with plasma Phe levels three times normal or higher performed significantly worse than all comparison groups (orthogonal contrasts: higher MHP vs. lower MHP $= 16.56$, $p < .0001$; higher MHP vs. norms $= 6.60$, $p = .005$; higher MHP vs. controls $= 6.35$, $p = .005$; higher MHP vs. siblings $= 12.02$, $p < .001$). Note that MHP infants with higher Phe levels were not protected here; their impairment was even more apparent than that of PKU infants.

The performance of PKU and MHP infants was comparable once concurrent Phe level was controlled for. Similarly, as a group, there were no significant differences between the performance of MHP infants with higher Phe levels and PKU infants with comparable Phe levels or between MHP infants with lower Phe levels and PKU infants with comparable Phe levels. Even though, as a group, the children with lower, more normal plasma Phe levels performed better and the children with higher Phe levels performed worse, no direct relation between concurrent Phe level (as a continuous variable) and performance in the front-open, large-box condition was found.

When, rather than concurrent Phe level, the mean plasma Phe level throughout the period of testing was used to assign participants to "higher" and "lower" Phe groups, we found that PKU participants whose mean Phe levels were three times normal or higher performed significantly worse than all other subject groups; however, MHP infants with mean Phe levels three times normal or higher performed comparably to all other subject groups ($F[6, 327] = 5.77$, $p < .0001$; orthogonal contrasts: higher PKU vs. lower PKU $= 17.07$, $p < .0001$; higher PKU vs. norms $= 29.83$, $p < .0001$; higher PKU vs. controls $= 11.70$, $p < .0005$; higher PKU vs. siblings $= 22.54$, $p < .0001$; no comparable comparisons for MHP infants with higher mean plasma Phe levels were significant).

Mean Phe level during the first month of life, on the other hand, was significantly and inversely related to performance among MHP participants ($F[1, 36] = 9.93$, $p < .004$) but not among PKU participants. Mean Phe level over the ages of 6–12 months was significantly and inversely related to the performance of the PKU participants ($F[1, 36] = 4.45$, $p < .05$) but not to that of the MHP participants. There was still no significant difference in the performance of PKU and MHP infants when either of these Phe level variables was controlled for.

Sex Differences

There were no significant sex differences and no significant sex × group interactions for the large box, front-open condition.

Side of the Box Open, Small Box

Group Differences: PKU and MHP Groups Combined

The group differences on the object retrieval task were particularly pronounced for the side-open, small-box condition because the intersubject variability was so small. By 8 months of age, almost all infants, except those whose Phe levels were toward the higher end of the acceptable range, were able to retrieve the toy from either the left or the right side of the small box when momentarily shown the toy through the box opening (see Figure 6c). Infants with Phe levels three times normal or higher could not do so until a month later (9 months of age).

Infants with higher Phe levels performed significantly worse than all other subject groups in the side-open, small-box condition ($F[4, 359] = 9.63$, $p < .0001$; orthogonal contrasts: higher Phe vs. lower Phe = 15.75, $p < .0001$; higher Phe vs. norms = 25.35, $p < .0001$; higher Phe vs. controls = 19.67, $p < .0001$; higher Phe vs. siblings = 34.91, $p < .0001$). None of the control groups differed significantly from one another.

The analyses presented above were based on plasma Phe levels immediately preceding testing. Results are similar for mean Phe level during the entire testing period (6–12 months of age), mean Phe level during the entire first year of life, mean Phe level during only the first month of life, and the percentage of the area under the Phe curve within the range of 2–6 mg/dl. In addition to the significant effect of group, there was a significant effect of age ($F[1, 357] = 421.51$, $p < .0000$).

Group Differences: PKU and MHP Groups Analyzed Separately

There were no significant differences in the performance of PKU and MHP infants on side-open, small-box trials once any measure of plasma Phe was controlled for. PKU infants whose mean Phe levels preceding each testing session were 6 mg/dl or higher performed significantly worse than other PKU participants with Phe levels closer to normal, the normative sample, matched controls, or siblings (F[6, 359] = 7.34, $p < .0001$; orthogonal contrasts: higher Phe vs. lower Phe = 17.34, $p < .0001$; higher Phe vs. norms = 25.79, $p < .0001$; higher Phe vs. controls = 23.49, $p < .0001$; higher Phe vs.

siblings = 34.29, $p < .0001$). MHP infants whose Phe levels were 6 mg/dl or higher for the 6 weeks before each testing session performed significantly worse than all comparison groups except other MHP infants with lower Phe levels (orthogonal contrasts: higher MHP vs. norms = 6.88, $p < .005$; higher MHP vs. controls = 7.36, $p < .005$; higher MHP vs. siblings = 13.10, $p < .0002$).

Similar results were obtained for mean Phe level during the period of 6–12 months of age, mean Phe level during the entire first year, mean Phe level during the first month of life, and percentage of the area under each child's Phe curve within the range of 2–6 mg/dl. For example, mean Phe levels for the first year of life were significantly and inversely related to performance on the small-box, side-open trials for both PKU infants and MHP infants ($F[1, 48] = 5.82$, $p < .03$, and $F[1, 48] = 6.80$, $p < .02$, respectively). Within individual infants, performance on the side-open, small-box condition covaried inversely with plasma Phe level; the correlation coefficients ranged from $-.76$ to $.32$, with a mean of $-.31$.

Sex Differences

There were no significant sex differences and no significant sex × group interactions for the small-box, side-open condition.

Side of the Box Open, Large Box

Group Differences: PKU and MHP Groups Combined

Performance improved significantly over age ($F[1, 324] = 211.48$, $p < .0001$; see Figure 6d). However, even controlling for age, infants with higher Phe levels performed worse than other infants with lower Phe levels, matched controls, and their siblings when the large box was used and the opening was at the left or right side ($F[4, 324] = 10.35$, $p < .0001$; orthogonal contrasts: higher Phe vs. lower Phe = 19.06, $p < .0001$; higher Phe vs. controls = 15.39, $p < .0001$; higher Phe vs. siblings = 31.97, $p < .0001$; see Figure 6d). As a group, infants from the general population performed significantly worse than siblings of the PKU and MHP participants (orthogonal contrast = 18.61, $p < .0001$). There were no group differences among PKU and MHP infants with Phe levels closer to normal, matched controls, and the siblings of the PKU and MHP participants. These results are based on Phe levels immediately preceding testing. Results are similar, although not quite as strong, for mean Phe level during the entire testing period (6–12 months of age) and for the percentage of the area under the Phe curve within the range of 2–6 mg/dl.

Group Differences: PKU and MHP Groups Analyzed Separately

There were no significant differences in the performance of PKU and MHP infants, controlling for any measure of plasma Phe. However, although MHP infants whose Phe levels were three times normal or higher during the 6 weeks prior to testing performed as poorly as PKU infants with comparable Phe levels, MHP infants whose mean Phe levels from 6–12 months of age were three times normal or higher performed better than PKU infants whose mean Phe levels were in the same range during that same period ($F[6, 322] = 7.67$, $p < .0001$; orthogonal contrast: higher PKU vs. higher MHP = 11.39, $p < .001$).

PKU infants whose mean Phe levels preceding each testing session were 6 mg/dl or higher performed significantly worse than all comparison groups ($F[6, 208] = 7.13$, $p < .0001$; orthogonal contrasts: higher PKU vs. lower PKU = 16.21, $p < .0001$; higher PKU vs. norms = 8.73, $p < .002$; higher PKU vs. controls = 16.25, $p < .0001$; higher PKU vs. siblings = 26.42, $p < .0001$). MHP infants whose mean Phe levels during the 6-week period before testing were 6 mg/dl or higher performed significantly worse than all comparison groups except the normative sample (orthogonal contrasts: higher MHP vs. lower MHP = 6.06, $p = .005$; higher MHP vs. controls = 6.66, $p < .005$; higher MHP vs. siblings = 15.06, $p < .0001$).

Level of Phe during the 6-week period before each testing session and the mean Phe level over the 6–12-month age period were significantly and inversely related to performance for infants with PKU ($F[1, 39] = 14.35$, $p < .0005$, and $F[1, 39] = 9.42$, $p < .004$, respectively). Mean Phe level throughout the first year of life and mean Phe level during the first month of life were significantly and inversely related to performance for MHP infants ($F[1, 48] = 15.22$, $p < .0003$, and $F[1, 48] = 35.58$, $p < .0001$, respectively).

Sex Differences

There was a significant sex × group interaction on trials with the large box open at the side ($F[6, 316] = 3.08$, $p < .01$). Among PKU and MHP infants with lower Phe levels, and among the siblings of PKU and MHP participants, boys performed better than girls (lower-Phe participants: $F[1, 44] = 3.82$, $p < .03$; siblings: $F[1, 71] = 5.64$, $p = .005$). There was no sex difference among matched control children or participants drawn from the general population.

For a summary of the results on the object retrieval task, see Table 7.

Spatial Discrimination

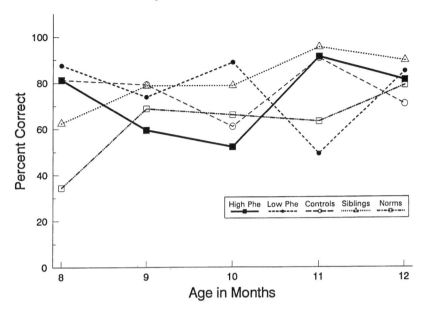

FIGURE 7.—Performance on the spatial discrimination task of infants in the five subject groups.

THE SPATIAL DISCRIMINATION TASK

Group Differences: PKU and MHP Groups Combined

The groups did not differ significantly overall in the percentage of correct responses on the spatial discrimination task. Infants with plasma Phe levels three to five times normal, or with more moderately elevated Phe levels, performed comparably to all comparison groups. No measure of plasma Phe yielded any significant group difference. There was little variation in performance on the spatial discrimination task, however, and little change in performance over age. In general, throughout the age range, group means varied between 60% and 85% correct (see Figure 7).

Group Differences: PKU and MHP Groups Analyzed Separately

Infants with PKU performed as well as all comparison groups regardless of Phe level or the Phe measure used. Similarly, MHP infants performed as well as all comparison groups regardless of their Phe level or of the time

89

period over which Phe levels were calculated. No relation between Phe level and performance was found. When the PKU and MHP subject groups were dichotomized by Phe level, no significant difference between PKU participants, between MHP participants, or between any of these groups and any comparison subject group was found.

Sex Differences

There were no significant sex differences and no significant sex × group interactions. For a summary of the results on the spatial discrimination task, see Table 7.

THE VISUAL PAIRED COMPARISON TASK

Briefest Presentation Times (15 Sec at 7 Months and 5 Sec at 10 Months)

Group Differences: PKU and MHP Groups Combined

Infants who need a longer sample presentation time might have a slower speed of processing and so need more time to encode information about the sample stimulus. The most likely presentation duration to produce any group difference would be the shortest presentation time. Hence, we looked at whether there were any differences in the percentage of infants choosing the novel stimulus (i.e., demonstrating recognition of the sample) using trials with 15-sec presentation times for 7-month-olds and 5-sec presentation times for 10-month-olds. No significant group differences emerged. There were no differences between any subject groups in performance at any sample presentation time regardless of the plasma Phe measure used to assign PKU and MHP participants to groups. However, even with only 5 sec to encode the stimulus, 10-month-old infants chose the novel stimulus more consistently than did 7-month-olds given three times as long with the stimulus ($F[1, 77] = 4.37$, $p = .03$).

Group Differences: PKU and MHP Groups Analyzed Separately

Dividing the PKU and MHP participants into "high" and "low" groups on the basis of their Phe concentrations during the 6 weeks immediately preceding testing yielded no significant group differences in performance. When PKU and MHP participants were assigned to groups on the basis of their mean Phe levels throughout the first year of life, there were still no significant differences between the performance of PKU infants and the performance

90

of any comparison group. MHP infants, whose mean Phe levels throughout the first year of life were three times normal or greater, tended to perform worse than PKU infants with comparable mean Phe levels and worse than most comparison groups, although none of these differences was significant at the .005 level (see Table 7). Dividing the PKU and MHP participants into two groups on the basis of the percentage of Phe levels within the range of 2–6 mg/dl still yielded no significant group differences in performance on the visual paired comparison task.

Phe levels immediately before testing were not significantly related to performance. However, the percentage of Phe levels between 6 and 12 months of age outside the range of 2–6 mg/dl was significantly and inversely related to performance (PKU infants: $F[1, 7] = 11.44$, $p < .02$; MHP infants: $F[1, 6] = 10.26$, $p < .02$). Mean plasma Phe concentration between 6 and 12 months of age was significantly and inversely related to performance among the infants with PKU ($F[1, 7] = 7.18$, $p < .04$), although not to performance among MHP infants. On the other hand, among infants with MHP, yet not among PKU infants, mean plasma Phe level between birth and 12 months of age and during the first month of life alone was significantly and inversely related to performance ($F[1, 6] = 19.61$, $p < .01$, and $F[1, 5] = 17.36$, $p < .02$, respectively).

No significant effects emerged for any other presentation time durations.

Sex Differences

There was no significant main effect for gender, nor were there any significant interactions.

Longest Delay (10 Min)

Group Differences: PKU and MHP Groups Combined

Adult patients and macaques who have sustained damage to the medial temporal lobe succeed on visual paired comparison and delayed nonmatching to sample tasks when there is only a brief delay but perform progressively worse than normal as the delays get longer. Therefore, the largest group differences, and the heaviest demands on memory, would be expected to occur at the longest delays. For this reason, we looked at whether there were group differences in performance at our longest delay, 10 min (600 sec). Infants with higher Phe levels were less likely to show that they remembered the sample after this delay than were infants drawn from the general population ($F[4, 82] = 3.32$, $p < .02$; orthogonal contrast: higher Phe vs. norms = 10.26, $p < .003$). No other comparisons reached statistical significance.

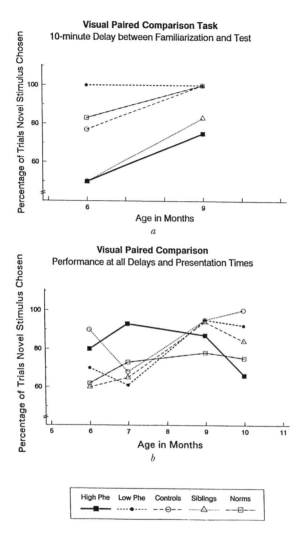

FIGURE 8.—Performance on the visual paired comparison task of infants in the five subject groups. *a*, Performance at the longest delay (10 min) between familiarization and test. *b*, Performance at all delays and presentation times.

At 6 months of age, infants with higher Phe levels chose the novel stimulus only 50% of the time after a delay of 10 min, whereas infants with less elevated Phe levels, infants in the normative sample, and infants matched to the PKU and MHP participants on a host of background characteristics selected the novel stimulus after a 10-min delay on 100%, 83%, and 77% of the trials, respectively (see Figure 8). By 9 months, infants in the lower-Phe, normative, and matched control groups selected the novel stimulus every time (100%), whereas infants with Phe levels three times normal or higher chose the novel stimulus only 75% of the time. The sibling group showed an intermediate level of performance.

Using any other measure of plasma Phe than concurrent levels yielded no significant difference between the higher- and the lower-Phe groups, leaving the differences between the normative sample and the higher-Phe groups as the only statistically significant differences. Across the groups, infants chose the novel stimulus more consistently as they grew older ($F[1, 42] = 5.91$, $p < .02$).

Group Differences: PKU and MHP Groups Analyzed Separately

There were no significant differences in the performance of PKU and MHP infants, controlling for any measure of plasma Phe. MHP infants with Phe levels three times normal or higher performed comparably to PKU infants with similar Phe levels, and PKU infants with lower Phe levels performed as well as MHP infants with comparable Phe levels.

PKU infants whose mean Phe levels preceding each testing session were 6 mg/dl or higher tended to perform worse than other infants with PKU who had lower Phe levels and than infants drawn from the general population; the same tendencies were found for MHP infants with higher Phe levels, who also tended to perform worse than matched controls. However, none of these differences was significant at $p \leq .005$ (see Table 7). There were no significant differences among the matched controls, siblings, the normative sample, and either PKU or MHP infants with lower Phe levels. No measure of plasma Phe, other than concurrent levels, yielded any differences among PKU infants or among MHP infants in performance on the visual paired comparison task with a 10-min delay.

Phe level during the 6 weeks immediately preceding testing was linearly and inversely related to performance for the PKU participants ($F[1, 6] = 11.07$, $p < .02$) but not for the participants with MHP. No other measure of plasma Phe showed any direct relation to performance. Within an infant over time, the correlation between performance at the 10-min delay and concurrent plasma Phe level varied from $-.51$ to $.56$; the mean was $r = -.16$.

Sex Differences

There were no significant sex differences and no significant sex × group interactions.

93

Performance at Other Presentation Times and Other Delays

We compared the performance of participants at each sample presentation duration (5, 15, 30, and 45 sec). No significant group differences at any sample presentation time were found, regardless of the plasma Phe measure used to assign PKU and MHP participants to groups. We also compared the subject groups in their performance at all delays (10, 15, 60, and 180 sec; results for the longest delay—600 sec—are presented above). There was no significant effect of subject group (higher PKU, lower PKU, higher MHP, lower MHP, norms, controls, and siblings) at any of these delays. Similarly, there was no effect of Phe level (regardless of the period over which plasma Phe was assessed) on performance at any of these delays.

One might expect group differences to be largest where participants had the least time to encode the sample (briefest presentation times) and the most demand on their memory (longest delays). Therefore, we looked at the performance of 7-month-olds on the trial where presentation time was 15 sec and the delay was 60 sec and at the performance of 10-month-olds on the trial where presentation time was 5 sec and the delay was 180 sec. No significant differences among the groups were found, although these analyses are based on only one trial per session and so are not as robust as those based on a more reliable measure of performance. For a summary of the results on the visual paired comparison task, see Table 7.

RELATIONS AMONG PERFORMANCE ON TASKS ADMINISTERED TO INFANTS

Some relations were found between performance on the $\overline{AB}$ and object retrieval tasks. No significant relations were found with performance on either the spatial discrimination or the visual paired comparison task and performance on any other task.

Performance on the $\overline{AB}$ task and on the small-box object retrieval trials (with either the front, the left, or the right side of the box open) was correlated within the age range of 8–9 months ($r[46] = .35, p < .01$). (Before 8 months, many infants could not be tested on $\overline{AB}$ because they could not uncover a hidden object; after 9 months, there were pronounced ceiling effects on small-box object retrieval trials.) Over the ages of 9–11 months, $\overline{AB}$ performance was correlated with performance on large-box object retrieval trials ($r[54] = .35, p < .01$). (Many participants could not be tested with the large box before the age of 9 months.) The correlation between performance on the $\overline{AB}$ task and performance on the small-box object retrieval trials was significant within the group of PKU and MHP infants and among infants from the general population ($r[13] = .54$, $p < .05$, and $r[24] = .49$, $p < .03$, respectively) but not among the sibling or matched control groups. The same was true for the correlation of performance on $\overline{AB}$ with performance on the large-box object retrieval trials (PKU and MHP infants: $r[15] = .68$, $p < .03$; norms: $r[24] = .41$, $p < .05$).

THE AB̄ TASK WITH INVISIBLE DISPLACEMENT

Group Differences: PKU and MHP Groups Combined

The critical trials on the AB̄-invisible task are the reversal trials, where the box containing the toy is moved to the side opposite to where the participant last found the toy. All groups of toddlers started out performing comparably on the reversal trials in the AB̄-invisible task. However, after 21 months, when all other groups started to improve, the performance of PKU and MHP toddlers with higher Phe levels leveled off or declined. Between 21 and 30 months, toddlers with PKU or MHP as a group performed significantly worse on the AB̄ task with invisible displacements than did their matched controls regardless of plasma Phe level ($F[1, 160] = 3.50$, $p < .01$; orthogonal contrast: PKU and MHP vs. controls $= 12.73$, $p < .0003$). There was no significant change in performance on the AB̄-invisible task with a 5-sec delay over the entire age range investigated, 15–30 months of age).

Phe level showed only a moderate effect on performance of the AB̄-invisible task. Between 21 and 30 months, toddlers with Phe levels toward the high end of what has been considered the safe range performed significantly worse on the task than did matched controls ($F[4, 150] = 2.60$, $p < .04$; orthogonal contrast: higher Phe vs. controls $= 7.51$, $p < .005$). The higher-Phe group also tended to perform worse than other PKU and MHP children with lower Phe levels and than their siblings, but these differences were not significant at $p < .005$ (see Figure 9). There were no significant differences in performance among PKU and MHP toddlers whose plasma Phe levels were under 6 mg/dl levels during the 6-week period preceding each testing session, children from the general population, children handpicked to match the PKU and MHP participants in demographic and health characteristics, and siblings of the PKU and MHP subjects.

Participants whose mean Phe levels during the first year of life had been 6 mg/dl or higher performed worse as 21–30-month-olds on the AB̄-invisible

A̅B̅ with Invisible Displacement - 5 Sec Delay

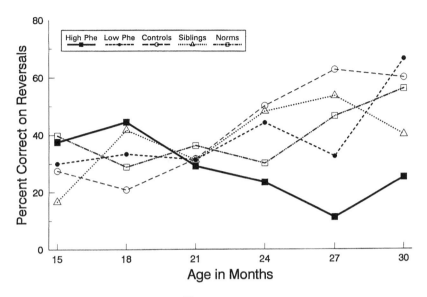

FIGURE 9.—Performance on the A̅B̅ task with invisible displacement (5-sec delay) of toddlers in the five subject groups.

task than did matched controls ($F[4, 150] = 3.57$, $p < .01$; orthogonal contrast: higher Phe vs. controls $= 13.18$, $p < .0003$). They also tended to perform worse than children from the general population and their own siblings (see Table 8).

There were few low-Phe participants for whom 20% or more of the area under the curve of their plasma Phe levels during the period of 12–30 months of age was outside the range of 2–6 mg/dl. Thus, most of the PKU and MHP participants were classified in the "low" within-range group. The performance of participants whose mean plasma Phe levels were under three times normal but whose Phe levels fluctuated so much that 20% or more of their blood tests revealed Phe levels three times normal or higher was significantly worse than all comparison groups ($F[4, 150] = 3.57$, $p < .01$; orthogonal contrasts: outside range vs. inside range $= 11.49$, $p < .0005$; outside range vs. norms $= 51.41$, $p < .0001$; outside range vs. controls $= 11.46$, $p < .0005$; outside range vs. siblings $= 12.66$, $p < .0003$).

Group Differences: PKU and MHP Groups Analyzed Separately

PKU and MHP participants performed comparably on the A̅B̅ task with invisible displacements, whether Phe concentration was controlled for or not.

TABLE 8

SUMMARY OF THE RESULTS ON THE FIVE COGNITIVE NEUROPSYCHOLOGICAL TESTS ADMINISTERED TO TODDLERS

	$\overline{A}\overline{B}$ WITH INVISIBLE DISPLACEMENT[a] [% Correct on Reversals]	
	[Concurrent Phe Level]	[Mean Phe during First Year]
High Phe vs. low Phe	.025, H < L	N.S.
High Phe vs. norms	N.S.	.025, H < N
High Phe vs. controls	*, H < C	***, H < C
High Phe vs. siblings	N.S.	.025, H < S
Low Phe vs. norms	N.S.	N.S.
Low Phe vs. controls	N.S.	N.S.
Low Phe vs. siblings	N.S.	N.S.
Controls vs. norms	.01, N < C	.01, N < C
Controls vs. siblings	N.S.	N.S.
Siblings vs. norms	N.S.	N.S.
High PKU vs. low PKU	N.S.	N.S.
High PKU vs. norms	N.S.	.025, H < N
High PKU vs. controls	*, H < C	*, H < C
High PKU vs. siblings	*, H < S	N.S.

98

Low PKU vs. N, C, S		N.S.
MHP vs. PKU		N.S.
High MHP vs. high PKU		N.S.
Low MHP vs. low PKU		N.S.
High MHP vs. low MHP		N.S.
High MHP vs. norms		N.S.
High MHP vs. controls		N.S.
High MHP vs. siblings	N.S.	N.S.
Low MHP vs. N, C, S	N.S.	N.S.
Other Phe measures showing a group difference	N.S.	
Phe measures directly, inversely related to performance for PKU subjects	N.S.	
Phe measures directly, inversely related to performance for MHP subjects	N.S.	None
Sex differences	None	

TABLE 8 (*Continued*)

THREE BOXES (Boxes Scrambled after Each Reach) [Concurrent Phe Level]

	[Number of Boxes Opened]	[Number of Reaches to Open All Boxes]	[Number of Reaches to First Error]	[Maximum Number of Consecutive Reaches to Same Position]
High Phe vs. low Phe	N.S.	N.S.	N.S.	*, H < L
High Phe vs. norms	N.S.	N.S.	N.S.	.025, H < N
High Phe vs. controls	N.S.	N.S.	N.S.	*, H < C
High Phe vs. siblings	N.S.	N.S.	N.S.	N.S.
Low Phe vs. norms	N.S.	N.S.	N.S.	N.S.
Low Phe vs. controls	N.S.	N.S.	N.S.	N.S.
Low Phe vs. siblings	N.S.	N.S.	N.S.	N.S.
Controls vs. norms	N.S.	N.S.	N.S.	N.S.
Controls vs. siblings	N.S.	N.S.	N.S.	N.S.
Siblings vs. norms	N.S.	N.S.	N.S.	N.S.
High PKU vs. low PKU	N.S.	N.S.	N.S.	N.S.
High PKU vs. norms	N.S.	N.S.	N.S.	N.S.
High PKU vs. controls	N.S.	N.S.	N.S.	N.S.
High PKU vs. siblings	N.S.	N.S.	N.S.	N.S.

Low PKU vs. N, C, S	N.S.	N.S.	N.S.	N.S.
MHP vs. PKU	N.S.	N.S.	N.S.	N.S.
High MHP vs. high PKU	N.S.	N.S.	N.S.	N.S.
Low MHP vs. low PKU	N.S.	N.S.	N.S.	N.S.
High MHP vs. low MHP	N.S.	N.S.	.05, H < L	.03, H < L
High MHP vs. norms	N.S.	N.S.	N.S.	N.S.
High MHP vs. controls	N.S.	N.S.	N.S.	N.S.
High MHP vs. siblings	N.S.	N.S.	N.S.	N.S.
Low MHP vs. N, C, S	N.S.	N.S.	N.S.	N.S.
Other Phe measures showing a group difference				
Phe measures directly, inversely related to performance for PKU subjects				
Phe measures directly, inversely related to performance for MHP subjects				
Sex differences	None	None	****, F < M	****, F < M
Among PKU				

TABLE 8 (*Continued*)

	THREE BOXES (Boxes Remain Stationary) [Concurrent Phe Level]			
	[Number of Boxes Opened]	[Number of Reaches to Open All Boxes]	[Number of Reaches to First Error]	[Maximum Number of Consecutive Reaches to Same Position]
High Phe vs. low Phe	N.S.	N.S.	N.S.	N.S.
High Phe vs. norms	N.S.	N.S.	N.S.	N.S.
High Phe vs. controls	N.S.	N.S.	N.S.	N.S.
High Phe vs. siblings	N.S.	N.S.	N.S.	N.S.
Low Phe vs. norms	N.S.	N.S.	N.S.	N.S.
Low Phe vs. controls	N.S.	N.S.	N.S.	N.S.
Low Phe vs. siblings	N.S.	N.S.	N.S.	N.S.
Controls vs. norms	N.S.	N.S.	N.S.	N.S.
Controls vs. siblings	N.S.	N.S.	N.S.	N.S.
Siblings vs. norms	N.S.	N.S.	N.S.	N.S.
High PKU vs. low PKU	N.S.	N.S.	N.S.	N.S.
High PKU vs. norms	N.S.	N.S.	N.S.	N.S.
High PKU vs. controls	N.S.	N.S.	N.S.	N.S.
High PKU vs. siblings	N.S.	N.S.	N.S.	N.S.

Low PKU vs. N, C, S	N.S.	N.S.	N.S.
MHP vs. PKU	N.S.	N.S.	N.S.
High MHP vs. high PKU	N.S.	N.S.	N.S.
Low MHP vs. low PKU	N.S.	N.S.	N.S.
High MHP vs. low MHP	N.S.	N.S.	N.S.
High MHP vs. norms	N.S.	N.S.	N.S.
High MHP vs. controls	N.S.	N.S.	N.S.
High MHP vs. siblings	N.S.	N.S.	N.S.
Low MHP vs. N, C, S	N.S.	N.S.	N.S.
Other Phe measures showing a group difference			
Phe measures directly, inversely related to performance for PKU subjects			
Phe measures directly, inversely related to performance for MHP subjects			
Sex differences	None	****, F < M	None
Among PKU			

TABLE 8 (*Continued*)

DELAYED NONMATCHING TO SAMPLE
[Concurrent Phe Level]

	30-Sec Delay [% Correct]	5-Sec Delay		
		[% Correct]	[Number of Errors to Criterion]	[Number of Trials to Criterion]
High Phe vs. low Phe	N.S.	N.S.	N.S.	N.S.
High Phe vs. norms	*, H < N	N.S.	*, H < N	.02, H < N
High Phe vs. controls	N.S.	N.S.	N.S.	N.S.
High Phe vs. siblings	N.S.	N.S.	N.S.	N.S.
Low Phe vs. norms	N.S.	.02, L < N	.04, L < N	.02, L < N
Low Phe vs. controls	N.S.	N.S.	N.S.	N.S.
Low Phe vs. siblings	N.S.	N.S.	N.S.	N.S.
Controls vs. norms	N.S.	N.S.	N.S.	N.S.
Controls vs. siblings	N.S.	N.S.	N.S.	N.S.
Siblings vs. norms	.03, S < N	N.S.	N.S.	N.S.
High PKU vs. low PKU	.01, H < L	N.S.	N.S.	N.S.
High PKU vs. norms	**, H < N	.01, H < N	N.S.	.04, H < N
High PKU vs. controls	N.S.	N.S.	N.S.	N.S.
High PKU vs. siblings	N.S.	N.S.	N.S.	N.S.

104

Low PKU vs. N, C, S	N.S.	.02, L < N	N.S.
MHP vs. PKU	N.S.	N.S.	N.S.
High MHP vs. high PKU	N.S.	N.S.	N.S.
Low MHP vs. low PKU	*, M < P	N.S.	N.S.
High MHP vs. low MHP	N.S.	N.S.	N.S.
High MHP vs. norms	N.S.	.04, H < N	N.S.
High MHP vs. controls	N.S.	N.S.	N.S.
High MHP vs. siblings	N.S.	N.S.	N.S.
Low MHP vs. N, C, S	.03, **, L < C, N	**, L < N	N.S.
Other Phe measures showing a group difference	Mean level during first month (L < H < N)	Mean level during first month	Mean level during first month
Phe measures directly, inversely related to performance for PKU subjects	Concurrent Phe level		
Phe measures directly, inversely related to performance for MHP subjects	None	None	None
Sex differences	None	None	None

TABLE 8 (*Continued*)

GLOBAL-LOCAL SPATIAL PROCESSING: PREFERENTIAL LOOKING
[Concurrent Phe Level]
[% Fixation to Novel Stimulus]

	All Stimuli	Global Stimuli	Local Stimuli
High Phe vs. low Phe	N.S.	N.S.	N.S.
High Phe vs. norms	N.S.	N.S.	N.S.
High Phe vs. controls	N.S.	N.S.	N.S.
High Phe vs. siblings	N.S.	N.S.	N.S.
Low Phe vs. norms	N.S.	N.S.	N.S.
Low Phe vs. controls	N.S.	N.S.	N.S.
Low Phe vs. siblings	N.S.	N.S.	N.S.
Controls vs. norms	N.S.	N.S.	N.S.
Controls vs. siblings	N.S.	N.S.	N.S.
Siblings vs. norms	N.S.	N.S.	N.S.
High PKU vs. low PKU	N.S.	N.S.	N.S.
High PKU vs. norms	N.S.	N.S.	N.S.
High PKU vs. controls	N.S.	N.S.	N.S.
High PKU vs. siblings	N.S.	N.S.	N.S.
Low PKU vs. N, C, S	N.S.	N.S.	N.S.

MHP vs. PKU	N.S.	N.S.	N.S.
High MHP vs. high PKU	N.S.	N.S.	N.S.
Low MHP vs. low PKU	N.S.	N.S.	N.S.
High MHP vs. low MHP	N.S.	N.S.	N.S.
High MHP vs. norms	N.S.	N.S.	N.S.
High MHP vs. controls	N.S.	N.S.	N.S.
High MHP vs. siblings	N.S.	N.S.	N.S.
Low MHP vs. N, C, S	N.S.	N.S.	N.S.
Other Phe measures showing a group difference		Mean level during first year	Mean level during first year
Phe measures directly, inversely related to performance for PKU subjects	Mean level during toddler period	Mean level during first year	
Phe measures directly, inversely related to performance for MHP subjects			Mean level during toddler period
Sex differences: Among PKU	**, F < M	.05, F < M	**, F < M

Note.—Dependent measures are given in square brackets, plasma Phe measures in curly braces. H = high Phe (plasma Phe levels 6–10 mg/dl); L = low Phe (plasma Phe levels 3–6 mg/dl); N = norms (children from the general population); C = controls (matched controls for the PKU and MHP participants with higher plasma Phe levels); S = siblings (siblings of the PKU and MHP participants); M = high/low MHP; P = high/low PKU. For sex differences only: M = male; F = female. N.S. = not significant. Concurrent Phe level = the mean plasma Phe level during the 6-week period preceding testing.

[a] The PKU and MHP toddlers as a group performed significantly worse than all three comparison groups (norms, matched controls, siblings) on the $\overline{AB}$ task with invisible displacement.

* $p < .005$.
** $p < .001$.
*** $p < .0005$.
**** $p < .0001$.

PKU children with higher plasma Phe levels performed significantly worse than the matched control and sibling groups ($F[6, 128] = 2.60$, $p < .04$; orthogonal contrasts: higher PKU vs. controls = 7.09, $p < .005$; higher PKU vs. siblings = 3.85, $p < .005$). No measure of Phe level, treated as a continuous variable, showed any significant relation to $\overline{AB}$-invisible performance.

Sex Differences

There were no significant sex differences and no significant sex × group interactions. For a summary of the results on $\overline{AB}$ with invisible displacement, see Table 8.

THE THREE BOXES TASK (BOXES SCRAMBLED AFTER EACH REACH)

Group Differences: PKU and MHP Groups Combined

Most toddlers of all ages were able to open all three boxes in only four or five reaches. Even so, toddlers needed fewer reaches to open all the boxes as they got older ($F[1, 224] = 5.85$, $p < .01$; see Figure 10). There were no significant group differences and no significant effect of plasma Phe level, regardless of Phe measure used, in (a) number of reaches to open all three boxes, (b) number of reaches to first error, (c) total number of boxes opened, or (d) maximum number of consecutive reaches to the same box. There was, however, a significant improvement over age ($F[1, 230] = 41.92$, $p < .0001$) and a significant group difference in the number of consecutive reaches back to the same location ($F[4, 230] = 2.50$, $p < .04$). PKU and MHP toddlers with higher Phe levels were more likely to perseveratively reach to the same position than were other PKU and MHP toddlers with lower Phe levels or matched controls (orthogonal contrasts: higher Phe vs. lower Phe = 6.82, $p < .005$; higher Phe vs. controls = 7.40, $p < .005$).

Group Differences: PKU and MHP Groups Analyzed Separately

There was no direct relation between plasma Phe level and perseverative position preferences when the PKU and MHP groups were combined or when the PKU group was considered alone. There were no significant differences between the performance of PKU toddlers, with higher or lower plasma Phe levels, and the performance of any comparison group. Among the MHP toddlers, those whose Phe levels were higher tended to show more consecutive reaches back to the same location than MHP toddlers with lower Phe levels ($F[1, 26] = 5.34$, $p < .02$).

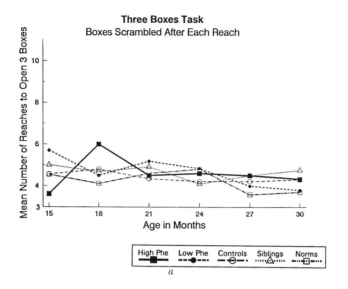

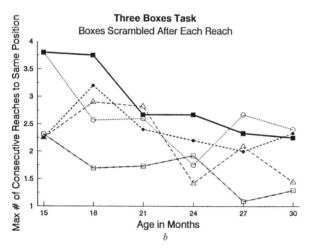

FIGURE 10.—Performance on the three boxes task (boxes scrambled after each reach) of toddlers in the five subject groups. *a,* Mean number of reaches to open three boxes. *b,* Maximum number of consecutive reaches to same position.

Sex Differences

When all the participants were included in the analysis, there was no significant difference between the performance of the boys and that of the girls. However, among just the participants with PKU, the boys performed better than the girls. This can be seen on all dependent measures, such as number of reaches to open all three boxes ($F[2, 63] = 21.52$, $p < .0001$) and number of consecutive reaches to the same location ($F[2, 80] = 27.44$, $p < .0001$). For a summary of the results on this task, see Table 8.

THE THREE BOXES TASK (BOXES REMAIN STATIONARY)

Group Differences: PKU and MHP Groups Combined

Performance tended to be worse when the boxes remained stationary than when they were scrambled after each reach, especially at the youngest age (15 months). This seemed to be because many toddlers erred by reaching back to the same place where they had last found a reward. Such position preferences always led to errors when the boxes were stationary, but in the scrambled-boxes condition a new, unopened box would sometimes be in that position, in which case the toddler would find another reward by reaching back to the same place. The number of consecutive reaches back to the same position when the boxes remained stationary declined markedly over age ($F[1, 231] = 135.17$, $p < .0001$), especially between 15 and 18 months for siblings (see Figure 11b). This decline was less evident among toddlers with higher Phe levels, as they tended to show *less* perseveration to position at the younger ages (see Figure 11b). There were no significant group differences and no significant effect of any plasma Phe variable on the number of reaches to open three boxes (Figure 11a), the number of reaches until the child's first error, or the maximum number of reaches to the same position.

Performance improved over age—on, for example, number of reaches to open all the boxes ($F[1, 232] = 62.61$, $p < .0001$). The older the toddler, the more likely he or she was to open all three stationary boxes ($F[1, 232] = 33.42$, $p < .0001$). Similarly, the difference between performance in the stationary and the scrambled-box versions decreased with age—as can be seen, for example, on number of reaches to open all three boxes (stationary trials vs. scrambled-box trials, $F[1, 231] = 29.74$, $p < .0001$).

Group Differences: PKU and MHP Groups Analyzed Separately

No significant differences on this task emerged between PKU and MHP participants, between either of these groups and any comparison groups, or within either group by plasma Phe level regardless of the measure of plasma Phe used.

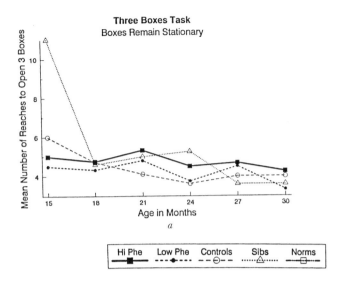

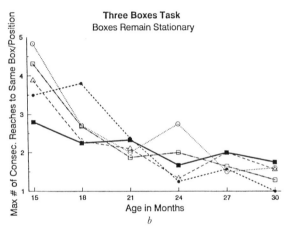

FIGURE 11.—Performance on the three boxes task (boxes remain stationary) of toddlers in the five subject groups. *a,* Mean number of reaches to open three boxes. *b,* Maximum number of consecutive reaches to same box/position.

Sex Differences

When all participants were included in the analysis, there was no significant difference in the performance of the boys compared to that of the girls. However, among just the participants with PKU, boys performed significantly better than girls—as can be seen, for example, on number of reaches to open

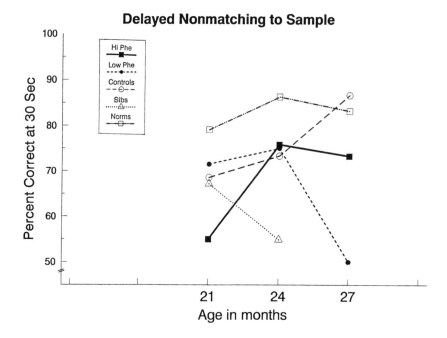

FIGURE 12.—Performance on the delayed nonmatching to sample task at the longest delay administered (30 sec) of toddlers in the five subject groups.

all three stationary boxes ($F[2, 69]$ = 44.13, $p < .0001$). For a summary of the results on this task, see Table 8.

THE DELAYED NONMATCHING TO SAMPLE TASK

Performance with Delays of 30 Sec

Group Differences: PKU and MHP Groups Combined

Human adults and macaques with medial temporal lobe damage succeed on the delayed nonmatching to sample task at brief delays but fail at longer delays. If any of our participant groups have problems in functions dependent on the medial temporal lobe, one would expect those participants to perform most differently from other participants at the longest delay (30 sec). We did find that PKU and MHP participants whose concurrent Phe levels were three times normal or higher performed worse than participants drawn from the general population ($F[4, 67]$ = 3.94, $p < .01$; orthogonal contrast: higher Phe vs. norms = 12.27, $p < .002$; see Figure 12). However, children with

112

higher Phe levels performed as well as children with lower Phe levels. Children with PKU or MHP performed comparably to their matched controls and siblings, regardless of whether their Phe levels were higher or lower than three times normal. Performance improved with age ($F[1, 71] = 2.15$, $p < .04$). The dip in performance at 27 months evident in Figure 12 is due to the fact that stimuli used at younger ages for delayed nonmatching to sample were used again at 27 months; that is, at 21 and 24 months the stimuli were novel, but at 27 months they were not.

Group Differences: PKU and MHP Groups Analyzed Separately

Toddlers with MHP whose Phe levels were 6 mg/dl or higher performed comparably to PKU participants with comparable Phe levels. However, MHP toddlers with lower Phe levels performed worse than did PKU toddlers with lower Phe levels ($F[6, 39] = 4.67$, $p < .002$; orthogonal contrast: lower MHP vs. lower PKU = 9.10, $p < .005$). MHP toddlers with Phe levels elevated *less* than three times normal also performed significantly *worse* than participants drawn from the general population and tended to perform *worse* than matched control subjects (orthogonal contrasts: lower MHP vs. norms = 13.35, $p < .001$; lower MHP vs. controls = 5.27, $p < .03$).

Among toddlers with PKU, level of Phe in the bloodstream during the 6 weeks immediately preceding testing was linearly and inversely related to performance ($F[1, 5] = 18.58$, $p < .004$). When the PKU participants were dichotomized, those whose Phe levels were three times normal or higher performed significantly worse than participants from the general population (orthogonal contrast = 13.77, $p < .001$) but not significantly worse than other PKU participants with lower Phe levels, matched controls, or siblings. Within a toddler over time, delayed nonmatching to sample performance tended to vary inversely with concurrent plasma Phe level; Pearson correlations ranged from −.66 to .42, with the mean being −.24. PKU participants with lower Phe levels and MHP participants with higher Phe levels did not differ significantly from controls, siblings, or norms in their performance at the 30-sec delay.

PKU toddlers whose Phe levels had been high during the first month of life performed significantly worse than participants from the general population ($F[6, 66] = 6.16$, $p < .0005$; orthogonal contrast: higher PKU vs. norms = 8.78, $p < .004$). PKU toddlers whose Phe levels had been *lower* during the first month performed significantly *worse* than children from the general population or matched controls (orthogonal contrasts: lower PKU vs. norms = 16.60, $p < .0001$; lower PKU vs. controls = 8.46, $p < .005$).

There was no significant linear relation between Phe levels during any other period of life and any measure of delayed nonmatching to sample performance.

Delayed Nonmatching to Sample

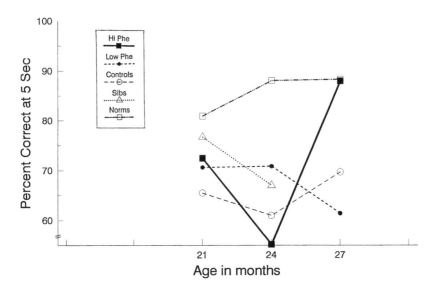

FIGURE 13.—Performance on the delayed nonmatching to sample task at the 5-sec delay of toddlers in the five subject groups.

Sex Differences

There were no significant sex differences and no significant sex × group interactions.

Performance at the 5-Sec Delay

Group Differences: PKU and MHP Groups Combined

Toddlers with higher Phe levels achieved percentages of correct responses comparable to all comparison groups (see Figure 13). There were no significant differences between subject groups in percentage of correct responses at the 5-sec delay.

Toddlers with higher Phe levels made more errors at the 5-sec delay than participants drawn from the general population ($F[4, 85] = 4.00$, $p < .01$; orthogonal contrast: higher Phe vs. norms = 10.35, $p < .003$). This was the only measure (and we looked at four: percentage of correct responses, number of errors to criterion, number of trials needed to pass criterion, and percentage of participants passing criterion) and the only comparison on this measure that yielded a difference significant at $p < .005$.

Regardless of plasma Phe level during the first month of life, PKU and MHP toddlers performed worse on the delayed nonmatching to sample task with a 5-sec delay than did the normative sample (orthogonal contrasts [number of trials to criterion]: higher Phe vs. norms = 12.59, p = .0005; lower Phe vs. norms = 9.01, p < .004; orthogonal contrasts [number of errors]: higher Phe vs. norms = 14.66, p < .0003; lower Phe vs. norms = 6.91, p < .01; orthogonal contrasts [percentage of correct responses]: higher Phe vs. norms = 18.20, p < .0001; lower Phe vs. norms = 8.12, p = .005).

Across groups, performance improved as participants grew older. This can be seen, for example, in the number of errors before passing criterion at the 5-sec delay ($F[1, 117]$ = 11.05, p = .001), number of trials to passing criterion ($F[1, 117]$ = 10.53, p < .002), and percentage of correct responses at the 5-sec delay ($F[1, 118]$ = 17.33, p < .0001).

Group Differences: PKU and MHP Groups Analyzed Separately

There were no significant differences between the PKU toddlers and the MHP toddlers on any measure of delayed nonmatching to sample performance at the 5-sec delay regardless of whether Phe level was controlled for.

Regardless of Phe level, toddlers with PKU did not show a significant difference in performance when compared to any group of participants on any dependent measure. Among participants with PKU, Phe level during the first month of life was significantly and directly related to the number of trials to criterion and inversely related to the percentage of correct reaches at the 5-sec delay ($F[1, 17]$ = 5.11, p < .04, and $F[1, 17]$ = 6.89, p < .02, respectively). Phe level was not significantly related to the number of errors at the 5-sec delay.

Among participants with MHP, those whose Phe levels were elevated *less* than three times normal achieved *lower* percentages of correct responses than participants from the general population ($F[6, 53]$ = 2.22, p = .05; orthogonal contrast: lower MHP vs. norms = 13.35, p < .001). Otherwise, regardless of Phe level, toddlers with MHP performed like other participants on all dependent measures. There was no significant linear relation between Phe level during any period of life and any measure of delayed nonmatching to sample performance for the MHP toddlers.

Sex Differences

There were no significant sex differences and no significant sex × group interactions. For a summary of the results on the delayed nonmatching to sample task, see Table 8.

THE GLOBAL-LOCAL SPATIAL PROCESSING TASK
(PREFERENTIAL LOOKING TECHNIQUE)

Group Differences: PKU and MHP Groups Combined

We investigated mean percentage of time fixating the novel stimulus, mean looking time during the test phase, and percentage of trials on which the novel or familiar stimulus was fixated more than chance. We investigated each of these once for global test trials, once for local test trials, and again for all trials combined. We investigated each of these when the test stimuli were small, medium, and large and when the test stimuli were the same size as the corresponding stimuli in the hierarchical figures (e.g., an H made up of S's tested by showing a large H and a small S) or opposite in size to the corresponding stimuli (e.g., an H made up of S's tested by showing a small H and a large S), and we looked at the interaction of this with the global/local condition. We also investigated the number of unusable trials for each participant within a given session. A trial was unusable if the child was so fidgety that we could not get him or her to look at the stimulus cards on that trial.

We found no significant difference among any of the subject groups on any of these dependent measures; however, at 15 and 18 months there were few usable sessions for the higher-Phe children because they were too fidgety and distractible, disinclined to sit still and look at our pictures. At 30 months most sessions for not only the children with higher Phe levels but also their siblings and matched controls were unusable for the same reason.

Toddlers tended to look to the familiar stimulus about 55% of the time regardless of their group membership (see Figure 14). Performance tended to be better (i.e., the difference in the amount of time spent looking at novel and familiar stimuli showed a larger difference) for the global features of the stimuli than for the local features. This difference was statistically significant at 18 and 27 months of age (percentage of fixation to the novel stimulus [global vs. local trials]: at 18 months, $t[1, 14] = 2.12$, $p < .05$; at 27 months, $t[1, 18] = 2.54$, $p = .02$).

Group Differences: PKU and MHP Groups Analyzed Separately

There were no significant differences between the performance of PKU and MHP toddlers on the global-local task, nor within either of these two groups did the toddlers with higher plasma Phe concentrations perform significantly differently than toddlers with lower Phe concentrations as a group. However, among PKU and MHP toddlers, mean level of Phe in the bloodstream was significantly related to the percentage of time a child fixated the

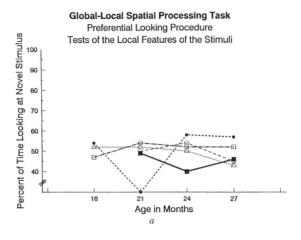

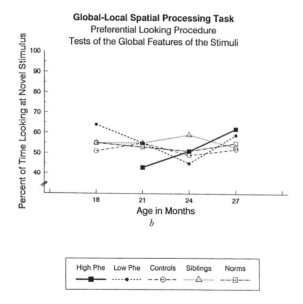

FIGURE 14.—Performance on the global-local spatial processing task (preferential look-ing procedure) of toddlers in the five subject groups. *a*, Tests of the local features of the stimuli. *b*, Tests of the global features of the stimuli.

novel stimulus on trials testing attention to the local features ($F[1, 9] = 12.15$, $p < .01$) and on all trials combined ($F[1, 9] = 11.28$, $p < .01$). That is, the higher the plasma Phe level during the 15 months of testing, the worse the toddler's performance, especially when attention to local details was tested. The toddlers who performed better spent more time looking at the familiar

117

stimuli than at the novel stimuli; the toddlers who performed worse divided their looking time more equally (i.e., we could discern no indication from their behavior that they recognized that one of the stimuli was familiar).

The mean plasma Phe level during the first year of life was significantly related to the percentage of time fixating the novel stimulus on global test trials ($F[1, 9] = 5.08$, $p < .05$) and over all trials combined ($F[1, 9] = 5.61$, $p < .03$). Participants with higher plasma Phe levels tended to be more fidgety and thus to have slightly fewer usable trials than participants with lower Phe levels, controlling for age ($F[1, 9] = 4.45$, $p = .06$).

Sex Differences

When all participants were included in the analysis, there was no significant difference in the performance of boys compared to that of girls. However, among the children with PKU, boys performed significantly better than girls (for global test trials, $F[1, 5] = 8.17$, $p < .05$; for local test trials, $F[1, 5] = 21.95$, $p < .001$). This was found at all individual ages for the local test trials but only at the youngest ages for the global test trials. For a summary of the results on this task, see Table 8.

RELATIONS AMONG PERFORMANCE ON THE TASKS ADMINISTERED TO TODDLERS

There were no significant interrelations between performance on any of the four tasks administered to the toddlers. Performance on three of these tasks did bear some relation to later IQ scores, however, although in general this relation was not strong. The strongest relation was between performance on the delayed nonmatching to sample task and later IQ (for linear regression of percentage correct at the 30-sec delay on IQ, $F[1, 12] = 4.61$, $p < .05$; percentage correct at the 5-sec delay on IQ, $F[1, 18] = 5.11$, $p < .04$; and errors to criterion at the 5-sec delay on IQ, $F[1, 18] = 8.18$, $p < .02$).

VII. RESULTS: YOUNG CHILDREN

THE DAY-NIGHT STROOP-LIKE TASK

Group Differences: PKU and MHP Groups Combined

Children with higher plasma Phe levels were correct on significantly fewer trials on the day-night task than was the normative sample or matched controls ($F[4, 306] = 2.54$, $p = .05$; orthogonal contrasts: higher Phe vs. norms = 7.29, $p < .005$; higher Phe vs. controls = 7.95, $p = .0025$; see Figure 15). They also tended to perform worse than other PKU and MHP children with lower plasma Phe levels or their own siblings, although these latter differences were not significant at $p < .005$ (see Table 9).

Regardless of group membership, children generally performed better on the task as they got older; the main effect for age was $F(1, 306) = 46.43$, $p < .0001$. Many of the youngest children ($3\frac{1}{2}$ years old) found it almost impossible to sustain good performance on the task after the first few trials. Most of the oldest children (7 years old) in all groups performed near ceiling. Hence, the group differences are even more striking between $4\frac{1}{2}$ and $6\frac{1}{2}$ years of age (participants tested longitudinally received only the control version of this task at 4 years).

Children of $4\frac{1}{2}$–$6\frac{1}{2}$ years of age whose Phe concentrations were 6 mg/dl or higher performed worse on the day-night task than other affected children with lower Phe levels, children from the general population, and matched controls ($F[4, 213] = 3.01$, $p < .02$; orthogonal contrasts: higher Phe vs. lower Phe = 7.85, $p < .005$; higher Phe vs. norms = 10.02, $p < .0025$; higher Phe vs. controls = 9.43, $p < .0025$). They also tended to perform worse than siblings (see Table 9).

Performance on the day-night task was significantly related to IQ test performance (linear regression, $F[1, 80] = 7.32$, $p < .008$). All group differences on the day-night task remained significant controlling for IQ.

The analyses presented above were based on sessions where participants had passed the pretest. Children with higher Phe levels were also significantly

119

Day-Night Stroop-Like Task

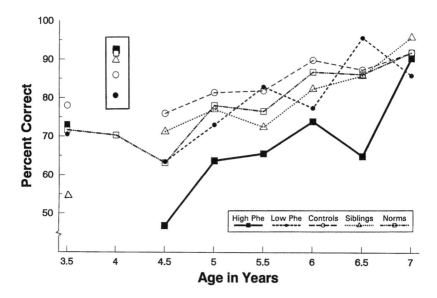

FIGURE 15.—Performance on the day-night Stroop-like task of children in the five sub-ject groups. The data points in the rectangle represent the results for the control condition of the task. The only condition administered to the children tested longitudinally at 4 years of age was the control condition. In the normative sample, which was tested cross-sectionally, some children received the control condition at age 4, while others received the experimen-tal condition.

more likely to fail the pretest ($F[4, 306] = 6.24$, $p < .0005$; orthogonal con-trasts: higher Phe vs. lower Phe $= 15.97$, $p < .0001$; higher Phe vs. norms $= 10.02$, $p < .0005$; higher Phe vs. controls $= 13.17$, $p < .0002$; higher Phe vs. siblings $= 6.70$, $p = .005$). No child with lower Phe levels and no matched control subject failed the pretest after the age of $3\frac{1}{2}$ years. By $4\frac{1}{2}$ years of age, 75% of both the siblings of the PKU and MHP participants and the chil-dren drawn from the general population were succeeding on the pretest; by 5 years, all such participants passed. On the other hand, only 50% of the children whose plasma Phe levels were three times normal or higher passed the pretest at age $4\frac{1}{2}$ years, and even by $5\frac{1}{2}$ years 20% of these participants were still unable to pass.

Other variables—such as response latency, response latency on just the first four or last four trials, or percentage correct on just the first four or last four trials—did not yield significant group differences. If children with higher Phe levels had performed more poorly because they were unable to sustain their attention over the 16 trials of the task, there should have been widening group differences in performance later and later in the testing sessions. This was not found. Children with higher Phe levels had more difficulty keeping the two rules in mind and inhibiting the predominant response throughout the testing session.

Children whose Phe levels were below 6 mg/dl performed very much like the children from the general population, matched controls, and siblings whether the children had PKU or MHP; no analyses yielded any significant differences between children whose Phe levels were low and any of the control groups on the day-night task. Similarly, there were no significant differences in performance on the day-night task or in the percentage of participants passing the pretest among any of the control groups.

When PKU and MHP children were divided into higher- and lower-Phe groups on the basis of their mean Phe level during the entire period from 3 to 7 years, results were comparable to those reported above. However, there were no significant differences in performance on the day-night Stroop-like task by Phe concentration during the first year of life or during the first month of life. Results were mixed for children whose Phe levels were outside the range of 2–6 mg/dl more than 20% of the time; they performed significantly worse than the matched controls or children from the general population ($F[4, 306] = 2.54$, $p < .04$; orthogonal contrasts: outside curve vs. controls $= 7.75$, $p < .005$; outside curve vs. norms $= 7.67$, $p = .005$) but comparably to other PKU and MHP children and to their own siblings.

Group Differences: PKU and MHP Groups Analyzed Separately

There was no significant difference in the performance of PKU and MHP children, controlling for any measure of plasma Phe level. There was also, however, no significant difference between the percentage of correct answers achieved by the MHP children, even those whose Phe levels were 6 mg/dl or higher, and that achieved by any of the comparison groups. MHP children with high levels of Phe in their bloodstreams showed a level of performance on the day-night task intermediate between that of the PKU children with high Phe levels and all other participants. However, only three MHP children had Phe levels classified as high; it is possible that the absence of any significant difference between their performance and that of other subject groups is due simply to the paucity of MHP participants in this age range with higher Phe levels.

Children with PKU whose plasma Phe levels were 6 mg/dl or higher succeeded on fewer trials than other PKU children with lower Phe levels, children from the general population, or matched controls ($F[6, 304] = 2.19$, $p < .05$; orthogonal contrasts: higher PKU vs. lower PKU $= 6.68$, $p = .005$; higher PKU vs. norms $= 9.96$, $p < .005$; higher PKU vs. controls $= 10.51$, $p = .005$). PKU children with higher Phe levels were also less likely to pass

TABLE 9

Summary of the Results on the Ten Cognitive Neuropsychological Tests Administered to Young Children

	Day-Night Stroop-like Task {Concurrent Phe Level}		Control Version of Day-Night Stroop-like Task {Concurrent Phe Level} [% Correct]
	[Passing Pretest]	[% Correct][a]	
High Phe vs. low Phe	****, H < L	*, H < L	N.S.
High Phe vs. norms	***, H < N	*, H < N	N.S.
High Phe vs. controls	***, H < C	*, H < C	N.S.
High Phe vs. siblings	*, H < S	.01, H < S	N.S.
Low Phe vs. norms	N.S.	N.S.	.05, L < N
Low Phe vs. controls	N.S.	N.S.	.02, L < C
Low Phe vs. siblings	N.S.	N.S.	N.S.
Controls vs. norms	N.S.	N.S.	N.S.
Controls vs. siblings	N.S.	N.S.	.03, S < C
Siblings vs. norms	N.S.	N.S.	.03, S < N
High PKU vs. low PKU	****, H < L	**, H < L	N.S.
High PKU vs. norms	***, H < N	***, H < N	N.S.
High PKU vs. controls	*, H < C	**, H < C	N.S.
High PKU vs. siblings	****, H < S	*, H < S	N.S.

122

Low PKU vs. N, C, S	N.S.	N.S.	.02, *, L < N, C
MHP vs. PKU	N.S.	N.S.	N.S.
High MHP vs. high PKU	N.S.	N.S.	N.S.
Low MHP vs. low PKU	N.S.	N.S.	N.S.
High MHP vs. low MHP	N.S.	N.S.	N.S.
High MHP vs. norms	N.S.	N.S.	N.S.
High MHP vs. controls	N.S.	N.S.	N.S.
High MHP vs. siblings	N.S.	N.S.	N.S.
Low MHP vs. N, C, S	N.S.	N.S.	.05, .01, L < N, C
Other Phe measures showing a group difference	Mean level throughout testing period (H < L, N, C, S); % of levels w/in 2–6 mg/dl (H < C, N)	Mean level throughout testing period (H < L, N, C, S); % of levels w/in 2–6 mg/dl (H < C, N)	
Phe measures directly, inversely related to performance for PKU subjects	*Every* measure	Concurrent Phe level	PKU and MHP: concurrent Phe level
Phe measures directly, inversely related to performance for MHP subjects	Concurrent Phe level	Concurrent Phe level	Concurrent Phe level
Sex differences	None	None	None

123

TABLE 9 (*Continued*)

TAPPING
{Concurrent Phe Level}

	[Passing Pretest]	[% Correct][a]	[% Correct][b]
High Phe vs. low Phe	*, H < L	*, H < L	.02, H < L
High Phe vs. norms	****, H < N	.02, H < N	****, H < N
High Phe vs. controls	****, H < C	.025, H < C	****, H < C
High Phe vs. siblings	***, H < S	.015, H < S	***, H < S
Low Phe vs. norms	N.S.	.01, L < N	N.S.
Low Phe vs. controls	N.S.	N.S.	N.S.
Low Phe vs. siblings	N.S.	N.S.	N.S.
Controls vs. norms	N.S.	N.S.	N.S.
Controls vs. siblings	N.S.	N.S.	N.S.
Siblings vs. norms	N.S.	N.S.	N.S.
High PKU vs. low PKU	***, H < L	.01, H < L	.02, H < L
High PKU vs. norms	****, H < N	.015, H < N	****, H < N
High PKU vs. controls	****, H < C	.015, H < C	****, H < C
High PKU vs. siblings	****, H < S	.01, H < S	**, H < S

124

Low PKU vs. N, C, S	N.S.	N.S.
MHP vs. PKU	N.S.	N.S.
High MHP vs. high PKU	N.S.	N.S.
Low MHP vs. low PKU	N.S.	N.S.
High MHP vs. low MHP	N.S.	N.S.
High MHP vs. norms	N.S.	N.S.
High MHP vs. controls	N.S.	N.S.
High MHP vs. siblings	N.S.	N.S.
Low MHP vs. N, C, S	N.S.	N.S.
Other Phe measures showing a group difference	Mean level throughout testing period	Mean level throughout testing period
Phe measures directly, inversely related to performance for PKU subjects	Concurrent Phe level	Concurrent Phe level
Phe measures directly, inversely related to performance for MHP subjects	Concurrent Phe level	Concurrent Phe level
Sex differences	None	.04, M < F

125

TABLE 9 (*Continued*)

	Three Pegs [Level at Which Succeeded in Tapping in Order Instructed]ᵃ {Concurrent Phe Level}	Corsi-Milner Test of Temporal Order Memory [% Correct] {Concurrent Phe Level}	
		Simple Black-and-White Stimuli	Complex Colored Stimuli
High Phe vs. low Phe	***, H < L	N.S.	N.S.
High Phe vs. norms	****, H < N	N.S.	N.S.
High Phe vs. controls	****, H < C	N.S.	N.S.
High Phe vs. siblings	***, H < S	N.S.	N.S.
Low Phe vs. norms	.03, L < C	N.S.	N.S.
Low Phe vs. controls	N.S.	N.S.	N.S.
Low Phe vs. siblings	N.S.	N.S.	N.S.
Controls vs. norms	.02, N < C	N.S.	N.S.
Controls vs. siblings	.01, S < C	N.S.	N.S.
Siblings vs. norms	N.S.	N.S.	N.S.
High PKU vs. low PKU	***, H < L	N.S.	N.S.
High PKU vs. norms	****, H < N	N.S.	N.S.
High PKU vs. controls	****, H < C	N.S.	N.S.
High PKU vs. siblings	**, H < S	N.S.	N.S.
Low PKU vs. N, C, S	N.S.	N.S.	N.S.

MHP vs. PKU	* P < M	N.S.	N.S.
High MHP vs. high PKU	N.S.	N.S.	N.S.
Low MHP vs. low PKU	N.S.	N.S.	N.S.
High MHP vs. low MHP	.05, H < L	N.S.	N.S.
High MHP vs. norms	.04, H < N	N.S.	N.S.
High MHP vs. controls	.01, H < C	N.S.	N.S.
High MHP vs. siblings	N.S.	N.S.	N.S.
Low MHP vs. N, C, S	N.S.	N.S.	N.S.
Other Phe measures showing a group difference	Mean level throughout testing period (H < N, C); every Phe measure (H < C)		
Phe measures directly, inversely related to performance for PKU subjects	Concurrent Phe level (p = .7); % of levels w/in 2–6 mg/dl		
Phe measures directly, inversely related to performance for MHP subjects			
Sex differences	.01, M < F	None	***, F < M
Among PKU			

TABLE 9 (*Continued*)

CORSI-MILNER TEST OF RECOGNITION MEMORY
[% Correct]
{Concurrent Phe Level}

	Simple Black-and-White Stimuli		Complex Colored Stimuli	
	Tested Immediately	Tested after 25-Min Delay	Tested Immediately	Tested after 25-Min Delay
High Phe vs. low Phe	N.S.	N.S.	N.S.	N.S.
High Phe vs. norms	N.S.	N.S.	N.S.	N.S.
High Phe vs. controls	N.S.	N.S.	N.S.	N.S.
High Phe vs. siblings	N.S.	N.S.	N.S.	N.S.
Low Phe vs. norms	N.S.	N.S.	N.S.	N.S.
Low Phe vs. controls	N.S.	N.S.	N.S.	N.S.
Low Phe vs. siblings	N.S.	N.S.	N.S.	N.S.
Controls vs. norms	N.S.	N.S.	N.S.	N.S.
Controls vs. siblings	N.S.	N.S.	N.S.	N.S.
Siblings vs. norms	N.S.	N.S.	N.S.	N.S.
High PKU vs. low PKU	N.S.	N.S.	N.S.	N.S.
High PKU vs. norms	N.S.	N.S.	N.S.	N.S.
High PKU vs. controls	N.S.	N.S.	N.S.	N.S.
High PKU vs. siblings	N.S.	N.S.	N.S.	N.S.

Low PKU vs. N, C, S	N.S.	N.S.	N.S.	N.S.
MHP vs. PKU	N.S.	N.S.	N.S.	N.S.
High MHP vs. high PKU	N.S.	N.S.	N.S.	N.S.
Low MHP vs. low PKU	N.S.	N.S.	N.S.	N.S.
High MHP vs. low MHP	N.S.	N.S.	N.S.	N.S.
High MHP vs. norms	N.S.	N.S.	N.S.	N.S.
High MHP vs. controls	N.S.	N.S.	N.S.	N.S.
High MHP vs. siblings	N.S.	N.S.	N.S.	N.S.
Low MHP vs. N, C, S	N.S.	N.S.	N.S.	N.S.
Other Phe measures showing a group difference				
Phe measures directly, inversely related to performance for PKU subjects				
Phe measures directly, inversely related to performance for MHP subjects				
Sex differences	None	None	None	None

129

TABLE 9 (*Continued*)

| | | Six Boxes (Boxes Scrambled after Each Reach) [Concurrent Phe Level] | | |
	[Number of Boxes Opened]	[Number of Reaches to Open All Boxes]	[Number of Reaches until First Error]	[Maximum Number of Consecutive Reaches to Same Box]
High Phe vs. low Phe	N.S.	N.S.	N.S.	N.S.
High Phe vs. norms	N.S.	N.S.	***, H < N	N.S.
High Phe vs. controls	N.S.	.02, C < H	N.S.	N.S.
High Phe vs. siblings	N.S.	N.S.	N.S.	N.S.
Low Phe vs. norms	N.S.	*, L < N	N.S.	N.S.
Low Phe vs. controls	N.S.	N.S.	N.S.	N.S.
Low Phe vs. siblings	N.S.	N.S.	N.S.	N.S.
Controls vs. norms	N.S.	.03, C < N	N.S.	N.S.
Controls vs. siblings	N.S.	N.S.	N.S.	N.S.
Siblings vs. norms	N.S.	N.S.	N.S.	N.S.
High PKU vs. low PKU	N.S.	N.S.	N.S.	N.S.
High PKU vs. norms	N.S.	N.S.	N.S.	N.S.
High PKU vs. controls	N.S.	N.S.	N.S.	N.S.
High PKU vs. siblings	N.S.	N.S.	N.S.	N.S.

Measure			
Low PKU vs. N, C, S	N.S.	N.S.	N.S.
MHP vs. PKU	N.S.	N.S.	N.S.
High MHP vs. high PKU	N.S.	N.S.	N.S.
Low MHP vs. low PKU	N.S.	N.S.	N.S.
High MHP vs. low MHP	N.S.	N.S.	N.S.
High MHP vs. norms	N.S.	N.S.	N.S.
High MHP vs. controls	N.S.	N.S.	N.S.
High MHP vs. siblings	N.S.	N.S.	N.S.
Low MHP vs. N, C, S	N.S.	N.S.	N.S.
Other Phe measures showing a group difference		None	
Phe measures directly, inversely related to performance for PKU subjects		Concurrent Phe level	
Phe measures directly, inversely related to performance for MHP subjects		Concurrent Phe level	
Sex differences	None	****, M < F	****, M < F

131

TABLE 9 (*Continued*)

	SIX BOXES (Boxes Remain Stationary) [Concurrent Phe Level]		
	[Number of Boxes Opened]	[Number of Reaches to Open All Boxes]	[Number of Reaches until First Error]	[Maximum Number of Consecutive Reaches to Same Box]
High Phe vs. low Phe	N.S.	N.S.	N.S.	N.S.
High Phe vs. norms	N.S.	N.S.	N.S.	N.S.
High Phe vs. controls	N.S.	N.S.	N.S.	N.S.
High Phe vs. siblings	N.S.	N.S.	N.S.	N.S.
Low Phe vs. norms	N.S.	N.S.	N.S.	N.S.
Low Phe vs. controls	N.S.	N.S.	N.S.	N.S.
Low Phe vs. siblings	N.S.	N.S.	N.S.	N.S.
Controls vs. norms	N.S.	N.S.	N.S.	N.S.
Controls vs. siblings	N.S.	N.S.	N.S.	N.S.
Siblings vs. norms	N.S.	N.S.	N.S.	N.S.
High PKU vs. low PKU	N.S.	N.S.	N.S.	N.S.
High PKU vs. norms	N.S.	N.S.	N.S.	N.S.
High PKU vs. controls	N.S.	N.S.	N.S.	N.S.
High PKU vs. siblings	N.S.	N.S.	N.S.	N.S.

132

Low PKU vs. N, C, S	N.S.	N.S.	N.S.	N.S.
MHP vs. PKU	N.S.	N.S.	N.S.	N.S.
High MHP vs. high PKU	N.S.	N.S.	N.S.	N.S.
Low MHP vs. low PKU	N.S.	N.S.	N.S.	N.S.
High MHP vs. low MHP	N.S.	N.S.	N.S.	N.S.
High MHP vs. norms	N.S.	N.S.	N.S.	N.S.
High MHP vs. controls	N.S.	N.S.	N.S.	N.S.
High MHP vs. siblings	N.S.	N.S.	N.S.	N.S.
Low MHP vs. N, C, S	N.S.	N.S.	N.S.	N.S.
Other Phe measures showing a group difference				
Phe measures directly, inversely related to performance for PKU subjects				
Phe measures directly, inversely related to performance for MHP subjects				
Sex differences	.01, M < F	*, M < F	.01, M < F	*, M < F

TABLE 9 (*Continued*)

GLOBAL-LOCAL SPATIAL PROCESSING: FORCED CHOICE
[Concurrent Phe Level]

	All		Global Features	
	[Reaction Time]	[% Correct]	[Reaction Time]	[% Correct]
High Phe vs. low Phe	N.S.	N.S.	N.S.	.05, H < L
High Phe vs. norms	N.S.	N.S.	N.S.	N.S.
High Phe vs. controls	N.S.	N.S.	N.S.	.01, H < C
High Phe vs. siblings	N.S.	N.S.	N.S.	N.S.
Low Phe vs. norms	N.S.	.02, L < N	N.S.	N.S.
Low Phe vs. controls	N.S.	N.S.	N.S.	N.S.
Low Phe vs. siblings	N.S.	.01, L < S	N.S.	N.S.
Controls vs. norms	N.S.	N.S.	N.S.	N.S.
Controls vs. siblings	N.S.	N.S.	N.S.	N.S.
Siblings vs. norms	N.S.	N.S.	N.S.	N.S.
High PKU vs. low PKU	N.S.	N.S.	N.S.	.02, H < L
High PKU vs. norms	N.S.	N.S.	N.S.	****, H < N
High PKU vs. controls	N.S.	N.S.	N.S.	****, H < C
High PKU vs. siblings	N.S.	N.S.	N.S.	**, H < S

134

Low PKU vs. N, C, S	N.S.	N.S.	N.S.	N.S.
MHP vs. PKU	N.S.	N.S.	N.S.	N.S.
High MHP vs. high PKU	N.S.	N.S.	N.S.	.04, P < M
Low MHP vs. low PKU	N.S.	N.S.	N.S.	N.S.
High MHP vs. low MHP	N.S.	N.S.	N.S.	N.S.
High MHP vs. norms	N.S.	N.S.	N.S.	*, H < N[c]
High MHP vs. controls	N.S.	N.S.	N.S.	*, H < C[c]
High MHP vs. siblings	N.S.	N.S.	N.S.	.01, H < S[c]
Low MHP vs. N, C, S	N.S.	N.S.	N.S.	N.S.
Other Phe measures showing a group difference				
Phe measures directly, inversely related to performance for PKU subjects				Concurrent Phe levels
Phe measures directly, inversely related to performance for MHP subjects				Concurrent Phe levels
Sex differences	None	None	None	None

TABLE 9 (*Continued*)

	GLOBAL-LOCAL SPATIAL PROCESSING: FORCED CHOICE: LOCAL {Concurrent Phe Level}		LINE BISECTION [% Deviation from Center of Line] {Concurrent Phe Level}
	[Reaction Time]	[% Correct]	
High Phe vs. low Phe	N.S.	N.S.	N.S.
High Phe vs. norms	N.S.	N.S.	N.S.
High Phe vs. controls	N.S.	N.S.	N.S.
High Phe vs. siblings	N.S.	N.S.	N.S.
Low Phe vs. norms	N.S.	$*$, L < N	N.S.
Low Phe vs. controls	N.S.	.04, L < C	N.S.
Low Phe vs. siblings	N.S.	$*$, L < S	N.S.
Controls vs. norms	N.S.	N.S.	N.S.
Controls vs. siblings	N.S.	N.S.	N.S.
Siblings vs. norms	N.S.	N.S.	N.S.
High PKU vs. low PKU	N.S.	N.S.	N.S.
High PKU vs. norms	N.S.	N.S.	N.S.
High PKU vs. controls	N.S.	N.S.	N.S.
High PKU vs. siblings	N.S.	N.S.	N.S.
Low PKU vs. N, C, S	$****$, L < $N,^{d}$ S	$**$, 0.4, $**$, L < N, C, S	N.S.
MHP vs. PKU	N.S.	N.S.	N.S.
High MHP vs. high PKU	N.S.	N.S.	N.S.
Low MHP vs. low PKU	N.S.	N.S.	N.S.

High MHP vs. low MHP	N.S.	N.S.	N.S.
High MHP vs. norms	N.S.	N.S.	N.S.
High MHP vs. controls	N.S.	N.S.	N.S.
High MHP vs. siblings	N.S.	N.S.	N.S.
Low MHP vs. N, C, S[d]	.04, .02 L < N, S[d]	.04, L < S	N.S.
Other Phe measures showing a group difference			
Phe measures directly, inversely related to performance for PKU subjects			
Phe measures directly, inversely related to performance for MHP subjects			
Sex differences	None	None	None

NOTE.—Dependent measures are given in square brackets, plasma Phe measures in curly braces. H = high Phe (plasma Phe levels 6–10 mg/dl); L = low Phe (plasma Phe levels 3–6 mg/dl); N = norms (children from the general population); C = controls (matched controls for the PKU and MHP participants with higher plasma Phe levels); S = siblings (siblings of the PKU and MHP participants); M = high/low MHP; P = high/low PKU. For sex differences only: M = male; F = female. N.S. = not significant. Concurrent Phe level = the mean plasma Phe level during the 6-week period preceding testing.

[a] The group differences are based on ages 4½–6½ years.
[b] Includes children who failed the pretest.
[c] Only when the test stimuli were intermediate in size.
[d] These group differences were found only when pictorial stimuli were used, not letters.
* $p < .005$.
** $p < .001$.
*** $p < .0005$.
**** $p < .0001$.

137

the pretest than any other group of children tested ($F[6, 304] = 4.69$, $p < .0004$; orthogonal contrasts: higher PKU vs. lower PKU = 18.80, $p < .0001$; higher PKU vs. norms = 12.65, $p < .0005$; higher PKU vs. controls = 7.90, $p < .005$; higher PKU vs. siblings = 17.02, $p < .0001$). These differences were even more pronounced between the ages of 4½ and 6½ years (i.e., the differences between PKU children and all other groups were even more pronounced if one omits the ages where ceiling and floor effects were found).

Percentage of correct responses on the day-night Stroop-like task was significantly and inversely related to level of Phe in the bloodstream only among MHP participants ($F[1, 5] = 16.49$, $p < .01$). Within individual MHP children, performance covaried significantly with plasma Phe level from $r = -.55$ to $r = -.94$, with a mean of $r = -.67$; within PKU children, the mean Pearson correlation of performance with Phe level was $-.12$. The percentage of children failing the pretest, on the other hand, was significantly and inversely related to every measure of plasma Phe among the PKU participants (e.g., concurrent Phe levels, $F[1, 41] = 20.37$, $p < .0001$; mean Phe levels between 3 and 7 years, $F[1, 65] = 5.97$, $p < .02$; area under the curve, $F[1, 65] = 8.12$, $p < .01$). Concurrent Phe levels were also directly and inversely related to pretest performance among participants with MHP ($F[1, 7] = 9.39$, $p < .04$).

Sex Differences

There were no significant sex differences and no significant sex × group interactions. For a summary of the results on the day-night Stroop-like task, see Table 9.

THE CONTROL CONDITION FOR THE DAY-NIGHT STROOP-LIKE TASK

At 4 years of age, children were asked to say "day" and "night" in response to two different abstract designs, rather than in response to images of the moon and the sun. All groups of children performed significantly better on this control version at 4 years than they did on the day-night task at either 3½ or 4½ years of age. No group of children averaged less than 80% correct on this control task, and most groups performed at about the 90% level (see Figure 15).

Group Differences: PKU and MHP Groups Combined

All groups of children performed relatively well on this control version of the day-night Stroop-like task (see Figure 15). PKU and MHP children with higher Phe levels performed no worse than any other group of children, regardless of the Phe measure used to dichotomize the PKU plus MHP group. Similarly, no significant difference in performance on the task was found among any of the comparison groups.

Group Differences: PKU and MHP Groups Analyzed Separately

There was no significant difference in the performance of PKU and MHP children, controlling for any measure of plasma Phe level. The only significant difference between the performance of PKU and MHP children and that of any comparison group was that PKU children with *lower* Phe levels performed *worse* than matched controls on this task ($F[6, 72] = 2.38$, $p < .04$; orthogonal contrast: lower PKU vs. controls $= 10.13$, $p < .003$). Among the PKU and MHP participants combined, and among the MHP participants alone, performance was linearly related to plasma Phe level ($F[1, 38] = 7.28$, $p = .01$, and $F[1, 14] = 6.56$, $p < .03$, respectively).

Sex Differences

There were no significant sex differences and no significant sex × group interactions. Performance on this task was not significantly related to IQ test performance. For a summary of the results on the control condition of the day-night Stroop-like task, see Table 9.

THE TAPPING TEST

Group Differences: PKU and MHP Groups Combined

There proved to be too little opportunity to demonstrate an understanding of the rules for the tapping test during pretesting. Only the fastest learners passed the pretest. Many children who went on to perform significantly better than chance on the test had not demonstrated an understanding of the task instructions during the pretest. There was a group difference in the percentage of children passing the tapping pretest. Significantly more children whose plasma Phe concentrations were 6 mg/dl or higher failed to pass the pretest ($F[4, 341] = 19.08$, $p < .0001$; orthogonal contrasts: higher Phe vs. lower Phe $= 6.88$, $p < .005$; higher Phe vs. norms $= 61.60$, $p < .0001$; higher Phe vs. controls $= 21.22$, $p < .0001$; higher Phe vs. siblings $= 11.26$, $p < .0005$). There was no group difference, however, in performance on the

139

first four test trials. This is consistent with the interpretation that the pretest was too brief for many children to demonstrate comprehension of the task instructions; their performance on the initial test trials, however, indicates that they did understand what they were being asked to do.

First, consider the test performance of only those children who passed the pretest. Looking at the entire age range from $3\frac{1}{2}$ to 7 years, there was no significant difference across the groups of children in percentage of correct responses on the tapping task. However, if one considers only the middle of the age range ($4\frac{1}{2}$–$6\frac{1}{2}$ years of age), clear group differences emerge.[7] Children with Phe concentrations of 6 mg/dl or higher performed significantly worse than other PKU and MHP children with lower Phe concentrations and tended to perform worse than the other comparison groups as well ($F[4, 201] = 3.86$, $p = .05$; orthogonal contrasts: higher Phe vs. lower Phe $= 6.85$, $p < .005$; high Phe vs. norms $= 4.13$, $p = .02$; higher Phe vs. controls $= 4.01$, $p < .03$; higher Phe vs. siblings $= 4.53$, $p < .02$).

Now, consider the performance of all children, even those who failed the pretest. Children with higher plasma Phe concentrations performed significantly worse than each comparison group, except siblings, if one considers the entire age range ($F[4, 341] = 8.06$, $p < .0001$; orthogonal contrasts: higher Phe vs. lower Phe $= 4.13$, $p = .02$; higher Phe vs. norms $= 28.48$, $p < .0001$; higher Phe vs. controls $= 16.12$, $p < .0001$; higher Phe vs. siblings $= 9.02$, $p < .0025$) and significantly worse than all comparison groups if one considers only the ages of $4\frac{1}{2}$–$6\frac{1}{2}$ years ($F[4, 210] = 9.39$, $p < .0001$; orthogonal contrasts: higher Phe vs. lower Phe $= 23.33$, $p < .0001$; higher Phe vs. norms $= 33.92$, $p < .0001$; higher Phe vs. controls $= 20.77$, $p < .0001$; higher Phe vs. siblings $= 26.41$, $p < .0001$). (See Figure 16.)

Children who had PKU or MHP but whose plasma Phe levels were under 6 mg/dl were as likely to pass the pretest as children from the general population, matched controls, or the siblings of PKU and MHP children. In general, they also performed as well on the tapping task itself.

Results are similar, although not quite as strong, when PKU and MHP children were assigned to higher- and lower-Phe groups on the basis of their mean levels throughout the $3\frac{1}{2}$–7-year age range, rather than on the basis of their Phe levels during the 6 weeks preceding each testing session. However, when group assignments were based on Phe levels during the first

---

[7] Performance on each task administered to young children was analyzed over the entire age range and across the middle of the age range ($4\frac{1}{2}$–$6\frac{1}{2}$ years). This was done because it is difficult to find a single measure that is appropriate for children as young as $3\frac{1}{2}$ and as old as 7 years. Hence, the tests were generally most discriminable within the middle of the age range, while being too easy for the oldest children and too difficult for the youngest children.

Tapping Task

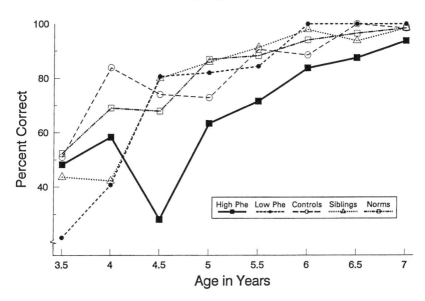

FIGURE 16.—Performance on the tapping task of children in the five subject groups

month or during the first year of life or on the area under the curve of the child's Phe levels, no significant differences were found among the groups.

There was no significant relation between performance on the tapping test and IQ when only the children who passed the pretest were included in the analysis. When children who failed the pretest were included in the analysis as well, percentage of correct responses on the tapping test was significantly related to IQ (linear regression, $F[1, 73] = 5.62$, $p < .02$). All group differences on the tapping test remained significant even controlling for IQ.

There were no significant differences among the performance of children from the general population, that of the matched controls, or that of the siblings of the PKU and MHP children in the percentage of children passing the pretest, performance of only those who passed the pretest, or performance including those who failed the pretest. Performance improved across all subject groups on all three of these measures as children grew older (percentage of children passing the pretest over age, $F[1, 341] = 41.14$, $p < .0001$; percentage of correct responses among children who passed the pretest, $F[1, 307] = 115.19$, $p < .0001$; percentage of correct responses including even children who failed the pretest, $F[1, 341] = 171.25$, $p < .0001$).

Other variables—such as response latency, response latency on just the earliest or latest trials, or percentage correct on the earliest or latest trials—did not yield any significant group differences.

Group Differences: PKU and MHP Groups Analyzed Separately

Children with PKU whose plasma Phe levels were 6 mg/dl or higher were significantly less likely to pass the pretest for the tapping task than children in any of the comparison groups ($F[6, 338] = 14.72$, $p < .0001$; orthogonal contrasts: higher PKU vs. lower PKU $= 10.10$, $p < .0005$; higher PKU vs. norms $= 29.96$, $p < .0001$; higher PKU vs. controls $= 14.41$, $p < .0001$; higher PKU vs. siblings $= 17.59$, $p < .0001$). When the children who failed the pretest were included in the analysis, the percentage of correct responses on the tapping task was significantly lower for PKU children whose Phe levels were 6 mg/dl or higher than for children from the general population, matched controls, or siblings and tended to be lower than the percentages for other PKU children with plasma Phe levels closer to normal ($F[6, 339] = 6.17$, $p < .0001$; orthogonal contrasts: higher PKU vs. norms $= 28.48$, $p < .0001$; higher PKU vs. controls $= 16.12$, $p = .0001$; higher PKU vs. siblings $= 9.02$, $p < .003$; higher PKU vs. lower PKU $= 4.13$, $p = .02$). Within the $4\frac{1}{2}$–$6\frac{1}{2}$-year age range, when the children who failed the pretest were included in the analysis, PKU children whose plasma Phe levels were three times normal or higher performed significantly worse than all comparison groups ($F[6, 208] = 9.39$, $p < .0001$; orthogonal contrasts: higher PKU vs. lower PKU $= 23.33$, $p < .0001$; higher PKU vs. norms $= 33.92$, $p < .0001$; higher PKU vs. controls $= 20.77$, $p < .0001$; higher PKU vs. siblings $= 26.41$, $p < .0001$).

MHP children whose plasma Phe levels were 6 mg/dl or higher performed at a level intermediate between that of PKU children with comparable Phe levels and the other groups of children. Regardless of the dependent measure or whether the entire age range or only the ages between $4\frac{1}{2}$ and $6\frac{1}{2}$ years were considered, no significant differences were found between the performance of MHP children with high levels of Phe and any other group of children, including PKU children with high plasma Phe levels.

Among those children who passed the pretest, performance on the tapping task did not show any direct relation with Phe level. Significant, inverse relations between performance on the tapping task and level of Phe in the bloodstream were found within the age range of $4\frac{1}{2}$–$6\frac{1}{2}$ years if the analysis included the children who had failed the pretest (PKU and MHP children combined, $F[1, 38] = 6.60$, $p < .02$; only those children with PKU, $F[1, 33] = 4.82$, $p < .04$; only MHP children, $F[1, 5] = 6.80$, $p < .05$). Within individual children, including even those children who failed the pretest, the relation between plasma Phe level and percentage of correct responses on the tapping task varied from $r = -.94$ to $r = .65$, with a mean of $r = -.43$.

Sex Differences

There were no significant sex differences or sex × group interactions in the percentage of children passing the pretest or in the performance of those who passed the pretest. However, in the percentage of correct answers including those participants who failed the pretest as well as those who passed, girls performed significantly better than boys (throughout the age range, $F[1, 341] = 4.43$, $p < .04$; within the age range of $4\frac{1}{2}$–$6\frac{1}{2}$ years, $F[1, 210] = 11.45$, $p < .001$). This sex difference was reversed (the boys performed better) among PKU and MHP children younger than 6 years of age whose plasma Phe levels were 6 mg/dl or higher ($F[2, 40] = 4.91$, $p < .05$). For a summary of the results on the tapping task, see Table 9.

THE THREE PEGS TASK

Group Differences: PKU and MHP Groups Combined

On the three pegs task, participants could succeed at any of three levels of difficulty—after verbal instructions alone, after a demonstration in addition to the verbal instructions, or after verbalizing the instructions themselves after having seen the demonstration and heard the verbal instructions—or fail despite all this help. Failure consisted of tapping the pegs in the order of their spatial arrangement, instead of in the order instructed. Performance improved dramatically on the task over age ($F[1, 343] = 130.30$, $p < .0001$). Children whose plasma Phe levels were 6 mg/dl or higher failed at levels of difficulty at which other children of the same age succeeded (see Figure 17). They performed significantly worse than all comparison groups ($F[4, 343] = 8.78$, $p < .0001$; orthogonal contrasts: higher Phe vs. lower Phe $= 10.97$, $p = .0005$; higher Phe vs. norms $= 23.97$, $p < .0001$; higher Phe vs. controls $= 33.23$, $p < .0001$; higher Phe vs. siblings $= 10.50$, $p = .0005$; all values are for the age range $4\frac{1}{2}$–$6\frac{1}{2}$ years of age). The difference between the performance of children with higher Phe levels and that of the other groups of children is also significant throughout the entire age range, despite the fact that most children reached ceiling on the task by about 6 years of age, as is evident from Figure 17.

Results are similar, although the group differences are not as pronounced, if one considers, not the most recent plasma Phe levels, but the children's mean Phe levels throughout the $3\frac{1}{2}$–7-year age range. Children whose mean Phe levels over the $3\frac{1}{2}$–7-year age range were 6 mg/dl or higher performed worse than the normative and matched control samples

Three Pegs Task

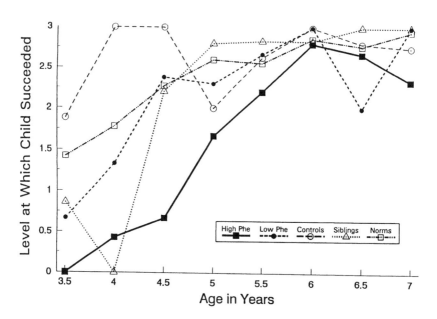

FIGURE 17.—Performance on the three pegs task of children in the five subject groups. Participants could succeed at any of three levels of difficulty—after verbal instructions alone (level 3), after a demonstration in addition to the verbal instructions (level 2), or after verbalizing the instructions themselves after having seen the demonstration and heard the verbal instructions (level 1). The more instructions subjects required, the lower the score their performance received.

$(F[4, 352] = 9.27, p < .005$; orthogonal contrasts: higher Phe vs. norms = 10.44, $p < .003$; higher Phe vs. controls = 19.04, $p < .0001$; values based on performance at ages $4\frac{1}{2}$–$6\frac{1}{2}$ years). They also tended to perform worse than the other two comparison groups, although the latter differences were not significant at $p < .005$ (see Table 9). Using all other Phe-level measures, such as mean Phe levels during the first month or the first year of life or the percentage of the area under the Phe curve within 2–6 mg/dl, children with higher Phe levels performed significantly worse than matched controls (e.g., using mean Phe levels during the first year, $F[4, 354] = 4.13$, $p < .003$; orthogonal contrast: higher Phe vs. controls = 13.69, $p = .0001$; values based on performance at $4\frac{1}{2}$–$6\frac{1}{2}$ years). There were no significant differences in performance on the three pegs task among the comparison groups. Children with Phe levels under 6 mg/dl (regardless of the time period over which Phe levels were calculated) performed as well as all other comparison groups.

Group Differences: PKU and MHP Groups Analyzed Separately

Children with PKU whose plasma Phe levels were 6 mg/dl or higher performed significantly worse than other PKU children with lower Phe levels, children from the general population, matched controls, and their own siblings ($F[6, 341] = 5.96$, $p < .0001$; orthogonal contrasts: higher PKU vs. lower PKU = 10.67, $p = .0005$; higher PKU vs. norms = 21.47, $p < .0001$; higher PKU vs. controls = 30.85, $p < .0001$; higher PKU vs. siblings = 9.72, $p < .001$; values based on performance at $4\frac{1}{2}$–$6\frac{1}{2}$ years). Children with MHP whose plasma Phe concentrations were 6 mg/dl or higher also showed some impairment on the three pegs task, although not as marked as for the children with PKU. The performance of MHP children whose Phe levels were 6 mg/dl or higher was similar to that of PKU children with comparable Phe levels and showed a tendency to be worse than other comparison groups, but none of the comparisons yielded differences that were statistically significant at the .005 level (see Table 9). Controlling for concurrent plasma Phe levels, PKU children performed significantly worse than MHP children ($F[1, 61] = 8.48$, $p = .005$).

The higher the level of plasma Phe, the worse performance on the three pegs task tended to be, although this just missed statistical significance ($F[1, 64] = 3.62$, $p = .06$). Within the same child over time, the correlation between plasma Phe level and performance on the three pegs task ranged from $-.92$ to .60, with a mean of $-.35$. No direct relation was found between mean Phe levels during $3\frac{1}{2}$–7 years of age, the first month of life, or the first year of life and performance on the three pegs task.

Sex Differences

Girls performed significantly better than boys on the three pegs test ($F[1, 343] = 7.73$, $p < .01$) at all ages and among all groups of participants. There was no significant interaction between sex and group. Performance was not significantly related to IQ test performance. For a summary of the results on the three pegs task, see Table 9.

THE CORSI-MILNER TEST OF RECOGNITION AND TEMPORAL ORDER MEMORY

This test included six conditions: immediate temporal order memory for black-and-white line drawings, immediate recognition memory for black-and-white line drawings, recognition memory for black-and-white line drawings after a 25-min delay, immediate temporal order memory for color paintings, immediate recognition memory for color paintings, and recognition memory for color paintings after a 25-min delay. Results for all these conditions are reported together because there were no significant group differences and no significant effect of plasma Phe level for any of the six conditions for any Phe measure.

Most children in all groups at all ages passed the temporal order memory pretest, demonstrating that they understood what they were being asked and that they could remember which of two stimuli they had last seen. However, at both 3½ and 4 years of age, roughly 10% of the children failed the recognition memory pretest and could not be included in analyses of recognition memory performance. They failed by consistently pointing to the new picture, rather than to the one they had just seen. Perhaps they had difficulty inhibiting their preference for novelty. There were no significant group differences on any pretest performance measure.

Whether the stimuli were simple black-and-white line drawings or complex colored paintings, mean performance in the temporal order memory conditions was rarely significantly better than chance until children reached 6½–7 years of age (see Figure 18). Children showed some improvement over age in immediate recognition memory, although even the youngest participants performed well (for simple black-and-white stimuli, $F[1, 133] = 12.76$, $p = .0005$; for complex color stimuli, $F[1, 91] = 6.67$, $p < .01$; see Figure 19). By 5½ years of age, most children were correct on at least 85% of the immediate recognition trials whether the stimuli were simple or complex.

When the simple, black-and-white line drawings were used, introducing a 25-min delay had no significant effect on recognition memory performance overall or at any age over 4 years (matched-pairs t test of immediate vs. delayed recognition of the black-and-white stimuli at 4 years of age, $t[37] = 2.05$, $p = .04$). The delay did have an effect, however, when complex color stimuli were used. At all ages, children's recognition memory performance for these stimuli was significantly worse after 25 min than after a minute or so (matched-pairs t test, $t[131] = 7.80$, $p = .0001$; see Figure 20). Performance improved over age at recognizing the stimuli after a 25-min delay (for simple black-and-white stimuli, $F[1, 115] = 40.44$, $p < .0001$; for complex color stimuli, $F[1, 94] = 6.34$, $p < .02$).

Sex Differences

There were no significant differences in the performance of the boys and that of the girls when black-and-white line drawings were used. However,

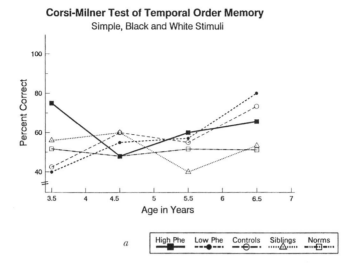

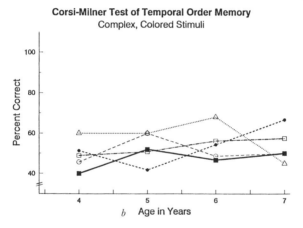

FIGURE 18.—Performance on the Corsi-Milner test of temporal order memory of children in the five subject groups. *a*, Simple black-and-white stimuli. *b*, Complex colored stimuli.

girls showed better immediate recognition memory of the complex color stimuli than did the boys ($F[1, 118] = 4.59$, $p < .03$). This difference also held within subject groups and ages but was most marked at the intermediate ages (between $4\frac{1}{2}$ and $6\frac{1}{2}$ years, $F[1, 54] = 6.70$, $p = .01$). Girls also tended to show better recognition memory for the colored stimuli after the 25-min delay, although this reached significance for only some of the subject groups. The strongest effect was found among the PKU and MHP participants with

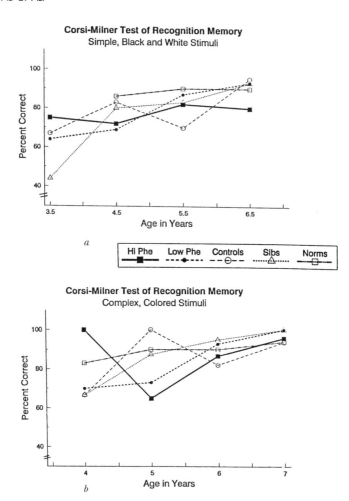

FIGURE 19.—Performance on the Corsi-Milner test of recognition memory of children in the five subject groups. *a*, Simple black-and-white stimuli. *b*, Complex colored stimuli.

lower plasma Phe levels ($F[1, 23] = 14.73$, $p < .0001$). When all the groups of participants were included in the analysis, there was no overall sex difference in the ability to remember the order in which the colored stimuli had been presented. However, among the children with PKU, boys showed much better temporal order memory for the colored stimuli than did the girls ($F[1, 23] = 11.31$, $p < .0004$). Performance on no condition of the Corsi-Milner tests correlated significantly with IQ test performance. For a summary of the results on the Corsi-Milner tests of temporal order memory and recognition memory, see Table 9.

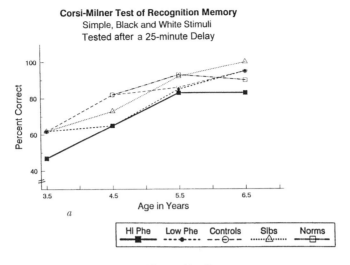

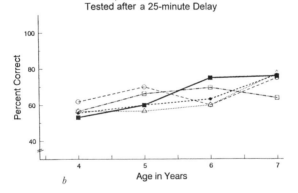

FIGURE 20.—Performance on the Corsi-Milner test of recognition memory with a 25-min delay of children in the five subject groups. *a*, Simple black-and-white stimuli. *b*, Complex colored stimuli.

THE SIX BOXES TASK (BOXES SCRAMBLED AFTER EACH REACH)

Number of Reaches Required to Find All Six Rewards

At 3½–4 years of age, children needed an average of 9.65 reaches to open all six boxes, whereas, by 6½–7 years, they needed 8.41 reaches on average (see Figure 21). This mild improvement in performance over age was not statistically significant. Children with higher Phe levels did not perform differently from any other comparison group. At the younger ages, other PKU

149

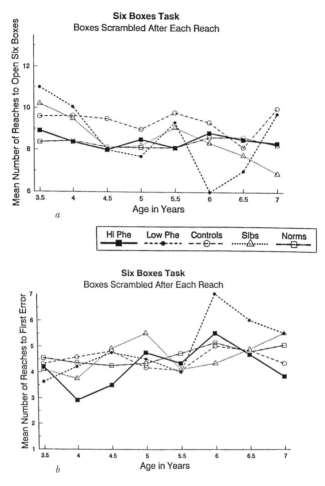

FIGURE 21.—Performance on the six boxes task (boxes scrambled after each reach) of children in the five subject groups. *a,* Mean number of reaches to open six boxes. *b,* Mean number of reaches to first error.

and MHP children, whose Phe levels were *lower* (closer to normal), required significantly *more* reaches to open all six boxes than did children from the general population ($F[4, 417] = 5.48$, $p = .0003$; orthogonal contrast: lower Phe vs. norms = 8.25, $p < .005$). The children with lower Phe levels showed the most improvement with increasing age ($F[1, 417] = 20.33$, $p < .0001$). Below 5 years of age, they performed *worse* than children with higher Phe levels or than children from the general population; above 5½ years, they performed better than all others except the sibling control group.

Among the PKU and MHP children with higher Phe levels, there was an inverse relation between concurrent level of Phe in the bloodstream and number of reaches to open all six boxes; all these children had Phe levels three times normal or higher, but those whose Phe levels climbed most performed worst ($F[1, 25] = 9.03$, $p < .01$). There were no other significant differences among the subject groups in the number of reaches required to find all six rewards. Within the same child over time, there was little relation between plasma Phe level and performance on the six boxes task. PKU and MHP infants with comparable plasma Phe levels performed comparably. Other plasma Phe measures were not significantly related to any measure of performance on the six boxes task.

Number of Reaches Until the First Error Occurred

Children erred later as they grew older. The youngest participants generally made their first error after they had successfully opened three of the boxes, whereas the oldest participants generally made their first error after successfully opening the fourth box ($F[1, 433] = 11.33$, $p < .001$; see Figure 22b). Children with higher Phe levels made their first error significantly earlier in a trial than did children from the general population ($F[4, 433] = 4.28$, $p < .002$; orthogonal contrast: higher Phe vs. norms $= 11.29$, $p < .0005$).

Other variables—such as number of different boxes opened, maximum number of consecutive reaches to the same box, and maximum number of consecutive reaches to the same location—did not yield any significant group differences or change over age, nor were they related to any plasma Phe measure. Children rarely reached to the same box more than two or three times in a row, even at the youngest ages tested.

Sex Differences

Among the participants with PKU or MHP, girls performed better than boys. Girls needed fewer trials to find all the rewards, that is, open all the boxes ($F[1, 115] = 98.6$, $p < .0001$). Boys were more likely to reach back perseveratively to the same box in which they had just searched ($F[1, 115] = 31.9$, $p < .0001$). No performance measure on this task correlated significantly with IQ. For a summary of the results on the six boxes task (boxes scrambled after each reach), see Table 9.

THE SIX BOXES TASK (BOXES REMAIN STATIONARY)

Performance in the stationary condition improved significantly with age (e.g., for number of reaches until the first error, $F[1, 482] = 4.64$, $p < .03$).

151

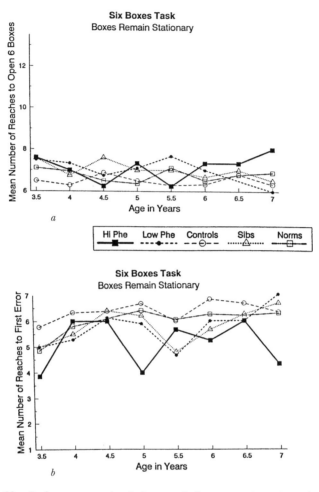

FIGURE 22.—Performance on the six boxes task (boxes remain stationary) of children in the five subject groups. *a*, Mean number of reaches to open six boxes. *b*, Mean number of reaches to first error.

However, no significant differences by subject group were found for any dependent measure: number of reaches to open all six boxes (i.e., to find all the rewards), number of rewards found (i.e., number of different boxes opened), number of reaches until the first error, or maximum number of consecutive reaches to the same box/location. The lack of any significant difference in performance across the groups can be seen in Figure 22. No measure of Phe in the bloodstream during any period of life was significantly related to any measure of performance in the stationary-box condition.

Performance in the stationary-box condition was significantly better than in the condition where the boxes were moved after each reach (performance when the boxes remained stationary vs. performance when the boxes were moved, paired $t[58]$ for number of reaches to open all boxes $= 5.79$, $p < .01$; paired $t[66]$ for number of reaches until first error $= 2.76$, $p < .04$). For example, when the boxes remained stationary, the children typically did not make a mistake until there was only one remaining unopened box.

Sex Differences

Girls performed significantly better than boys in the stationary-box condition. This was true across all subject groups and within the group of participants with PKU or MHP (e.g., for the number of reaches to find all six rewards, $F[1, 482] = 8.16$, $p < .005$, and $F[1, 110] = 6.78$, $p < .01$, respectively). No sex $\times$ condition interactions were found. No performance measure on this task correlated significantly with IQ. For a summary of the results on the six boxes task (boxes remain stationary), see Table 9.

THE GLOBAL-LOCAL SPATIAL PROCESSING TASK
(FORCED CHOICE PROCEDURE)

We analyzed mean reaction time and percentage of correct responses for all the trials together, just the global test trials, just the local test trials, all trials where the stimuli were pictures, just the global picture trials, just the local picture trials, all trials where the stimuli were letters or numbers, just the global letter/number trials, just the local letter/number trials, all trials where the test stimuli were the same size as the sample stimuli, all trials where the test stimuli were opposite in size from the sample stimuli, all trials where the stimuli were intermediate in size, and the interaction of global/local feature with size of the test stimuli.

Group Differences: PKU and MHP Groups Combined

Reaction Time across All Trials

There was no significant change over age in reaction time on any condition of this task. The only significant group difference we found for reaction time was for local feature, picture trials. Here, PKU and MHP children with *lower* Phe levels took *longer* to respond than did children from the general population ($F[4, 161] = 2.17$, $p = .08$; orthogonal contrast: lower Phe vs. norms $= 8.26$, $p < .005$). On no reaction time measure did the children with higher Phe levels differ from the other groups of children, nor did the other comparison groups differ from one another.

Reaction Times on Trials Where the Child Responded Correctly

With increasing age, the children were better able to combine accuracy with speed. Younger children took significantly longer to respond on trials where they were correct than did older children ($F[1, 216] = 4.28$, $p < .0003$). There were no significant differences among the different groups of participants, or by any measure of plasma Phe levels, in reaction time on correct trials, however.

Percentage of Correct Responses over All Trials Combined

As the children grew older, they improved significantly in their accuracy on the task ($F[1, 233] = 44.49$, $p < .0001$). Percentage of correct responses improved from roughly 60% at 3½–4 years to roughly 90% at 7 years of age. There were no significant differences in performance among children with higher Phe levels and any other group of participants or among the children with lower Phe levels and any other group.

Percentage of Correct Responses on Trials Testing the Global Features of the Stimuli

Performance improved as the children grew older ($F[1, 235] = 72.15$, $p < .0001$)—from chance at 3½ years to roughly 90% correct at 7 years, with most of the improvement occurring between 3½ and 5½ years of age. No significant differences in performance among the groups emerged using the concurrent Phe measure or any other measure (see Figure 23).

Percentage of Correct Responses on Trials Testing the Local Features of the Stimuli

There was a significant main effect for age ($F[1, 231] = 94.13$, $p < .0001$) primarily because of the improvement in the performance of siblings and children from the general population as they grew older (see Figure 24). Children with PKU and MHP started out performing better than the other groups of children, but those whose Phe levels were three to five times normal showed little improvement over age. Using Phe levels during the 6-week period preceding each testing session, PKU and MHP children with *lower* Phe levels were significantly *worse* at identifying the local feature in our hierarchi-

154

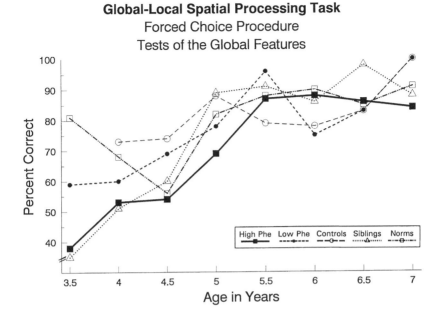

FIGURE 23.—Performance on the global-local spatial processing task: forced choice procedure (tests of the global features) of children in the five subject groups.

cal stimuli, when small test stimuli were used, than children from the general population or than siblings ($F[4, 235] = 4.49$, $p < .002$; orthogonal contrasts: lower Phe vs. norms = 13.33, $p = .003$; lower Phe vs. siblings = 13.61, $p = .003$). (Small test stimuli match the original local feature in size.) When medium-size or large test stimuli were used, no significant group differences emerged. No significant group differences were found using other Phe measures.

Percentage of Correct Responses with Opposite Size Stimuli

Opposite size stimuli are small test stimuli used to test the global feature of the hierarchical model stimuli and large test stimuli used to test the local feature of the hierarchical model stimuli. Performance with these stimuli improved over age ($F[1, 65] = 6.01$, $p < .0001$). PKU and MHP children with *lower* plasma Phe levels performed *worse* than the sibling group on trials with opposite size stimuli and showed a similar tendency in comparison with the other subject groups ($F[4, 65] = 2.55$, $p < .05$; orthogonal contrasts: lower Phe vs. siblings = 8.98, $p < .004$; lower Phe vs. higher Phe = 6.24, $p < .02$;

155

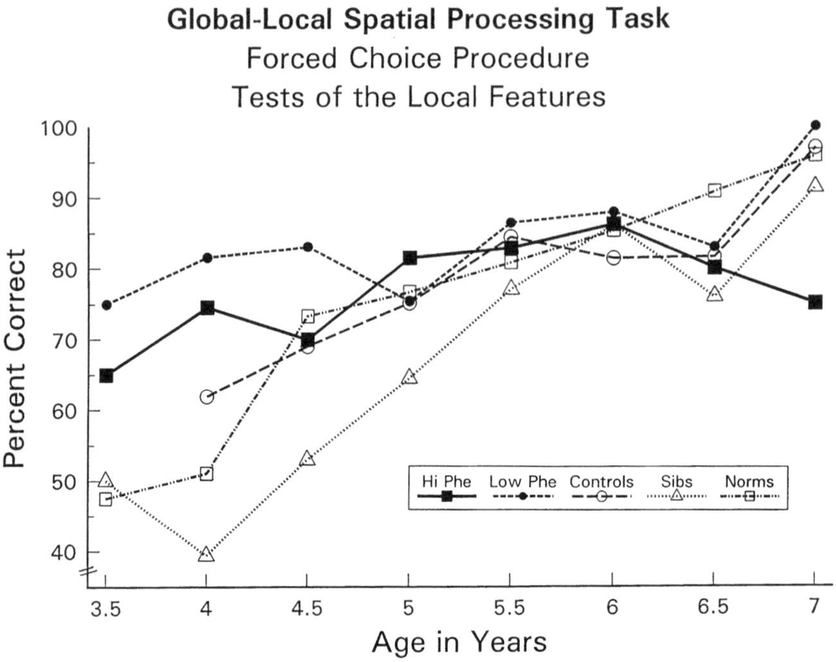

Global-Local Spatial Processing Task
Forced Choice Procedure
Tests of the Local Features

FIGURE 24.—Performance on the global-local spatial processing task: forced choice procedure (tests of the local features) of children in the five subject groups.

lower Phe vs. norms = 6.09, $p < .02$; lower Phe vs. controls = 4.95, $p < .03$). No other group differences were found. Regardless of the plasma Phe measure used, there were no significant differences in performance among children with higher Phe levels and any other group of children. The same effect of age and the same difference between the performance of children with lower Phe levels and that of other subject groups were also found when only those trials with pictorial stimuli were included in the analysis. No age or group differences were found when performance with opposite size stimuli was analyzed for only those trials where letters had been used as the stimuli.

Percentage of Correct Responses When the Test Stimuli Were Small

Small test stimuli are the same size as the local feature in the models and opposite in size from the global feature in the models. Performance improved over age ($F[1, 167] = 3.21$, $p < .003$). When pictures served as the stimuli, performance with small test stimuli was significantly *worse* among the PKU and MHP children with *lower* Phe levels than among children from the general population or the siblings of PKU and MHP children ($F[4, 167]$

156

= 3.10, $p < .02$; orthogonal contrasts: lower Phe vs. norms = 8.99, $p < .004$; lower Phe vs. siblings = 11.04, $p < .002$; lower Phe vs. higher Phe = 3.79, $p < .05$; lower Phe vs. controls = 4.15, $p < .05$).

Group Differences: PKU and MHP Groups Analyzed Separately

Reaction Time

There were no significant differences in speed of responding between the PKU and the MHP children, controlling for plasma Phe levels. Level of plasma Phe was directly and negatively related to reaction time only when the children were tested on the local features of pictorial stimuli. On local picture trials, PKU children with *lower* Phe concentrations were significantly *slower* to respond than children from the general population or the group of siblings ($F[5, 172]$ = 5.43, $p < .0001$; orthogonal contrasts: lower PKU vs. norms = 18.36, $p < .0001$; lower PKU vs. siblings = 18.24, $p < .0001$).

Percentage of Correct Responses over All Trials Combined

There were no significant differences between the accuracy of PKU children and that of MHP children controlling for blood level of Phe and no significant differences within these groups by the blood level of Phe for any Phe measure.

Percentage of Correct Responses on Trials Testing the Global Features of the Stimuli

PKU children with higher concurrent Phe concentrations were significantly less likely than children from the general population, matched control subjects, or siblings to identify the global features of the stimuli correctly ($F[6, 228]$ = 2.18, $p < .05$; orthogonal contrasts: higher PKU vs. norms = 32.93, $p < .0001$; higher PKU vs. controls = 19.51, $p < .0001$; higher PKU vs. siblings = 11.59, $p < .001$). When the test stimuli were intermediate in size, MHP children whose concurrent Phe levels were 6 mg/dl or higher were significantly less likely to identify the global features of the stimuli correctly than were children from the general population or matched controls ($F[6, 233]$ = 2.33, $p < .03$; orthogonal contrasts: higher MHP vs. norms = 9.69, $p < .002$; higher MHP vs. controls = 10.03, $p < .002$). Within the PKU and MHP groups combined, and within the MHP group alone, performance on the global trials was significantly and inversely related to concurrent Phe levels (for PKU plus MHP, $F[1, 50]$ = 4.71, $p < .04$; for MHP alone, $F[1, 5]$ = 8.41, $p < .04$). Children with PKU performed significantly worse than children with MHP, even controlling for concurrent Phe levels ($F[1, 99] = 5.56$, $p = .02$). No significant differences between groups or by Phe level were found. No significant relation between performance and Phe level was found.

Percentage of Correct Responses on Trials Testing the Local Features of the Stimuli

There were no significant differences between the performance of PKU and that of MHP children, and no significant effect of plasma Phe level, when local features were tested. PKU children with lower concurrent Phe levels performed worse than their siblings and worse than the normative sample ($F[5, 233] = 3.00$, $p < .002$; orthogonal contrasts: lower PKU vs. siblings = 12.14, $p < .001$; lower PKU vs. norms = 11.09, $p < .001$). No significant group differences were found when any other measure of plasma Phe levels was used.

Sex Differences

There were no significant sex differences and no significant sex × group interactions. No performance measure on this task correlated significantly with IQ. For a summary of the results on the global-local task (forced choice procedure), see Table 9.

THE LINE BISECTION TASK

Group Differences: PKU and MHP Groups Combined

On the line bisection task, children were asked to indicate the exact middle of each of a set of lines differing in length and position on the page. We calculated mean percentage deviation from the midpoint for each child by dividing the distance of each response from the midpoint by the length of its line and then averaging across these. Children improved on the task between 3½ and 5 years of age ($F[1, 241] = 3.80$, $p < .05$; see Figure 25). At 3½ years, their mean deviation from the midpoint was over 20%; by 5 years, most children showed a deviation from the midpoint of only about 5%. There were no significant differences in performance among the groups of participants. There was also no significant effect of the level of Phe in the bloodstream, regardless of the Phe measure used or the time period over which it was calculated. There were no significant sex differences and no significant sex × group interactions. Performance on the line bisection task was not

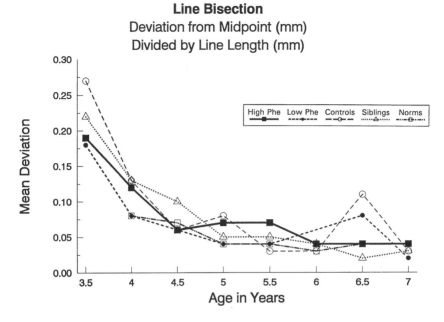

Line Bisection
Deviation from Midpoint (mm)
Divided by Line Length (mm)

FIGURE 25.—Performance on the line bisection test (deviation from midpoint [mm] divided by line length [mm]) of children in the five subject groups.

significantly related to IQ test performance. For a summary of the results on the line bisection test, see Table 9.

RELATIONS AMONG PERFORMANCE ON TASKS
ADMINISTERED TO CHILDREN 3½–7 YEARS OF AGE

Performance on the tapping task, the three pegs task, and the day-night Stroop-like task was correlated (tapping and three pegs tasks, $r[144] = .53$, $p = .0001$; tapping and day-night tasks, $r[144] = .35$, $p = .0001$; day-night and three pegs tasks, $r[151] = .20$, $p = .01$). The relation was strongest between performance on the tapping task and that on the three pegs task. The correlation between mean performance on these two tasks was significant among PKU children ($r[22] = .59$, $p < .01$), MHP children ($r[11] = .58$, $p < .05$), their siblings ($r[12] = .78$, $p < .01$), and children from the general population ($r[95] = .47$, $p < .0001$). Performance on the tapping and day-night tasks was significantly correlated for children from the general population ($r[95] = .27$, $p = .02$), siblings ($r[12] = .60$, $p = .05$), and matched controls ($r[15] = .67$, $p < .01$) but not for PKU or MHP children. Although performance on the day-night and three pegs tasks was significantly correlated overall, the only subgroup for whom this correlation was significant was children with PKU ($r[22] = .44$, $p < .05$).

Performance on none of the other tasks administered to young children—the control condition for the Stroop-like task, the Corsi-Milner test of recognition memory (immediate or after a delay), the Corsi-Milner test of temporal order memory, the line bisection task, the six boxes task (boxes stationary), the six boxes tasks (boxes scrambled after each reach), or the global-local spatial processing task (any condition)—was significantly related to performance on any other task.

VIII. CONCLUSIONS

The conclusions chapter is organized around what we see as the major findings of the study.

When both working memory and inhibitory control were required, children with plasma Phe levels roughly 6–10 mg/dl performed worse than other children. Performance on these tasks covaried linearly and inversely with plasma Phe level; the higher a child's Phe level, the worse that child's performance tended to be on tasks that required working memory plus inhibitory control. The effect of elevated Phe levels in the bloodstream appeared to be acute, rather than chronic, as performance covaried most consistently with concurrent Phe levels rather than with mean Phe levels over a more extended period or earlier Phe levels.

The deficits on tasks that required working memory plus inhibitory control were evident in both the youngest and the oldest age ranges; they appeared early and appeared to remain, at least through the ages we investigated. On the other hand, children with Phe levels of 6–10 mg/dl performed as well as other children when only working memory, but not inhibitory control, was required or when recognition memory or spatial analyses were required. That is, the ability to hold information in mind while at the same time resisting a prepotent response, dependent on dorsolateral prefrontal cortex, appeared to be affected, while the abilities dependent on parietal cortex, the medial temporal lobe, and even other regions of prefrontal cortex appeared to be spared.

Although all participants had IQs above 80, children with higher plasma Phe levels obtained lower IQ scores than other groups of children, and IQ scores varied inversely with plasma Phe level. IQ tests are global measures, however, and group differences here were not as marked as they were on measures designed to focus specifically on working memory and inhibitory control. Other children born with PKU, whose Phe levels had been kept between 2 and 6 mg/dl, performed comparably to other children on our tasks. Thus, at least in this subgroup of PKU children, deficits in the ability to exercise working memory and inhibitory control simultaneously did not appear to be a necessary, unavoidable consequence of being born with PKU.

Finally, the cognitive performance of girls seemed to be more adversely affected than that of boys by mild plasma Phe elevations in the range of 6–10 mg/dl.

AN IMPAIRMENT WHEN REQUIRED TO USE BOTH WORKING MEMORY AND INHIBITORY CONTROL

We found that phenylketonuric children who have been on a low-Phe diet since the first month of life but who have moderately elevated plasma Phe levels (levels roughly three to five times normal; 6–10 mg/dl, or 360–600 mol/l) were impaired on all six tests that required the working memory and inhibitory abilities dependent on dorsolateral prefrontal cortex. These six tasks were A$\overline{B}$, object retrieval, A$\overline{B}$ with invisible displacement, the day-night Stroop-like task, tapping, and three pegs.

Summary of the Evidence

No comparison or control group is perfect, so we included several. On each task, the performance of children with higher plasma Phe levels (levels three to five times normal; mean = 7.86 mg/dl) was compared to that of four other groups of participants: (*a*) other PKU and MHP children with lower plasma Phe levels (levels three times normal or lower; mean = 4.45 mg/dl); (*b*) their own siblings; (*c*) matched controls; and (*d*) children from the general population. The deficit in the working memory and inhibitory control abilities dependent on dorsolateral prefrontal cortex of children with plasma Phe concentrations of 6–10 mg/dl was evident in relation to each comparison group, although all four comparisons did not yield significant differences on every task.

We used two alternative procedures to help summarize the many comparisons across groups and across tasks. With the first we counted each behavioral task equally and looked at the results on one dependent measure per task. Because for most tasks there is not general agreement on the one best dependent measure, for each task (the control tasks as well as those that required working memory plus inhibitory control) we selected the dependent measure that yielded the strongest between-group differences on that particular task. This gave each task the best possible opportunity to yield a difference between our subject groups, whether we had predicted group differences or not. Of the 24 comparisons between the group of PKU and MHP children with higher plasma Phe levels and the four other groups of children on these six tasks dependent on working memory plus inhibitory control (6 tasks $\times$ 4 comparisons per task), the children with higher Phe levels performed significantly worse than the comparison groups on 75% of these comparisons using the stringent criterion of $p \leq .005$ for each test to correct for multiple comparisons (see Table 10). This pattern of 18 of 24 comparisons in the predicted direction would be most unlikely to occur by chance ($p < .01$, binomial distribution). Thus, as a group, the PKU and MHP children with plasma Phe levels three to five times higher than normal were impaired on these tasks. The results are similar if the children with MHP are omitted from the analyses: PKU children with higher Phe levels performed significantly worse than the four comparison groups on 19 of the 24 comparisons, a pattern of performance that is significant at $p < .004$ (binomial distribution).

With the second procedure we considered all the dependent measures listed in the summary tables (Tables 7, 8, and 9 above). This was done to address concerns that selecting one measure per task might bias the summary of the results. The reader should be aware, however, that, when all dependent measures are considered, those behavioral tasks with more dependent measures are counted more heavily. Luckily, both methods for summarizing the findings yielded very similar results; we present both to satisfy readers who might feel that one procedure or the other might have unfairly biased the summaries obtained.

The second method for summarizing the results yielded 56 comparisons between the group of PKU and MHP children with higher plasma Phe levels and the other children on these six tasks dependent on working memory plus inhibitory control (14 dependent measures $\times$ 4 comparisons per dependent measure). The children with higher Phe levels performed significantly worse than the comparison groups on 66% of these comparisons (see Table 10). This pattern of 37 of 56 comparisons in the predicted direction would be most unlikely to occur by chance ($p < .03$, z distribution). Thus, as a group, the PKU and MHP children with plasma Phe levels three to five times higher than normal were impaired on these tasks. The results are similar if the children with MHP are omitted from the analyses: PKU children with higher Phe levels performed significantly worse than the four comparison groups on 39 of the 56 comparisons, a pattern of performance that is significant at $p < .02$ (z distribution).

Both procedures for comparing performance across the subject groups lead to the same basic conclusion—that, on the tasks that require the working memory and inhibitory control functions dependent on dorsolateral prefrontal cortex, the impairment of the PKU children whose plasma Phe levels were three to five times above normal was clear and consistent. By following all participants longitudinally (except the normative sample), we were able to obtain a more accurate indication of each child's ability and developmental trajectory than is possible when participants are tested only once. These re-

TABLE 10

PAIRWISE COMPARISONS BETWEEN PARTICIPANT GROUPS SIGNIFICANT AT $p \leq .005$

	The Six Tasks That Required the Working Memory and Inhibitory Control Abilities Dependent on Dorsolateral Prefrontal Cortex	The 13 Control Tasks
Comparisons performed using one dependent measure per behavioral task:		
PKU and MHP children whose plasma Phe levels were three to five times normal performed significantly worse than the other groups of children on	18 of 24 comparisons (75%)	4 of 52 comparisons (8%)
PKU children whose plasma Phe levels were three to five times normal performed significantly worse than the other groups of children on	19 of 24 comparisons (79%)	4 of 52 comparisons (8%)
The other groups of children performed significantly differently from one another on	2 of 36 comparisons (5%)	3 of 78 comparisons (4%)
Comparisons performed using all dependent measures:		
PKU and MHP children whose plasma Phe levels were three to five times normal performed significantly worse than the other groups of children on	37 of 56 comparisons (66%)	6 of 164 comparisons (4%)
PKU children whose plasma Phe levels were three to five times normal performed significantly worse than the other groups of children on	39 of 56 comparisons (69%)	4 of 164 comparisons (2%)
The other groups of children performed significantly differently from one another on	3 of 84 comparisons (4%)	3 of 246 comparisons (1%)

NOTE.—The .005 significance level was chosen to correct for multiple comparisons. This is similar to what a Bonferroni correction would do.

peated observations over time provided our statistical analyses with enough power to detect group differences despite the fact that the number of participants in our groups was not large.

The poor performance of PKU children whose plasma Phe levels were three to five times above normal on tasks that required both holding information in mind (working memory) and acting counter to one's initial tendency (inhibitory control) was evident even when controlling for IQ, sex, health variables, and background characteristics. IQ was correlated with performance on delayed nonmatching to sample, the day-night Stroop-like task, and the tapping task. Controlling for IQ reduced the size of group differences on these tasks, but all results that had been significant without controlling for IQ remained significant. The variance common to the IQ measure and these other tests may well be attributable to the fact that the IQ measure, in part, required the medial temporal lobe and dorsolateral prefrontal cortex functions tapped by these tasks.

Comparison with Findings from Other Studies

Our finding of deficits in the cognitive abilities dependent on dorsolateral prefrontal cortex in PKU children whose plasma Phe levels are mildly elevated (three to five times normal) is consistent with the results of a number of other studies. The most relevant are those by Smith, Klim, Mallozzi, and Hanley (1996) and Welsh et al. (1990), as these investigators used cognitive tasks tailored to the functions of dorsolateral prefrontal cortex. They report deficits very much in accord with those reported here. Other studies have found deficits in similar functions, although those studies were not designed to investigate a "frontal lobe" hypothesis (e.g., Brunner et al., 1983; Faust et al., 1986; Krause et al., 1985; Pennington et al., 1985; Ris, Williams, Hunt, Berry, & Leslie, 1994).

No study is perfect. Each of the studies cited above was plagued by one or more of the following problems: plasma Phe levels well above five times normal among many of the PKU participants (e.g., mean Phe levels as high as 25 mg/dl in Smith et al., 1996; even in Welsh et al., 1990, over one-third of the PKU participants had Phe levels over five times normal); PKU participants who had been off the low-Phe diet for a number of years even if they were currently back on diet; delayed diet initiation among many of the PKU participants (i.e., after the first month of life); small numbers of participants (e.g., only five PKU participants in Pennington et al., 1985); few measures (if any) empirically linked to prefrontal cortex function; and few or no control measures. Because of problems with any given study, the converging evidence across the mounting number of studies, each with its own strengths and weaknesses, is impressive and important. With a few exceptions (notably, Mazzocco, Nord, van Doorninck, Greene, & Kovar, 1994), the picture that is emerging is clear and consistent.

Discussion of the Importance and Implications

We have found deficits in the cognitive abilities dependent on dorsolateral prefrontal cortex in children who have plasma Phe levels within the range that has been considered clinically acceptable. Plasma levels of Phe up to 10 mg/dl had been thought to be safe. Our findings call into question the safety of plasma Phe levels of 6–10 mg/dl (three to five times normal). Readers are reminded that, when clinicians talk about "high" plasma Phe levels in PKU patients, they are typically referring to Phe levels 10–30 times normal. None of the children we studied had Phe levels in that range. When we refer to children with "higher Phe levels," we mean only higher than the Phe levels of our other subjects, that is, toward the high end of what has been the standard range of control; we do not mean "high" in the sense of being outside that range.

It has been widely believed that "early diagnosis and proper dietary therapy result in normal development [for PKU children]" (Koch & Wenz, 1987, p. 118), and proper dietary therapy has been considered to have been followed if "blood Phe levels neither exceed 10 mg/100 ml nor fall below 2 mg/100 ml" (Williamson et al., 1981, p. 165). Yet, despite the fact that the PKU children we studied were diagnosed early, began dietary treatment early, have been maintained on the low-Phe diet ever since, and have blood Phe concentrations that have, on average, remained under 10 mg/dl and over 2 mg/dl, we found significant and consistent cognitive deficits.

The cognitive deficits in participants who have been treated for PKU that have been documented in other studies can be explained away by saying (*a*) that the plasma Phe levels of many of the PKU participants were outside the "safe" range (i.e., five times normal or higher), (*b*) that, even if concurrent Phe levels were not excessively elevated, earlier Phe levels had been (during the years the PKU participants were off the low-Phe diet), or (*c*) that the low-Phe diet had been started too late to avert early brain damage. However, none of these disclaimers is applicable to the results reported here. The present study included only children whose mean plasma Phe levels were roughly 10 mg/dl or less, who had remained continuously on diet, and who had been placed on a low-Phe diet at or before 4 weeks of age.

It is still common practice in the United States to consider plasma Phe concentrations up to five times normal ($\leq$ 10 mg/dl) acceptable in children with PKU. Perhaps the United States should follow the example of a number of European countries, which had previously considered plasma Phe elevations up to five times normal acceptable and have recently changed that guideline to Phe elevations no higher than three times normal (e.g., in Britain, Medical Research Council Working Party on Phenylketonuria, 1993). Plasma Phe levels three to five times normal do not appear to be as benign as once thought.

A NEGATIVE, LINEAR RELATION BETWEEN PHE LEVEL AND PERFORMANCE ON TASKS THAT REQUIRE WORKING MEMORY AND INHIBITORY CONTROL

The higher a child's Phe level, the worse that child's performance tended to be on the behavioral tasks dependent on the memory plus inhibition measures dependent on dorsolateral prefrontal cortex. We found a direct, inverse relation between plasma Phe levels and performance on five of these six tests (the exception being $\overline{AB}$ with invisible displacement).

Summary of the Evidence

This was consistently true for children with PKU, although only sometimes true for children with MHP. On the $\overline{AB}$ task, Phe levels covaried significantly with performance whether the PKU or the MHP groups were considered. On the object retrieval task, the performance of MHP infants varied as a direct, inverse function of their plasma Phe levels only for the harder, large-box conditions. On both the day-night Stroop-like task and the tapping task, PKU and MHP children whose Phe levels were higher tended to be unable to inhibit the dominant response even during pretesting. On the day-night task, percentage of correct responses varied directly and inversely with plasma Phe level among children with MHP, but this relation was not significant for children with PKU. On the other hand, on the three pegs task, plasma Phe levels showed some relation to performance among PKU children but not among MHP children.

Comparison with Findings from Other Studies

Smith et al. (1996) and Welsh et al. (1990) found performance on dorsolateral prefrontal cortex measures to be significantly and negatively correlated with plasma Phe levels—results consistent with our findings. The relation we found between plasma Phe level and performance is particularly impressive because of the truncated range of Phe levels; all PKU children in our study were on a dietary regimen to keep their Phe levels from climbing too high. Smith and Beasley (1989) and Welsh et al. (1990) found this relation between Phe level and intellectual performance despite the fact that the Phe levels of

167

their participants were generally within the "acceptable" range—again, results consistent with our findings.

ACUTE, RATHER THAN CHRONIC, EFFECT OF PHE LEVEL

Cognitive performance was most strongly and consistently related to concurrent plasma Phe levels.

Summary of the Evidence

One might have expected that, over a wide age range, during the first weeks of life (before diet initiation, when Phe levels can be so high), or during the first year of life (when the brain is undergoing the most dramatic postnatal changes), chronic plasma Phe levels might have been most strongly related to performance. However, the plasma Phe measure most strongly and most consistently related to performance was concurrent Phe levels (the average level of Phe in the child's bloodstream during the 6 weeks prior to each cognitive testing session, including the day of testing but not limited to that day alone). As current Phe levels varied, so too, inversely, did behavioral performance on the tasks dependent on the working memory and inhibitory control abilities subserved by dorsolateral prefrontal cortex. Indeed, over time, changes in plasma Phe levels within the same child were accompanied by concomitant, inverse changes in performance on these cognitive tasks.

Comparison with Findings from Other Studies

There appears to be unanimity in the literature that, among children treated early for PKU, current performance reflects current plasma Phe levels rather than earlier ones. For example, Smith et al. (1996) and Welsh et al. (1990) report that performance on measures of dorsolateral prefrontal cortex function was strongly correlated with concurrent Phe levels and less so with lifetime Phe levels. Brunner et al. (1983) found that cognitive neuropsychological performance was significantly correlated with concurrent Phe levels but not with Phe levels during infancy. Using IQ and school achievement as the outcome measures, Dobson et al. (1976) also found a significant, negative correlation with concurrent plasma Phe levels and a much weaker association with Phe levels earlier in life.

The only contrary finding we have seen is the report of de Sonneville, Schmidt, Michel, and Batzler (1990) that Phe levels during the 2 years preceding cognitive testing were a better predictor of speed of responding on a continuous performance test than were concurrent Phe levels. Because participants in the present study were followed longitudinally, we are able to present evidence for the first time that performance on tasks requiring the working memory and inhibitory control functions of dorsolateral prefrontal cortex covaried inversely with Phe levels in the same child over time.

Discussion of the Importance and Implications

The finding that performance is most closely tied to current plasma Phe levels bodes well for the possible reversibility of the kinds of cognitive deficits documented here. Had Phe levels early in life (during the first month or the first year) best predicted performance, that would have suggested that something irreversible might have happened during early infancy (especially during the first weeks of life, before a PKU infant is placed on a low-Phe diet, when Phe levels can be extraordinarily high). Instead, we found that performance was most sensitive to Phe levels around the time of testing.

Indeed, where investigators have tried to reverse cognitive deficits in patients with PKU by reducing Phe intake, the results have been quite promising. Krause et al. (1985) manipulated Phe intake during three 1-week periods in a triple-blind, crossover design. They found that cognitive performance covaried with plasma Phe concentrations. Schmidt et al. (1994) placed PKU adults back on diet for 4–5 weeks. They found that, when plasma Phe levels were lower, the patients were better able to maintain sustained attention and had quicker reaction times, although the patients never performed as well as control subjects.

Although we did not intervene to manipulate Phe levels, we had hoped that there might be enough naturally occurring variation in plasma Phe levels over the 4 years of the study to obtain preliminary evidence of the possible reversibility of the cognitive deficits. Unfortunately, while some children's Phe levels fluctuated a good deal, it was rare for a participant's Phe levels to be brought stably down. Over the period of the study, several children's Phe levels gradually climbed higher, but no child who was brought under better dietary control continued to follow the improved regimen. This speaks to how difficult it is to impose a more restrictive diet on a child who has grown accustomed to a less restrictive one. If our hypothesis is correct that the problem is in the moderate imbalance between Phe and Tyr in the bloodstream, which reduces dopamine metabolism in prefrontal cortex, then it may be possible to reverse the cognitive deficits in PKU children, even when their plasma Phe levels are three to five times normal, by providing supplemental Tyr or by increasing the level or efficacy of available dopamine (perhaps with low doses of L-dopa or ritalin).

The finding that cognitive performance covaried with children's current plasma Phe levels is also consistent with the biological mechanism that we have proposed as the cause of the cognitive deficits. We have proposed a biochemical explanation based on the level of dopamine metabolism in prefrontal cortex, which should vary directly with changes in the Phe:Tyr ratio in plasma, as opposed to an explanation based on structural, neuroanatomical changes, which might less flexibly react to changes in the current level of Phe in the bloodstream.

DEFICITS SEEN IN THE YOUNGEST AND OLDEST AGE RANGES TESTED

The impairment of the PKU children with higher Phe levels in the exercise of working memory and inhibitory control could be seen throughout the age range tested. It was as evident in our oldest age range ($3\frac{1}{2}$–7 year olds) as it was in our youngest (6–12 month olds). Thus, when age-appropriate tasks were used, there was little evidence of any narrowing of the gap between higher-Phe PKU children and their same-aged peers, at least from 6 months through 6 years of age.

Summary of the Evidence

The present study provides the first evidence of cognitive impairments in *infants* treated early and continuously for PKU. On A$\overline{B}$ and object retrieval (the two tasks requiring memory plus inhibition administered to infants), PKU and MHP infants as a group and PKU infants alone (all of whose plasma Phe levels were three to five times normal) performed significantly worse than the four comparison groups (other affected children with lower plasma Phe levels, children from the general population, matched controls, or siblings) on seven of these eight comparisons (using one dependent measure per task; $p < .04$, binomial distribution). (When all dependent measures for the A$\overline{B}$ and object retrieval tasks are considered, PKU children with higher Phe levels performed significantly worse than the other subject groups on 17 of the 24 comparisons [71%]; $p < .04$.)

On the day-night Stroop-like task, the tapping task, and the three pegs task (the three tasks requiring memory plus inhibition administered to young children), PKU plus MHP children as a group and PKU children alone (all of whose average concurrent plasma Phe levels were three to five times normal) performed significantly worse than the four comparison groups on 10 and 11, respectively, of 12 comparisons (using one dependent measure per task; $p < .02$, and $p < .003$, respectively, binomial distribution). (When all dependent measures for the day-night, tapping, and three pegs tasks are considered, PKU children with higher Phe levels performed significantly worse than the other subject groups on 19 of the 24 comparisons [79%]; $p < .004$, using one measure per task, or 39 of 56 comparisons [70%]; $p < .005$, z distribution.)

The results are strongest at the youngest and oldest age ranges tested and weakest for toddlers, probably because of the lack of good tasks for this age range (15–30 months).

Discussion of the Importance and Implications

Although prefrontal cortex is probably not fully mature until puberty or later, it is already subserving important cognitive functions during the first year of life. Our present results indicate that the cognitive functions dependent on dorsolateral prefrontal cortex seem to be acutely sensitive to the level of dopamine in prefrontal cortex even during infancy and early childhood. This extends previous results that had shown that these cognitive functions are acutely sensitive to the level of dopamine in dorsolateral prefrontal cortex in adult monkeys and human adults (Brozoski et al., 1979; Luciana, Depue, Arbisi, & Leon, 1992; Sawaguchi & Goldman-Rakic, 1991).

Are the cognitive deficits we have observed indicative of a developmental delay or of absolute, lasting deficits? On the one hand, all children, even PKU children with higher Phe concentrations, improved over time on our tasks. On the other hand, the impression that PKU children may "catch up" to other children is probably misleading. In almost all cases, such catching up was due to ceiling effects because the same tasks were administered over a wide age range and these tasks were often too easy for children at the upper end of an age range. Many tests, such as IQ measures, get around this problem by increasing the difficulty of the test as children get older, although the test may be called by the same name throughout. We have repeatedly found that, when all groups of children appeared to be performing comparably because all were near ceiling, the differences between the groups reappeared when we went to the next battery of tasks for the next age range.

We stopped studying children at 7 years of age. One cannot tell from this study whether sometime after 7 years PKU children whose plasma Phe levels remain only moderately elevated might no longer show the kinds of cognitive deficits we have documented, as Mazzocco et al. (1994) have suggested. Many studies of elementary school–age PKU children have found cognitive deficits (e.g., Smith & Beasley, 1989; Weglage, Pietsch, Fünders, Koch, & Ullrich, 1995; Welsh et al., 1990); recent studies by Ris et al. (1994) and Smith et al. (1996) report deficits in the cognitive abilities dependent on prefrontal cortex in young adults with PKU. However, dietary compliance tends to become progressively more lax after children enter school, and these

171

studies have therefore included participants whose plasma Phe levels were outside what has been the acceptable limit for young children (≤ 10 mg/ dl). What would happen if plasma Phe levels were maintained at three to five times normal? Would the cognitive deficits eventually disappear? The data do not presently exist to answer that question.

Amino acid uptake across the blood-brain barrier changes during development, offering more protection against plasma Phe elevations as children get older (Greengard & Brass, 1984; Lajtha, Sershen, & Dunlop, 1988). Thus, it is quite possible that the plasma Phe levels we found to be detrimental during infancy and early childhood might be benign in later childhood or adolescence. Indeed, Smith, Beasley, and Adee (1991) found a weaker relation between plasma Phe levels and IQ in children over 8 years of age than in younger children.

Early cognitive deficits or developmental delays, especially when they extend over a period as long as we have documented here (6 years), are likely to have profound and enduring effects, even if the cognitive deficits themselves are subsequently resolved and the developmental gap closed. Children who have inordinate difficulty when a change in thinking is required, when presented with a new problem, or when trying something for the first time may come to avoid facing new problems or confronting new situations out of fear. Their frustration and discouragement at the difficulty they have with cognitive tasks that come so much easier to other children may lead them to dislike school or cognitively demanding situations; they might stop trying even if, when they are older, those tasks are no longer so difficult for them.

Children who have repeatedly seen themselves struggle with cognitive tasks that their peers find easy come to believe themselves to be less able and less intelligent and may continue to see themselves in this way long after the ability gap may have narrowed. Similarly, others around the child (parents, teachers, and peers) will expect the child to perform as he or she always has, and it is well known that people often perform as others expect them to perform. Thus, to label a young child as not as sharp as others can have a lifelong effect on him or her, even if objective measures later show that the cognitive gap has been closed. Also, PKU children whose Phe concentrations are moderately elevated appear to have difficulty getting their actions to reflect their intentions or their knowledge because they can sometimes get stuck in behavioral ruts from which they cannot easily extricate themselves, and they may therefore be considered bad, intentionally difficult, or willful, judgments that can affect a child for life.

Consequently, although we do not know whether the cognitive gap that we have demonstrated closes at a later age, we would contend that, even if it does, its presence early in life is likely to have powerful effects thereafter.

DO OUR WORKING MEMORY PLUS INHIBITORY CONTROL TASKS REALLY REQUIRE DORSOLATERAL PREFRONTAL CORTEX?

How clear is the evidence that the impairment we have found is in the functions of dorsolateral prefrontal cortex? Empirical evidence does not yet exist on the neural system subserving performance on all six of the tasks that we claim require the working memory and inhibitory control abilities dependent on dorsolateral prefrontal cortex. However, the results are the same if you consider only the three tasks for which such empirical evidence already exists ($A\overline{B}$, object retrieval, and tapping).

Summary of the Evidence

PKU children with higher plasma Phe levels were impaired on the $A\overline{B}$, object retrieval, and tapping tasks whether they were compared to other PKU children with lower Phe levels, their own siblings, matched controls, or children from the general population. $A\overline{B}$ and object retrieval have been shown empirically to depend on dorsolateral prefrontal cortex (Diamond & Goldman-Rakic, 1985, 1989; Diamond et al., 1989). Tapping has been shown empirically to depend on the prefrontal system; however, this is based on human patients who had massive lesions of the frontal lobe (Luria, 1980).

Discussion of the Importance and Implications

Most neuropsychological testing with young children has been conducted with modifications of tests used with adults or animals, without evidence that the modified test requires the hypothesized neural system, or with tests justified on theoretical grounds alone. This is also true of some of the tests we have used here. However, wherever possible, we have tried to use, not modifications of existing tests, but exactly the same task that has been linked to one or another neural system. This is important because investigators have often been wrong in their hypotheses about the neural system required for success on a behavioral task and because seemingly minor modifications in a task can change which neural regions are recruited for its performance. We have also tried to use diverse tasks thought to require the working memory and inhibitory abilities dependent on dorsolateral prefrontal cortex in order to obtain converging evidence. The fact that we found similar group differences on tasks superficially as different as $A\overline{B}$ and object retrieval (both of which require working memory and inhibitory control) yet not on a task as superficially similar to $A\overline{B}$ as spatial discrimination (which requires reference memory but not working memory or inhibition) gives us added confidence in our conclusions.

It should be noted, however, that the empirical evidence linking the $\overline{\text{AB}}$, object retrieval, and tapping tasks to prefrontal cortex is based on results in nonhuman primates and human adults. We are assuming here that the neural basis for successful performance on these tasks is the same in children, but that has not yet been tested empirically.

The strongest output projection from dorsolateral prefrontal cortex is to the caudate nucleus (which is one of the structures that make up the striatum or basal ganglia). The striatum matures earlier than does prefrontal cortex. Could the cognitive deficits that we have documented here be caused by dysfunction in the striatum rather than in prefrontal cortex? Yes, it is certainly possible. The striatum participates in the "prefrontal neural system," and there is considerable overlap in the cognitive deficits produced by damage to prefrontal cortex or to the caudate nucleus.

We think it unlikely that the critical structure affected is the striatum rather than prefrontal cortex, however, because, unlike the prefrontal dopamine projection (which originates in the ventral tegmental area), the striatal dopamine projection (which originates in the substantia nigra) is extremely robust in the face of reduced availability of Tyr (e.g., Bradberry et al., 1989; Roth, 1984). Indeed, in our animal model of early and continuously treated PKU, we found that, while dopamine metabolism in prefrontal cortex was markedly reduced, dopamine metabolism in the striatum was not significantly reduced. There is a known mechanism that could produce a selective effect on prefrontal cortex function (moderately reduced CNS levels of Tyr can cause this), and there are known mechanisms that could produce a global effect across brain regions,[8] but we know of no mechanism that could produce a selective effect on striatal function in PKU children. (For evidence of the selectivity of the cognitive deficits, see the section "Selective, Rather than Global, Cognitive Deficits" below.)

EFFECT ON IQ

Early and continuously treated PKU children with plasma Phe levels roughly three to five times normal had significantly lower IQ scores than con-

---

[8] Mechanisms that could produce a global effect across brain regions include (*a*) excessive amounts of Phe reaching the brain (which would have a global toxic effect), (*b*) reductions in the levels of Trp as well as Tyr reaching the brain (which would affect serotonergic systems as well as dopaminergic systems), or (*c*) a dramatic reduction in CNS Tyr levels (which would affect dopamine and norepinephrine systems throughout the brain).

trol subjects, although all scored within the normal range (IQs ≥ 80). IQ was found to be inversely related to plasma Phe concentrations.

Comparison with Findings from Other Studies

Lower IQ scores among PKU children than control groups and a direct, negative relation between IQ scores and PKU children's plasma Phe levels are well-replicated findings (e.g., Costello et al., 1994; Dobson et al., 1976; Smith & Beasley, 1989; Smith et al., 1991)—although here, as with most of the other findings on the cognitive performance of early treated PKU children, not every study has found this effect (e.g., Welsh et al., 1990).

In agreement with our results, Dobson et al. (1976) found early plasma Phe levels to be much more weakly related to later IQ scores than concurrent Phe levels. The results of Costello et al. (1994) also suggest that it is concurrent Phe levels, rather than the early, grossly elevated Phe concentrations, that are responsible for the diminution of IQ. In their study of children with mild atypical PKU, who never had grossly elevated blood concentrations of Phe early in life, Costello et al. (1994) found below-normal IQ scores and a negative and significant association between IQ and Phe level, using the same IQ measure as used here (the Stanford-Binet test) administered at the same age (4 years).

Discussion of the Importance and Implications

As have others, we found that the IQs of PKU children whose plasma Phe levels were three to five times normal were in the 80s and 90s. This is comparable to the IQ scores of people after prefrontal cortex excision (see, e.g., Stuss & Benson, 1986, 1987). The effect on IQ scores of PKU children may be due to that portion of the IQ test that taps dorsolateral prefrontal cortex functions. IQ tests, by design, are gross measures of cognitive functioning, as they are designed to tap many functions. Thus, an overall IQ score is not a sensitive measure of dysfunction specific to one neural system, affecting one kind of ability.

SELECTIVE, RATHER THAN GLOBAL, COGNITIVE DEFICITS

Children treated early and continuously for PKU whose plasma Phe levels were three to five times normal and who were impaired on all six tasks dependent on the working memory plus inhibitory control abilities dependent on dorsolateral prefrontal cortex performed normally on all 13 control

175

tasks, which tapped other cognitive abilities dependent on other neural systems.

Summary of the Evidence

In contrast to the consistency of the deficits we observed in the working memory and inhibitory control functions dependent on dorsolateral prefrontal cortex, PKU children whose Phe levels were three to five times normal only occasionally performed poorly on the other 13 tests administered, which required recognition memory, visuospatial processing, rule learning, and working memory but not also inhibitory control. On each of the 13 control tasks, the performance of children with higher plasma Phe levels was compared with four comparison groups: other PKU and MHP children with lower plasma Phe levels, their own siblings, matched controls, and children from the general population. This yielded a total of 52 pairwise comparisons using one dependent measure per task (13 tasks × 4 comparisons per task). On these 52 comparisons, PKU and MHP children with higher Phe levels performed significantly worse on only four (8%; see Table 10 above). If the MHP children are omitted from the analyses, PKU children with higher Phe levels similarly performed worse on only four of the 52 comparisons (8%).

On the other hand, on the six tasks dependent on the working memory and inhibitory control functions dependent on dorsolateral prefrontal cortex, PKU and MHP children with higher Phe levels performed worse on 18 of the 24 comparisons (75%). PKU children with higher Phe levels performed worse on 19 of the 24 comparisons (79%). The consistency of the deficits of the PKU children with higher plasma Phe levels on the memory and inhibition tasks and of the scarcity of their deficits on all other tasks is extremely unlikely to be a chance occurrence (67 of 76 comparisons in the predicted direction [88%], $p < .0001$, z distribution). Indeed, over all 19 tasks, 175 of the 190 pairwise comparisons (92%) yielded the predicted results ($p < .0001$, z distribution).

If performance on all dependent measures is considered, the results are as follows. On the 13 control tasks, PKU and MHP children with higher Phe levels performed significantly worse on only six of the 164 comparisons (4%). If the MHP children are omitted from the analyses, PKU children with higher Phe levels similarly performed worse on only four of the 164 comparisons (2%). On the other hand, on the six tasks dependent on the working memory and inhibitory control functions dependent on dorsolateral prefrontal cortex, PKU and MHP children with higher Phe levels performed worse on 37 of the 56 comparisons (66%). PKU children with higher Phe levels performed worse on 39 of the 56 comparisons (69%). The likelihood of finding 195 of 220 comparisons in the predicted direction (89%, for higher-Phe PKU and

MHP participants vs. the other subject groups) or of finding 199 of 220 comparisons in the predicted direction (91%, for higher-Phe PKU participants vs. the other subject groups) by chance is extremely low (for both 89% and 91%, $p < .0001$, z distribution). Indeed, over all 19 tasks, 519 of the 550 pairwise comparisons (94%) yielded the predicted results ($p < .0001$, z distribution).

Performance on some of the control tasks (delayed nonmatching to sample, visual paired comparison, global-local spatial processing, and the control condition of the day-night Stroop-like task) covaried with plasma Phe levels. However, on these tasks, which do not require dorsolateral prefrontal cortex, only one Phe measure was typically related to performance, and which Phe measure related to performance varied from task to task. For example, on the delayed nonmatching to sample task, performance was directly related to current Phe levels, while performance on the toddler global-local task was directly related to what the average Phe level had been during the first year of life.

Tasks Dependent on Other Regions of Prefrontal Cortex

Three boxes (boxes scrambled after each reach), six boxes (boxes scrambled after each reach), and the Corsi-Milner test of temporal order memory also tax working memory and also require the functions of prefrontal cortex, but they do not tax inhibitory control as well, and they do not require precisely the same region of prefrontal cortex as do tasks that tax both working memory and inhibitory control. Similarly, learning the delayed nonmatching to sample rule, as opposed to being able to remember the sample over lengthy delays, may well be dependent on ventrolateral prefrontal cortex (see the discussion of this in Chapter III above). Learning delayed nonmatching to sample apparently requires being able to understand the symbolic relation between stimulus object and reward; it does not tax inhibitory control. On only four of the 16 comparisons between the PKU and the MHP children with higher plasma Phe levels and the other groups of children on these four tasks (4 tasks × 4 comparisons per task) did the children with higher Phe levels perform significantly worse than the comparison groups. (Comparable numbers when all dependent measures were included are 4 of 52 comparisons, i.e., less than 8%.)

Similarly, when plasma Phe level was treated as a continuous variable, only one significant relation was found between plasma Phe levels and any measure of performance on these four tasks: Phe level during the first month of life was related to performance on the training delay in the delayed nonmatching to sample task. Thus, in general, neither PKU nor MHP children with higher plasma Phe levels were impaired on these other prefrontal tasks, which required memory but not inhibitory control, and no direct relation was found between current Phe level and performance on any of these tasks. The other subject groups did not differ from one another on any of these tasks either.

Tasks Dependent on the Medial Temporal Lobe

The visual paired comparison task, delayed nonmatching to sample task (with a 30-sec delay), and Corsi-Milner test of recognition memory require the recognition memory ability dependent on the medial temporal lobe. Of the 12 comparisons between the children with higher plasma Phe levels and the other groups of children on these three tasks (3 tasks × 4 comparisons per task), children with higher Phe levels performed significantly worse than the comparison groups on only two of these 12 comparisons. (Comparable numbers when all dependent measures were included are 2 of 32 comparisons, i.e., less than 6%.) Thus, as a rule, PKU and MHP children with higher plasma Phe levels performed comparably to other participants on the three tasks dependent on the functions of the medial temporal lobe.

The two significant effects were that PKU and MHP children with higher Phe levels performed worse than children from the general population in the longest delay condition on the visual paired comparison task and on the delayed nonmatching to sample task. More significant effects might have been found, however, had there been more trials in the visual paired comparison task or if delayed nonmatching to sample had been tested at more ages. Plasma Phe levels covaried inversely with performance on the visual paired comparison task among infants with PKU but not among MHP infants.

Tasks Dependent on Parietal Cortex

The global-local task (administered to toddlers as a preferential looking task and to preschoolers as a forced choice reaction time task) and the line bisection task are sensitive to dysfunction in parietal cortex. On none of the 12 comparisons between the PKU and MHP children with higher plasma Phe levels and the other groups of children on these three parietal tasks (3 tasks × 4 comparisons per task [one dependent measure per task]) did children with higher Phe levels perform significantly worse than the comparison groups. PKU participants with higher Phe levels performed significantly worse on 3 of the 12 comparisons with the other subject groups. Comparable numbers when all dependent measures were included are 0 of 40 (for the PKU and MHP groups combined) and 3 of 40 (when the participants with MHP were omitted). Thus, in general, subject groups did not differ from one another in their performance on tasks dependent on parietal cortex function, nor did performance covary by Phe level on any of these tasks.

During the preschool period, however, PKU participants whose Phe levels were higher performed worse than children from the general population, matched controls, or siblings of PKU children when tested on the global features of the hierarchical stimuli in the forced choice version of the global-local task. MHP preschoolers with higher Phe levels also performed significantly worse than the normative or matched control groups on the global features, but only when the test stimuli were intermediate in size. In contrast to their performance on tests of the global features, $3^{1}/_{2}$–5-year-old PKU and MHP children with higher Phe levels perform better when tested on the small, local features than the group of children from the general population or the group of siblings of MHP and PKU participants. Perhaps children with higher Phe levels are less likely to take in the big picture because they focus too narrowly on one little part of the larger whole. That would be consistent with a frontal lobe impairment (e.g., Luria, 1980). This result might be worth further exploration and attempted replication in other studies.

Comparison with Findings from Other Studies

Consistent with the findings reported here, Smith et al. (1996) and Welsh et al. (1990) found (*a*) that young children (Welsh et al., 1990) and young adults (Smith et al., 1996) treated early and continuously for PKU whose plasma Phe levels were moderately elevated were more impaired on tasks dependent on prefrontal cortex function than on tasks dependent on parietal cortex or the medial temporal lobe and (*b*) that performance on the prefrontal cortex tasks, but not on the other tasks, was significantly and negatively associated with plasma Phe level. For example, Welsh et al. (1990) found normal recognition memory (a skill dependent on the medial temporal lobe) among PKU children with moderately elevated plasma Phe levels.

On the global-local forced choice task, we found that, compared to other children of the same age, $3^{1}/_{2}$–5-year-old PKU children whose Phe levels were three to five times normal were impaired in processing the global feature of stimuli and may have been a bit facilitated in processing the local feature of the stimuli. There are two possible interpretations of this finding. The first is that it might reflect a laterality effect. We had not predicted any laterality effects and, in general, did not design our tasks to investigate that. However, this pattern of performance on the global-local forced choice task would be consistent with an impairment in the functions of the right hemisphere, and a possible left hemisphere advantage, among the PKU children with moderately elevated plasma Phe levels. Pennington et al. (1985) also report finding similarities between the performance of PKU children and patients with right hemisphere damage (e.g., problems with visuospatial tasks). However, Craft, Gourovitch, Dowton, Swanson, and Bonforte (1992) found effects in their PKU participants that suggested more compromise in left hemisphere functioning. Hemispheric differences in the density of the dopaminergic innervation (e.g., Glick, Jerussi, & Zimmerberg, 1977) might account for differential effects in the two cerebral hemispheres.

The second interpretation—which is most consistent with our other findings, however—is that the higher-Phe PKU children's impaired attention to the global, overall form and excellent attention to the small, recurrent detail of which the overall form was composed may reflect impaired prefrontal cortex functioning. "A patient with a frontal lobe syndrome examines only one detail of the picture shown to him. . . . He perceives a single detail, does not move on to any further details, [and does not attempt] to correlate the details of the picture" (Luria, 1966, pp. 270–272). Goldstein (1944) similarly observed that damage to frontal cortex renders a person unable "to grasp the entirety of a complex situation," focusing on one aspect rather than the whole. This can be conceived of as a failure of inhibition; the patient's attention is captured by one salient feature, and the patient is unable to inhibit that pull and thus move his or her attention around. On the global-local task, focusing on only one detail would result in focusing on the local feature of the stimulus, and it would not matter where on the stimulus one looked because the same local feature was displayed throughout the stimulus. However, focusing on only one detail would impair one's ability to perceive the global gestalt. Children of 3 years display a similar tendency to look at only a few points on a novel object rather than more thoroughly examining the entire object (e.g., Zinchenko, Chzhi-Tsin, & Tarakanov, 1963). Whereas most children show this tendency much less after 3 years, PKU children with higher plasma Phe levels seem to continue to display it for another year or more.

Discussion of the Importance and Implications

Our results suggest that PKU children whose plasma Phe levels are three to five times normal have a selective cognitive deficit. Their deficit appears to be limited principally to one neural system. They have difficulty holding information in mind and at the same time resisting or overriding a strong response tendency. This conclusion is based on converging evidence obtained from six different measures. So far as we have been able to discern, the results from 13 different measures indicate that the functions of the medial temporal lobe, of parietal cortex, and, indeed, of other regions of prefrontal cortex appear to be spared. PKU children who had been treated early and continuously, even those whose Phe levels were 6–10 mg/dl, could hold information in mind (when they did not need to exercise inhibitory control at the same time), recognize pictures or objects they have seen before, and perform spatial analyses.

This finding of deficit in the functions of dorsolateral prefrontal cortex, but not in the functions of other neural systems, is consistent with the biological mechanism we have proposed as the cause of the cognitive deficits. We had predicted that dopamine metabolism would be affected because, since Phe and Tyr compete to cross the blood-brain barrier, less Tyr reaches the brain if the ratio of Phe:Tyr increases in the blood. Tyr is an essential precursor of dopamine. We predicted that a moderate imbalance in the Phe:Tyr ratio in plasma (as when Phe levels are three to five times normal in PKU children) would have a more adverse effect on the dopamine projection to prefrontal cortex than on other dopamine systems in the brain because the high firing and high dopamine turnover rates of the prefrontally projecting dopamine neurons make them unusually vulnerable to modest reductions in the level of Tyr reaching the brain. If the Phe:Tyr ratio in plasma is only modestly elevated, the corresponding reduction in Tyr reaching the brain would only be modest.

High levels of Phe in the brain can have toxic effects, particularly on glia and myelin (e.g., Dyer, Kendler, Philibotte, Gardiner, Cruz, & Levy, 1996; Hommes, 1990). Such effects are seen in untreated PKU. When PKU is treated, high levels of Phe do not enter the brain because the plasma elevation in Phe is kept to a moderate level. At most, the increase in the level of Phe reaching the brain is moderate; there is no evidence that such modest Phe increases adversely affect the brain, although it is certainly possible. The specificity of the deficits that we have observed leads us to reason that the cause of those deficits is probably too little Tyr in the brain, rather than too much Phe reaching the brain, because all neural regions should be equally vulnerable to the negative effects of too much Phe; the functions of dorsolateral prefrontal cortex should not be disproportionately affected. If the cause of the cognitive deficits were too much Phe in the CNS, we would have expected the cognitive deficits to be global, rather than limited to one neural system.

Finally, Trp, which is the precursor of serotonin, also competes with Phe to cross the blood-brain barrier. We predicted that the level of Trp in the brain would be less affected than the level of Tyr when plasma Phe levels are five times normal or lower (*a*) because Trp competes more successfully with Phe for access to the protein carriers at the blood-brain barrier than does Tyr (the transport proteins have a very high affinity for Phe, a rather low affinity for Tyr, and an intermediate affinity for Trp) and (*b*) because the level of Tyr in the bloodstream is reduced in children with PKU (since the conversion of Phe to Tyr is disrupted) but the level of Trp in the bloodstream is normal. If the cause of the cognitive deficits were too little Trp in the CNS, we would have expected the cognitive deficits to be global, or more reflective of the functions of other neural systems, rather than limited to the functions subserved by dorsolateral prefrontal cortex. However, we found some effect on the serotonergic system in the brain in our initial animal model of early and continuously treated PKU (Diamond, Ciaramitaro, et al., 1994); it is possible that the behavioral effects that we document in this *Monograph* may be caused by reductions in both Tyr and Trp in the CNS and perhaps by increased Phe as well.

Our conclusion must be twice tempered. First, some of the tasks on which we saw no group differences had ceiling or floor effects, some showed little variability in performance over age, sex, or other variables, and some had only a handful of test trials within a given session. It is certainly possible that, had more sensitive measures been used, we might have found the performance of PKU children with Phe levels of 6 mg/dl or higher to be worse than that of other children on still other cognitive functions, in addition to the deficit we found when working memory and inhibitory control were required.

Second, the mechanism that we have proposed to explain the cause of the cognitive deficits in children treated early and continuously for PKU rests, in part, on the special properties of the dopamine neurons that project to prefrontal cortex. We were surprised, therefore, that the performance of our PKU children was largely unaffected on tasks that required remembering what choices one had already made or remembering the order in which stimuli had been presented (the three and six boxes tasks and the Corsi-Milner test of temporal order memory), tasks that have been shown empirically to depend on prefrontal cortex function. PKU children with moderately elevated Phe levels were impaired only on the subclass of prefrontal cortex tasks that required both holding information in mind and resisting a prepotent action tendency. We had not predicted this, and we are not sure why we found it. Why should a moderately elevated ratio of Phe to Tyr in the bloodstream adversely affect performance on certain tasks dependent on prefrontal cortex (those that require the ability simultaneously to hold information in mind and to resist or override a strong response tendency) but leave performance on other tasks that require other cognitive functions dependent on prefrontal cortex unaffected?

One possibility is that there may be a dissociation in the regions within dorsolateral prefrontal cortex required by these different tasks (Passingham, 1995, 1996) and that different subregions may be more or less sensitive to a decrease in dopamine. The information on the dopamine projection that we have thus far is limited, as it comes from rats who do not have enough dorsolateral prefrontal cortex to parcelate it into separate subregions. However, that information as of now provides no evidence of regional differentiation within dorsolateral prefrontal cortex in the properties of the dopamine projection; prefrontal cortex in general is innervated by dopamine neurons whose cell bodies lie in the A10 cell group within the ventral tegmental area (VTA). As a class, these neurons have a higher baseline firing rate and a higher rate of dopamine turnover than the dopamine neurons in the substantia nigra.

On the other hand, dorsolateral prefrontal cortex consists primarily of Areas 9 and 46. In the rhesus macaque, Area 9 is much more densely innervated by dopamine than is Area 46 (Lewis, Campbell, Foote, & Morrison, 1986; Lewis & Morrison, 1989). The tasks on which we found no effect are more strongly linked to Area 9 than to Area 46 (Petrides 1995, 1996; Petrides, Alivisatos, Evans, & Meyer, 1993). Perhaps the subregion of dorsolateral prefrontal cortex that enables us to hold information in mind and inhibit interfering actions or thoughts is more acutely sensitive to any small fluctuations in dopamine because it has so relatively little dopamine to start with and hence might need all its allotment all the time.

Another possibility is suggested by the fact that the prefrontal tasks on which we found no effect do not require memory of spatial information, and it has been proposed that dorsolateral prefrontal cortex is specialized specifically to hold spatial information in mind (Goldman-Rakic, 1987). However, not all the tasks on which we found an effect require memory of spatial information—the day-night Stroop-like task and the tapping task do not.

Perhaps our tasks that required working memory but not inhibition were too easy. That may have been the case. Two of the tasks that required working memory but not inhibition—six boxes (boxes scrambled) and Corsi-Milner temporal order memory—appear, however, to have been at least as difficult as the six tasks on which children with higher Phe levels were impaired, judging by measures such as the percentage of correct responses.

Perhaps no effects were found on the tasks that required working memory but not inhibition because of a combination of ceiling effects on some tasks and floor effects on others. There was probably a floor effect on the Corsi-Milner temporal order memory task. Certainly, there appear to have been ceiling effects on the three boxes task. On the prefrontal tasks on which we found strong group differences, there were clear improvements in performance over the age range studied. On the prefrontal tasks on which we found no effect, and on A̅B̅ with invisible displacement (where we found little effect), the age × performance gradient was relatively flat. It is very possible that there was too little variation in performance among participants for us to be able to detect differences in performance among the subject groups on those tasks.

Robbins and his colleagues (e.g., Robbins, 1996) and Mangels (1997) have found that prefrontal cortex is not required for memory of the choices one has already made or for temporal order memory when that information is processed incidentally, rather than intentionally, or when the task does not lend itself to the use of a strategy. It is possible that the versions of the self-ordered and temporal memory tasks that we have used here might not require prefrontal cortex involvement because they did not lend themselves to the use of a strategy. Certainly, on the Corsi-Milner test of memory for temporal order, there was no meaningful order to the stimuli; they told no story, reflected no underlying organizing principles, and in general did not relate one to another. Perhaps a group difference would have emerged had there been a reason to remember the order in which the stimuli were being presented other than the fact that one would be tested on that.

Milner and her colleagues (Milner et al., 1991) found that patients with prefrontal cortex excisions were impaired on the temporal order test on which we found no impairment, but the excisions in their patients extended across subregions within prefrontal cortex and were not restricted to Areas 46 and 9. Robbins (1996) found that prefrontal cortex was critically involved in remembering which stimuli one had already chosen when normal participants were able to apply a strategy to the task. However, in a condition very much like our multiple boxes tasks, where the boxes were scrambled after each reach, they found that participants were not able to develop a strategy to solve the task, and prefrontal cortex did not appear to be required. However, Petrides (1995) found that monkeys were impaired on the three boxes tasks (boxes scrambled after each reach) after lesions of dorsolateral prefrontal cortex. Thus, the literature is contradictory on this point. The possibility exists that we might have found an impairment among participants with high plasma Phe levels had we included a test where temporal order memory, or memory of responses already made, was more amenable to the use of a strategy.

In short, we are not sure why children with higher Phe levels were impaired on the tasks that required working memory and inhibitory control but not on other tasks that also are linked to prefrontal cortex. We have suggested that the boxes and Corsi-Milner tasks may have failed to show an effect (*a*) because of ceiling and floor effects, (*b*) because they did not lend themselves to the use of a strategy (the boxes tasks) or because the stimuli were presented in random order (Corsi-Milner), (*c*) because taxing inhibitory control alone or in combination with a working memory load is critical, or (*d*) because these tasks depend on a different region of prefrontal cortex and there are regional differences within prefrontal cortex in the density of dopaminergic innervation and perhaps in the tolerance for mildly reduced Tyr availability.

Is it critical that both working memory and inhibitory control be taxed for PKU children with mildly elevated plasma Phe levels to show a deficit? Would deficits be found if only one of those abilities were taxed?

The tasks that PKU children with plasma Phe levels three to five times normal failed all require two things. (1) Participants must act on the basis of information that is not perceptually present, information that is held in mind. That is, the tasks require participants to keep information in working memory or keep their attention focused on information (sustained attention). (2) Participants must act in a way that is counter to their initial inclination. In other words, participants must inhibit a predisposition to act a certain way and instead do something else; they have to exercise control over their behavior, instead of acting unthinkingly or reflexively. We found that, when PKU children whose plasma Phe levels were 6–10 mg/dl had to use information they were holding in mind to act counter to their predilections, they too often gave the prepotent response rather than the considered one.

The working memory and inhibitory control requirements of these tasks are probably complexly intertwined. On the one hand, by concentrating especially hard on the information you are holding in mind, you increase the likelihood that that information will guide your behavior, and you decrease the likelihood of mistakenly emitting the "default," or normally prepotent, response. On the other hand, in order to be able to keep your mind focused on the relevant information, you must inhibit both internal and external distractions. (Some of these issues are discussed at the end of Chapter III.)

Working memory is required for the visual paired comparison, delayed nonmatching to sample, three and six boxes, Corsi-Milner, and global-local tasks. Few deficits were found on these tasks. Indeed, the control condition of the day-night Stroop-like task posed the same working memory requirement as its companion task (participants had to keep two rules in mind), but, unlike the companion task, the control condition did not also require response inhibition. PKU children with higher Phe levels were impaired on the companion task (with white-sun and black-moon cards) but not on the control condition (where abstract designs appeared on the cards). Perhaps we would have found an impairment when working memory, but not inhibitory control, was taxed if we had administered delayed nonmatching to sample to younger children or in more testing sessions, if we had included more trials on the visual paired comparison task, or if the recognition memory portion of the Corsi-Milner test had been more challenging or the temporal order memory portion less challenging. We cannot be sure. We also cannot rule out the possibility that other tasks that require working memory alone might reveal a problem where we have found none. However, thus far there is no evidence that PKU children with moderately elevated Phe levels perform any worse than other children when working memory is taxed if inhibitory control is not taxed as well.

None of the tasks on which the children with mildly elevated plasma Phe levels succeeded required inhibitory control. However, we included no task that required inhibitory control without also requiring working memory. PKU children with higher Phe levels sometimes also have attention deficit disorder (ADD) or attention deficit hyperactivity disorder (ADHD). For example, 13% of the early treated PKU patients studied by Craft et al. (1992) were also

185

diagnosed with ADHD. More commonly, PKU children have ADD- or ADHD-like symptoms or behavior problems, rather than full-blown ADHD. That is, despite dietary treatment, PKU children are sometimes unusually easily distracted and can have difficulty concentrating or maintaining their attention; they can be unusually fidgety, restless, irritable, or lacking in impulse control (e.g., Anderson, Siegel, Fisch, & Wirt, 1969; Berry et al., 1979; Dobson, Williamson, Azen, & Koch, 1977; Smith, Beasley, Wolff, & Ades, 1988).

Perhaps the function most affected in these children is the ability to control their behavior. We might have found an impairment on tasks that required inhibitory control alone had we included any such tasks. On the other hand, these children might be able to exercise inhibitory control and to hold information in mind, but not be able to do both at the same time; it may be critical that both abilities are taxed. The present data do not permit us to distinguish between these two possibilities, but the data do point to the centrality of inhibitory control functions, either alone or in combination with working memory. Indeed, the one measure on the three boxes task that yielded group differences (the number of consecutive reaches back to the same position) is sensitive to difficulties in inhibitory control. Participants having such difficulties tend to repeat their last rewarded response.

Is it simply that children with higher Phe levels were impaired on the more difficult tests? Were the control tasks too easy?

Some of the control tasks were easy. There were ceiling effects on the three and six boxes tasks (boxes remaining stationary), the control condition of the day-night Stroop-like task, and the Corsi-Milner test of immediate recognition memory. However, there do not appear to have been ceiling effects on the visual paired comparison, delayed nonmatching to sample, global-local spatial processing (with either preferential looking or forced choice reaction time), six boxes (boxes scrambled after each reach), Corsi-Milner temporal order memory, or line bisection tasks. These tasks appear to have been as difficult, or more so, for our participants than the tasks that required working memory and inhibitory control, yet the children with higher Phe levels generally performed as well as other children on the control tasks.

The control groups differed from one another on 4%–5% of the comparisons on the working memory and inhibition tasks and on 1%–4% of the comparisons on the control tasks (depending on the method of comparison used; see Table 10 above). Had there been a large discrepancy in difficulty, one might have expected to find more differences among the four control groups on the more difficult tasks, but such a discrepancy was not found.

The question of difficulty level should not be dismissed too easily, however. Tasks sensitive to prefrontal cortex function, in general, tend to be more difficult than tasks not dependent on that neural system. It remains to be seen whether group differences are still found primarily on the tasks dependent on the functions of dorsolateral prefrontal cortex when researchers control for difficulty more rigorously than we have done here.

GOOD PERFORMANCE WHEN PHE LEVELS ARE UNDER 6 MG/DL

PKU children whose plasma Phe levels were closer to normal (under three times above normal) performed comparably to all control groups on our cognitive neuropsychological tests.

Summary of the Evidence

On the 57 comparisons across all 19 tasks between children with lower Phe levels, on the one hand, and matched controls, siblings, and children from the general population, on the other hand (19 tasks [one dependent measure per task] × 3 comparisons per task), lower-Phe children performed significantly worse on only three pairwise comparisons (5%); on one comparison, they performed better than children from the general population (see Tables 7, 8, and 9 above). Indeed, only 5 of the 114 pairwise comparisons among all control groups (PKU children with lower plasma Phe levels, children from the general population, matched controls, and siblings of the PKU children) on these 19 tasks (19 tasks × 6 comparisons per task) yielded a significant difference (see Table 10 above). (When all the dependent measures were considered, PKU and MHP children whose Phe levels were under three times normal performed worse than the matched control, normative, and sibling groups on 3 of the 165 comparisons [2%]; only 3 of the 330 pairwise comparisons among all control groups yielded significant differences [1%].) Thus, in general, all these groups of children performed comparably to one another.

Comparison with Findings from Other Studies

The generally good performance we found on our 19 tasks among PKU children whose Phe levels were under 6 mg/dl is consistent with other recent reports. For example, de Sonneville et al. (1990) found that performance differences between PKU children and controls were due solely to the subgroup of PKU children whose Phe levels were over 9.5 mg/dl. In our study, as in others, PKU children with "lower" Phe levels did not have Phe levels lower than normal; on the contrary, by and large their Phe levels were elevated above normal, but the elevations were relatively small compared to other PKU children.

187

Discussion of the Importance and Implications

For the children who have some residual phenylalanine hydroxylase activity or who are able to follow a very restrictive diet, our results look very promising. In general, PKU children whose Phe levels were less than three times normal looked very much like other healthy, normal children. Parents of children with PKU or MHP who generally keep their children's Phe levels below three times normal (below 6 mg/dl) should take comfort from these results.

The results on the $\overline{AB}$ task demonstrate the importance of maintaining plasma Phe levels within the acceptable range (2–6 mg/dl), rather than allowing Phe levels to vary widely even if their mean value is acceptable: those infants who had mean Phe levels under three times normal but who on 20% of their Phe tests showed levels under 2 or over 6 mg/dl performed as poorly on $\overline{AB}$ as infants whose mean Phe levels were high (three to five times normal). On the other hand, those PKU and MHP infants whose plasma Phe levels were maintained consistently between 2 and 6 mg/dl performed fully as well as children from the general population, matched controls, and our group of siblings.

These results provide hope that the cognitive deficits that we have observed in PKU children whose Phe levels are three to five times normal may be preventable. If plasma Phe levels do not rise above 6 mg/dl, the working memory and inhibitory control functions dependent on dorsolateral prefrontal cortex (as well as the other cognitive functions) appear to be normal. It had long been thought that a diet sufficiently low in Phe to keep plasma Phe levels from reaching 6 mg/dl or more was so restrictive and burdensome that children would not comply with it. However, in clinics in Denmark, Ireland, the United Kingdom, and the United States, and across the Netherlands and Switzerland, it has been demonstrated that compliance can be obtained when children are placed on a strict diet from the beginning and are told that there is no acceptable alternative. Compliance is problematic where children have been on a more lax regimen and are later asked to give up foods that were previously permitted or where strict dietary compliance is presented as an ideal that the child is not really expected to achieve. (It is also important that families realize that plasma Phe levels below 2 mg/dl are also detrimental to PKU children, as several earlier studies have demonstrated, and that, depending on the particular mutation on chromosome 12 causing the PKU, some children cannot bring their plasma Phe level down into the 2–6 mg/dl range even if they follow a low-Phe diet rigorously.)

If our hypothesis is correct—if the problem is indeed in the moderate imbalance between Phe and Tyr in the bloodstream, which reduces dopamine metabolism in prefrontal cortex—then it may be possible to prevent cognitive deficits in PKU children, even when their plasma Phe levels are three to five times normal, by providing supplemental Tyr or by increasing the level or efficacy of available dopamine (perhaps with low doses of L-dopa or ritalin).

INTERMEDIATE PERFORMANCE OF MHP CHILDREN

In general, the performance of children with MHP whose plasma Phe levels were three to five times normal was intermediate between that of PKU children with comparable plasma Phe levels and that of the comparison groups. MHP children with higher plasma Phe levels performed almost as well as all control groups but also almost as poorly as children with PKU whose Phe levels were similarly moderately elevated.

Summary of the Evidence

If one compares the performance of the MHP children with higher plasma Phe levels to that of matched controls, siblings of PKU and MHP children, or children from the general population, the conclusion would be that MHP children look fine; they perform almost as well as other children. On the other hand, if one compares the performance of these MHP children to that of PKU children whose Phe levels are similarly 6–10 mg/dl, the conclusion would be that there are grounds for concern; PKU children with plasma Phe levels three to five times normal have a clear deficit, and MHP children with comparable Phe levels perform almost as poorly. Although the means show intermediate levels of performance, the number of MHP children with higher Phe levels within each individual age range in our study was small; more significant differences between the performance of MHP children and that of other subject groups might have emerged had we been able to include more higher-Phe MHP participants in our study.

Comparison with Findings from Other Studies

Our findings are in agreement with those from other studies insofar as we found that MHP children were generally not significantly impaired on our tests even if their Phe levels are within the range of 6–10 mg/dl. Lang, Koch, Fishler, and Baker (1989) and Weglage, Schmidt, Fünders, Pietsch, and Ullrich (1996) report similar results.

Among the MHP children we tested, we found a direct, inverse relation between plasma Phe level and performance on a number of our tasks as well as on IQ. Similar results are reported by the Medical Research Council (1993). Indeed, that report indicates a significant deficit in IQ among chil-

dren with MHP. Lang et al. (1989), however, did not find a significant relation between plasma Phe level and IQ among their participants with MHP.

Discussion of the Importance and Implications

MHP children did not perform significantly worse than other normal,
healthy children even when their plasma Phe levels were three to five times
above normal. On the other hand, our results also provide a cautionary note:
MHP children with moderately elevated Phe levels did not perform on an
even par with other children; they were just not significantly worse. Their
performance was not significantly better than that of PKU children with moderate plasma Phe elevations, who were significantly impaired. It may *not* be
true that MHP children can eat a diet rich in Phe with impunity. After all,
we found that their performance on a number of our tasks, as well as on our
IQ measure, suffered in direct proportion to how high their plasma Phe levels
rose (even though the variation was within the range that has been considered clinically acceptable, 2–10 mg/dl).

Because they can hydroxylate Phe to some extent, MHP children tend
to have near normal plasma Tyr levels. The fact that cognitive deficits were
clear among children with PKU whose Phe levels were three to five times
normal, while marginal for MHP children with similar Phe levels, is consistent
with our hypothesis that it may be the ratio of Phe to Tyr in the bloodstream
that is critical, not just the level of Phe.[9] We regret that the absence of plasma
Tyr measurements on many of the children prevented us from investigating
this hypothesis more directly.

Clinical opinion has generally considered a low-Phe diet sufficient treatment for PKU. However, blood Phe levels often cannot be maintained at fully
normal levels because of the body's need for protein. If the problem is the
plasma Phe:Tyr ratio, it might be possible to ameliorate the cognitive deficits
in PKU children who are under moderately good dietary control through the
oral administration of supplemental Tyr. If the Tyr supplements succeed in
raising the level of Tyr in the bloodstream (and hence reducing the plasma
Phe:Tyr imbalance), and if the added Tyr succeeds in reaching the brain,
the result should be normal, or near normal, cognitive performance—if our
hypothesis is correct.

There have been studies of the effect of Tyr supplementation on the
cognitive performance of PKU patients. Generally, however, the amount of
Tyr administered was insufficient to raise plasma Tyr levels (Mazzocco et al.,
1992) or the plasma Phe:Tyr ratio (Smith et al., 1996) significantly, or the

---

[9] For the subset of children in our study for whom we had plasma Tyr measurements,
we found what most others have found: MHP children have roughly normal levels of Tyr in
their bloodstreams.

PKU children had relaxed their dietary compliance, and their plasma Phe levels were therefore much greater than five times normal (Pietz et al., 1995; Smith et al., 1996), resulting in a marked plasma Phe:Tyr imbalance despite the added Tyr. Smith et al. (1996) did find, however, that performance on the self-ordered pointing task designed by Petrides and Milner (1982) and on a one-back continuous performance task was significantly correlated with plasma Tyr levels. Lou, Lykkelund, Gerdes, Udesen, and Bruhn (1987) report that cognitive neuropsychological performance improved when a low-Phe diet was supplemented by high Tyr intake, but this study included few participants. Güttler and Lou (1986) report a beneficial effect from Tyr supplementation even when PKU patients were eating a regular diet, which appears to contradict the results of other studies.

In short, the data are not yet available to evaluate our prediction that supplementing a low-Phe diet with added Tyr should ameliorate the cognitive impairments in PKU children whose plasma Phe levels are kept under five times normal if the additional Tyr remains in the bloodstream rather than being quickly urinated out and if the added Tyr is able to reach the brain.

Our data do not permit us to rule out three other possible interpretations of why cognitive deficits were clear among PKU children with Phe levels three to five times normal while marginal among MHP children with comparable plasma Phe levels: (1) MHP children eat a normal diet; PKU children cannot. We cannot rule out the possibility that the PKU diet somehow contributes to the clearer cognitive deficits among the children with PKU. (2) PKU children have extremely high neonatal Phe levels until they are placed on the low-Phe diet; MHP children never have such high Phe levels. We cannot rule out the possibility that extremely high Phe levels at such a critical time during early development contributes to the more pronounced cognitive deficits found among the children with PKU. (3) Within each age range, our numbers of MHP participants with higher Phe levels were very small. Points 1 and 2, however, apply equally well to the PKU children with lower Phe levels, in whom we found normal cognitive performance.

SEX DIFFERENCE

We found the cognitive performance of girls with PKU to be more adversely affected than that of boys with PKU. PKU boys tended to outperform PKU girls.

Summary of the Evidence

On four different tasks, among the children with PKU only, girls did not perform as well as boys; on *none* of these tasks was a similar sex difference found in any of the other four subject groups. On one task $(\overline{AB})$, among all other subject groups (MHP, matched controls, siblings, and norms), the girls could withstand significantly longer delays than the boys. This sex difference was reversed among participants with PKU—PKU boys could withstand significantly longer delays than PKU girls. Girls in all subject groups received higher IQ scores than boys, but this sex difference was smallest among the children with PKU. On no task did PKU girls outperform PKU boys.

Discussion of the Importance and Implications

We had not predicted a sex difference and are not sure why we found it. We do not know of other reports of differential effects of PKU or of plasma Phe elevations on girls. Craft et al. (1992) report greater cognitive deficits in PKU males than in PKU females. However, research on another inborn error of metabolism, galactosemia, has found girls to be disproportionately affected (Fishler, 1993). Galactosemic girls were found to score six points lower than boys on the Stanford-Binet test and 14 points lower on the WAIS-R, where the performance of girls trailed most strongly on the performance subscales. On the WAIS-R, galactosemic boys consistently performed within the normal range, whereas several scores among galactosemic girls were below average.

OVERALL SUMMARY

In conclusion, we have found that PKU children with plasma Phe levels of 6–10 mg/dl perform worse than other children of the same age when the working memory and inhibitory control abilities dependent on dorsolateral prefrontal cortex are required. This deficit was evident in both the youngest and the oldest subjects and showed no evidence of subsiding with age. It was evident regardless of the group to which the children were compared—other PKU children with lower Phe levels, children from the general population, matched controls, or their own siblings—and it remained significant even when IQ, gender, health variables, and background variables were controlled. The cognitive deficit appears to be selective in that weaknesses were not found in other cognitive abilities, dependent on other neural regions. The finding that other PKU children whose plasma Phe levels did not rise as much above normal performed normally across all 19 cognitive tasks provides hope that the cognitive deficits observed in other PKU children with higher Phe levels might be preventable. The finding that performance on the tasks requiring working memory and inhibitory control was most strongly related to concurrent plasma Phe levels, rather than to chronic Phe levels or to Phe levels earlier in life, provides hope that the cognitive deficits reflect current biochemical levels, rather than structural damage, and hence might be reversible.

These findings, plus those from our work on an animal model of early and continuously treated PKU (Diamond, Ciaramitaro, et al., 1994) and our work on visual contrast sensitivity (Diamond & Herzberg, 1996), provide support for the biological mechanism we have hypothesized to underlie the observed cognitive deficits. The mechanism that we have hypothesized is that, when the ratio of Phe to Tyr in the bloodstream is moderately elevated, the amount of Tyr that can reach the brain from the bloodstream is moderately reduced; those dopamine neurons that fire most quickly and turn over dopamine most quickly (i.e., the dopamine neurons that project to prefrontal cortex and that are in the retina) are disproportionately affected by a moderate reduction in available Tyr.

Since we think that we understand the biological mechanism causing the deficits, we think that we might be able to correct them. We take heart that the cognitive deficits documented here might be preventable or reversible by keeping children on low-Phe diets strict enough to maintain plasma Phe levels between 2 and 6 mg/dl and, where that is not possible (and some children's metabolism is such that it is not possible), by giving the children Tyr or low doses of L-dopa or ritalin.

REFERENCES

Anderson, V. E., Siegel, F. S., Fisch, R. O., & Wirt, R. D. (1969). Responses of phenylketonuric children on a continuous performance test. *Journal of Abnormal Psychology, 74,* 358–362.

Bachevalier, J. (1990). Ontogenetic development of habit and memory formation in primates. In A. Diamond (Ed.), *The development and neural bases of higher cognitive functions. Annals of the New York Academy of Sciences,* **608,** 457–484.

Bachevalier, J., Brickson, M., & Hagger, C. (1993). Limbic-dependent recognition memory in monkeys develops early in infancy. *Neuroreport,* **4,** 77–80.

Bachevalier, J., & Mishkin, M. (1984). An early and a late developing system for learning and retention in infant monkeys. *Behavioral Neuroscience,* **98,** 770–778.

Bachevalier, J., & Mishkin, M. (1986). Visual recognition impairment follows ventromedial but not dorsolateral prefrontal lesions in monkeys. *Behavioral Brain Research,* **20,** 249–261.

Balamore, U., & Wozniak, R. H. (1984). Speech-action coordination in young children. *Developmental Psychology,* **20,** 850–858.

Bannon, M. J., Bunney, E. B., & Roth, R. H. (1981). Mesocortical dopamine neurons: Rapid transmitter turnover compared to other brain catecholamine systems. *Brain Research,* **218,** 376–382.

Barbizet, J. (1970). Prolonged organic amnesias. In J. Barbizet (Ed.), *Human memory and its pathology* (D. K. Jardine, Trans.). San Francisco: W. H. Freeman.

Bättig, K., Rosvold, H. E., & Mishkin, M. (1960). Comparison of the effects of frontal and caudate lesions on delayed response and alternation in monkeys. *Journal of Comparative Physiology,* **53,** 400–404.

Bauer, R. H., & Fuster, A. H. (1976). Delayed-matching and delayed-response deficit from cooling dorsolateral prefrontal cortex in monkeys. *Journal of Comparative and Physiological Psychology,* **90,** 293–302.

Bench, C. J., Frith, C. D., Grasby, P. M., Friston, K. J., Paulesu, E., Frackowiak, R. S., & Dolan, R. J. (1993). Investigations of the functional anatomy of attention using the Stroop test. *Neuropsychologia,* **31,** 907–922.

Benton, A. L. (1969). Disorders of spatial orientation. In P. Vincken & G. Bruyn (Eds.), *Handbook of clinical neurology* (Vol. **3**). Amsterdam: North-Holland.

Benton, A. L., & Hamsher, K. deS. (1976). *Multilingual aphasia examination manual (revised).* Iowa City: University of Iowa Press.

Berry, H. K., O'Grady, D. J., Perlmutter, L. J., & Bofinger, M. K. (1979). Intellectual development and achievement of children treated early for phenylketonuria. *Developmental Medicine and Child Neurology,* **21,** 311–320.

Bessman, S. P. (1979). The justification theory: The essential nature of the non-essential amino acids. *Nutrition Reviews*, **37**, 209–220.

Bickel, H., Beckers, R. G., Wamberg, E., Schmid-Rüter, E., Feingold, J., Cahalane, S. F., Bottine, E., Jonxis, J. H. P., Colombo, J. P., & Carson, N. (1973). Collective results of mass screening for inborn errors in eight European countries. *Acta Paediatrica*, **62**, 413–416.

Bickel, H., Gerrard, J., & Hickmans, E. M. (1954). The influence of phenylalanine intake on the chemistry and behavior of a phenylketonuric child. *Acta Paediatrica*, **43**, 64–77.

Bodis-Wollner, I. (1988). Altered spatio-temporal contrast vision in Parkinson's disease and MPTP-treated monkeys: The role of dopamine. In I. Bodis-Wollner & M. Piccolino (Eds.), *Dopaminergic mechanisms in vision*. New York: Alan Liss.

Bodis-Wollner, I. (1990). Visual deficits related to dopamine deficiency in experimental animals and Parkinson's disease patients. *Trends in Neural Science*, **13**, 296–302.

Bodis-Wollner, I., Marx, M. S., Mitra, S., Bobak, P., Mylin, L., & Yahr, M. (1987). Visual dysfunction in Parkinson's disease: Loss in spatiotemporal contrast sensitivity. *Brain*, **110**, 1675–1698.

Borkowski, J. G., Benton, A. L., & Spreen, O. (1967). Word fluency and brain damage. *Neuropsychologia*, **5**, 135–140.

Bradberry, C. W., Karasic, D. H., Deutch, A. Y., & Roth, R. H. (1989). Regionally-specific alterations in mesotelencephalic dopamine synthesis in diabetic rats: Association with precursor tyrosine. *Journal of Neural Transmission*, **78**, 221–229.

Brass, C. A., & Greengard, O. (1982). Modulation of cerebral catecholamine concentrations during hyperphenylalaninaemia. *Biochemical Journal*, **208**, 765–771.

Brody, B. A., Ungerleider, L. G., & Pribram, K. H. (1977). The effects of instability of the visual display on pattern discrimination learning by monkeys: Dissociation produced after resections of frontal and inferotemporal cortex. *Neuropsychologia*, **15**, 439–448.

Brozoski, T. J., Brown, R. M., Rosvold, H. E., & Goldman, P. S. (1979). Cognitive deficit caused by regional depletion of dopamine in prefrontal cortex of rhesus monkey. *Science*, **205**, 929–932.

Brunner, R. L., Berch, D. B., & Berry, H. (1987). Phenylketonuria and complex spatial visualization: An analysis of information processing. *Developmental Medicine and Child Neurology*, **29**, 460–468.

Brunner, R. L., Jordan, M. K., & Berry, H. K. (1983). Early-treated phenylketonuria: Neuropsychologic consequences. *Journal of Pediatrics*, **102**, 831–835.

Brush, E. S., Mishkin, M., & Rosvold, H. E. (1961). Effects of object preferences and aversions on discrimination learning in monkeys with frontal lesions. *Journal of Comparative and Physiological Psychology*, **54**, 319–325.

Bubser, M., & Schmidt, W. J. (1990). 6-hydroxydopamine lesion of the rat prefrontal cortex increases locomotor activity, impairs acquisition of delayed alternation tasks, but does not affect uninterrupted tasks in the radial maze. *Behavioral Brain Research*, **37**, 157–168.

Bugbee, N. M., & Goldman-Rakic, P. S. (1981). Functional 2-deoxyglucose mapping in association cortex: Prefrontal activation in monkeys performing a cognitive task. *Society for Neuroscience Abstracts*, **7**, 239.

Burgess, P. W., & Shallice, T. (1996). Response suppression, initiation and strategy use following frontal lobe lesions. *Neuropsychologia*, **34**, 263–273.

Butters, N., Pandya, D., Sanders, K., & Dye, P. (1969). Behavioral deficits in monkeys after selective lesions within the middle third of sulcus principalis. *Journal of Comparative and Physiological Psychology*, **76**, 8–14.

Casey, B. J., Cohen, J. D., Noll, D. C., Forman, S., & Rapoport, J. L. (1993). Activation of the anterior cingulate during the Stroop conflict paradigm using functional MRI. *Society for Neuroscience Abstracts*, **19**, 1285.

Chirigos, M., Greengard, P., & Udenfriend, S. (1960). Uptake of tyrosine by rat brain in vivo. *Journal of Biological Chemistry,* **235,** 2075–2079.

Churchland, A., & Diamond, A. (1996). Solving the riddle of the late appearance of success on the delayed nonmatching to sample task. *Society for Neuroscience Abstracts,* **22,** 281.

Cohen, J. D., Forman, S., Braver, T. S., Casey, B. J., Servan-Schreiber, D., & Noll, D. C. (1994). Activation of prefrontal cortex in a non-spatial working memory task with functional MRI. *Human Brain Mapping,* **1,** 293–304.

Cohen, L. B., & Gelber, E. R. (1975). Infant visual memory. In L. B. Cohen & P. Salapatek (Eds.), *Infant perception: From sensation to cognition* (Vol. 1). New York: Academic.

Corsi, P. M. (1972). *Human memory and the medial temporal regions of the brain.* Unpublished doctoral dissertation, McGill University.

Costello, P. M., Beasley, M. G., Tillotson, S. L., & Smith, I. (1994). Intelligence in mild atypical phenylketonuria. *European Journal of Pediatrics,* **153,** 260–263.

Cowie, V. A. (1971). Neurological and psychiatric aspects of phenylketonuria. In H. Bickel, F. Hudson, & L. Woolf (Eds.), *Phenylketonuria and some other inborn errors of amino acid metabolism.* Stuttgart: Georg Thiese.

Craft, S., Gourovitch, M. L., Dowton, S. B., Swanson, J. M., & Bonforte, S. (1992). Lateralized deficits in visual attention in males with developmental dopamine depletion. *Neuropsychologia,* **30,** 341–351.

Deiber, M.-P., Passingham, R. E., Colebatch, J. G., Friston, K. J., Nixon, P. D., & Frackowiak, R. S. J. (1991). Cortical areas and the selection of movement: A study with positron emission tomography. *Experimental Brain Research,* **84,** 393–402.

de Sonneville, L. N. J., Schmidt, E., Michel, U., & Batzler, U. (1990). Preliminary neuropsychological test results. *European Journal of Pediatrics,* **149**(Suppl. 1), S39–S44.

Diamond, A. (1981). Retrieval of an object from an open box: The development of visual-tactile control of reaching in the first year of life. *Society for Research in Child Development Abstracts,* **3,** 78.

Diamond, A. (1985). Development of the ability to use recall to guide action, as indicated by infants' performance on AB̄. *Child Development,* **56,** 868–883.

Diamond, A. (1990a). Developmental time course in human infants and infant monkeys, and the neural bases, of inhibitory control in reaching. In A. Diamond (Ed.), *The development and neural bases of higher cognitive functions.* Annals of the New York Academy of Sciences, **608,** 637–676.

Diamond, A. (1990b). The development and neural bases of memory functions as indexed by the AB̄ and delayed response tasks in human infants and infant monkeys. In A. Diamond (Ed.), *The development and neural bases of higher cognitive functions.* Annals of the New York Academy of Sciences, **608,** 267–317.

Diamond, A. (1990c). Rate of maturation of the hippocampus and the developmental progression of children's performance on the delayed non-matching to sample and visual paired comparison tasks. In A. Diamond (Ed.), *The development and neural bases of higher cognitive functions.* Annals of the New York Academy of Sciences, **608,** 394–426.

Diamond, A. (1991a). Frontal lobe involvement in cognitive changes during the first year of life. In K. R. Gibson & A. C. Petersen (Eds.), *Brain maturation and cognitive development: Comparative and cross-cultural perspectives.* New York: Aldine de Gruyter.

Diamond, A. (1991b). Neuropsychological insights into the meaning of object concept development. In S. Carey & R. Gelman (Eds.), *The epigenesis of mind: Essays on biology and knowledge.* Hillsdale, NJ: Erlbaum.

Diamond, A. (1995). Evidence of robust recognition memory early in life even when assessed by reaching behavior. *Journal of Experimental Child Psychology,* **59,** 419–456.

Diamond, A., Ciaramitaro, V., Donner, E., Djali, S., & Robinson, M. (1994). An animal model of early-treated PKU. *Journal of Neuroscience,* **14,** 3072–3082.

Diamond, A., Ciaramitaro, V., Donner, E., Hurwitz, W., Lee, E., Grover, W., & Minarcik, C. (1992). Prefrontal cortex cognitive deficits in early treated PKU: Results of a longitudinal study in children and of an animal model. *Society of Neuroscience Abstracts*, **18**, 1063.

Diamond, A., & Doar, B. (1989). The performance of human infants on a measure of frontal cortex function, the delayed response task. *Developmental Psychobiology*, **22**, 271–294.

Diamond, A., & Goldman-Rakic, P. S. (1985). Evidence for involvement of prefrontal cortex in cognitive changes during the first year of life: Comparison of performance of human infant and rhesus monkeys on a detour task with transparent barrier. *Society for Neuroscience Abstracts*, **11**, 832.

Diamond, A., & Goldman-Rakic, P. S. (1986). Comparative development in human infants and infant rhesus monkeys of cognitive functions that depend on prefrontal cortex. *Society for Neuroscience Abstracts*, **12**, 742.

Diamond, A., & Goldman-Rakic, P. S. (1989). Comparison of human infants and rhesus monkeys on Piaget's $\overline{AB}$ task: Evidence for dependence on dorsolateral prefrontal cortex. *Experimental Brain Research*, **74**, 24–40.

Diamond, A., & Herzberg, C. (1996). Impaired sensitivity to visual contrast in children treated early and continuously for PKU. *Brain*, **119**, 523–538.

Diamond, A., & Lee, E. (in preparation). *Early success on the delayed nonmatching to sample task when the act of reaching for the stimulus immediately produces the reward.*

Diamond, A., & Taylor, C. (1996). Development of an aspect of executive control: Development of the abilities to remember what I said and to "Do as I say, not as I do." *Developmental Psychobiology*, **29**, 315–334.

Diamond, A., Towle, C., & Boyer, K. (1994). Young children's performance on a task sensitive to the memory functions of the medial temporal lobe in adults, the delayed nonmatching to sample task, reveals problems that are due to non–memory related task demands. *Behavioral Neuroscience*, **108**, 1–22.

Diamond, A., Zola-Morgan, S., & Squire, L. (1989). Successful performance by monkeys with lesions of the hippocampal formation on $\overline{AB}$ and object retrieval, two tasks that mark developmental changes in human infants. *Behavioral Neuroscience*, **103**, 526–537.

DiLella, A. G., Marvit, J., Lidsky, A. S., Güttler, F., & Woo, S. L. C. (1986). Tight linkage between a splicing mutation and a specific DNA haplotype in phenylketonuria. *Nature*, **322**, 799–803.

Dobson, J. C., Kushida, E., Williamson, M. L., & Friedman, E. G. (1976). Intellectual performance of 36 phenylketonuric patients and their non-affected siblings. *Pediatrics*, **58**, 53–58.

Dobson, J. C., Williamson, M. L., Azen, C., & Koch, R. (1977). Intellectual assessment of 111 four-year-old children with phenylketonuria. *Pediatrics*, **60**, 822–827.

Drewe, E. A. (1975). An experimental investigation of Luria's theory on the effects of frontal lobe lesions in man. *Neuropsychologia*, **13**, 421–429.

Dyer, C. A., Kendler, A., Philibotte, T., Gardiner, P., Cruz, J., & Levy, H. L. (1996). Evidence for central nervous system glial cell plasticity in phenylketonuria. *Journal of Neuropathology and Experimental Neurology*, **55**, 795–814.

Eslinger, P. J., & Grattan, L. M. (1993). Frontal lobe and frontal-striatal substrates for different forms of human cognitive flexibility. *Neuropsychologia*, **31**, 17.

Fagan, J. F., III. (1970). Memory in the infant. *Journal of Experimental Child Psychology*, **9**, 217–266.

Fagan, J. F., III. (1973). Infants' delayed recognition memory and forgetting. *Journal of Experimental Child Psychology*, **16**, 424–450.

Fantz, R. L. (1964). Visual experience in infants: Decreased attention to familiar patterns relative to novel ones. *Science*, **146**, 668–670.

Faust, D., Libon, D., & Pueschel, S. (1986). Neuropsychological functioning in treated phenylketonuria. *International Journal of Psychiatry in Medicine,* **16,** 169–177.

Fernstrom, J. D., & Fernstrom, M. H. (1988). Tyrosine availability and dopamine synthesis in the retina. In I. Bodis-Wollner & M. Piccolino (Eds.), *Dopaminergic mechanisms in vision.* New York: Alan Liss.

Fernstrom, M. H., Baker, R. L., & Fernstrom, J. D. (1989). In vivo tyrosine hydroxylation rate in retina: Effects of phenylalanine and tyrosine administration in rats pretreated with *p*-chlorophenylalanine. *Brain Research,* **499,** 291–298.

Fernstrom, M. H., Volk, E. A., & Fernstrom, J. D. (1986). In vivo inhibition of tyrosine uptake into rat retina by large neutral, but not acidic, amino acids. *American Journal of Physiology,* **251,** E393–E399.

Fishler, K. (1993). Intellectual development in galactosemia. In G. N. Donnell (Ed.), *Galactosemia: New frontiers in research.* Washington, DC: National Institutes of Health.

Følling, A. (1934). Uber Ausscheidung von Phenylbrenztraubensäure in der harn als Stoffwechselanomalie in verbindung mit imbezillität. *Hoppe-Seyler's Ztschr. Physiol. Chem.,* **227,** 169.

Fuster, J. M. (1973). Unit activity in prefrontal cortex during delayed-response performance: Neuronal correlates of transient memory. *Journal of Neurophysiology,* **36,** 61–78.

Fuster, J. M., & Alexander, G. E. (1970). Delayed response deficit by cryogenic depression of frontal cortex. *Brain Research,* **20,** 85–90.

Fuster, J. M., & Alexander, G. E. (1971). Neuron activity related to short-term memory. *Science,* **173,** 652–654.

Gaffan, D., Gaffan, E. A., & Harrison, S. (1984). Effects of fornix transection on spontaneous and trained non-matching by monkeys. *Quarterly Journal of Experimental Psychology,* **36,** 285–303.

Gerstadt, C., Hong, Y., & Diamond, A. (1994). The relationship between cognition and action: Performance of 3½–7 year old children on a Stroop-like day-night test. *Cognition,* **53,** 129–153.

Glick, S. D., Jerussi, T. P., & Zimmerberg, B. (1977). Behavioral and neuropharmacological correlates of nigrostriatal asymmetry in rats. In S. Haenad et al. (Eds.), *Lateralization of the nervous system.* New York: Academic.

Goldman, P. S., & Rosvold, H. E. (1970). Localization of function within the dorsolateral prefrontal cortex of the rhesus monkey. *Experimental Neurology,* **27,** 291–304.

Goldman, P. S., & Rosvold, H. E. (1972). The effects of selective caudate lesions in infant and juvenile rhesus monkeys. *Brain Research,* **43,** 53–66.

Goldman-Rakic, P. S. (1987). Circuitry of primate prefrontal cortex and regulation of behavior by representational memory. *Handbook of Physiology,* **5,** 373–417.

Goldstein, K. (1944). The mental changes due to frontal lobe damage. *Journal of Psychology,* **17,** 187–208.

Greengard, O., & Brass, C. A. (1984). Developmental changes of cerebral phenylalanine uptake from severely elevated blood levels. *Neurochemical Research,* **9,** 837–847.

Greengard, O., Yoss, M. S., & DelValle, J. A. (1976). α-methylphenylalanine, a new inducer of chronic hyperphenylalaninemia in suckling rats. *Science,* **192,** 1007–1008.

Guitton, D., Buchtel, H. A., & Douglas, R. M. (1985). Frontal lobe lesions in man cause difficulties in suppressing reflexive glances and generating goal-directed saccades. *Experimental Brain Research,* **58,** 455–472.

Guthrie, R. (1996). The introduction of newborn screening for phenylketonuria: A personal history. *European Journal of Pediatrics,* **155,** S4–S5.

Guthrie, R. E., & Susi, A. (1963). A simple phenylalanine method for detecting phenylketonuria in large populations of newborn infants. *Pediatrics,* **32,** 338–343.

Güttler, F. (1988). Epidemiology and natural history of phenylketonuria and other hyperphenylalaninemias. In R. J. Wurtman & E. Ritter-Walker (Eds.), *Dietary phenylalanine and brain function*. Boston: Birkhäuser.

Güttler, F., & Lou, H. C. (1986). Dietary problems of phenylketonuria: Effect on CNS transmitters and their possible role in behaviour and neuropsychological function. *Journal of Inherited Metabolic Disease*, **9**, 169–177.

Harlow, H. F. (1950). Analysis of discrimination learning by monkeys. *Journal of Experimental Psychology*, **40**, 26–39.

Holtzman, N. A., Kronmal, R. A., van Doorninck, W., Azen, C., & Koch, R. (1986). Effect of age at loss of dietary control on intellectual performance and behavior of children with phenylketonuria. *New England Journal of Medicine*, **314**, 593–598.

Hommes, F. A. (1990). Demyelination in hyperphenylalaninemia. *Annals of the New York Academy of Sciences*, **605**, 449–452.

Hommes, F. A., & Moss, L. (1992). Myelin turnover in hyperphenylalaninemia: A re-evaluation with the HPH-5 mouse. *Journal of Inherited Metabolic Disease*, **15**, 243–251.

Hsia, D. Y.-Y. (1970). Phenylketonuria and its variants. *Progress in Medical Genetics*, **7**, 29–68.

Hudson, F. P., Mordaunt, V. L., & Leahy, I. (1970). Evaluation of treatment begun in the first three months of life in 184 cases of phenylketonuria. *Archives of Disease in Childhood*, **45**, 5–12.

Huether, G., Kaus, R., & Neuhoff, V. (1982). Brain development in experimental hyperphenylalaninemia: Myelination. *Neuropediatrics*, **13**, 177–182.

Ikeda, M., Levitt, M., & Udenfriend, S. (1967). Phenylalanine as substrate and inhibitor of tyrosine hydroxylase. *Archives of Biochemistry and Biophysics*, **120**, 42–47.

Irie, K., & Wurtman, R. J. (1987). Release of norepinephrine from rat hypothalamic slices: Effects of desipramine and tyrosine. *Brain Research*, **432**, 391–394.

Iuvone, P. M., Galli, C. L., Garrison-Gund, C. K., & Neff, N. H. (1978). Light stimulates tyrosine hydroxylase activity and dopamine synthesis in retinal amacrine neurons. *Science*, **202**, 901–902.

Iuvone, P. M., Tigges, M., Fernandes, A., & Tigges, J. (1989). Dopamine synthesis and metabolism in rhesus monkey retina: Development, aging, and the effects of monocular visual deprivation. *Visual Neuroscience*, **2**, 465–471.

Jacobsen, C. F. (1936). Studies of cerebral function in primates: 1. The functions of the functional association areas in monkeys. *Comparative Psychology Monographs*, **13**, 3–60.

Jacobsen, C. F., & Nissen, H. W. (1937). Studies of cerebral function in primates: The effects of frontal lobe lesions on the delayed alternation habit in monkeys. *Journal of Comparative Physiological Psychology*, **23**, 101–112.

Jenkins, I. H., Brooks, D. J., Nixon, P. D., Frackowiak, R. S. J., & Passingham, R. E. (1994). Motor sequence learning: A study with positron emission tomography. *Journal of Neuroscience*, **14**, 3775–3790.

Katz, I., Lloyd, T., & Kaufman, S. (1976). Studies on phenylalanine and tyrosine hydroxylation by rat brain tyrosine hydroxylase. *Biochemica et Biophysica Acta*, **445**, 567–578.

Kaufman, S., Berlow, S., Summer, G. K., Milstein, S., Schulman, J. D., Orloff, S., Spielberg, S., & Pueschel, S. (1978). Hyperphenylalaninemia due to a deficiency of biopterin: A variant of phenylketonuria. *New England Journal of Medicine*, **299**, 673–679.

Kaufman, S., Kapatos, G., McInnes, R. R., Schulman, J. D., & Rizzo, W. B. (1982). Use of tetrahydropterins in the treatment of hyperphenylalaninemia due to defective synthesis of tetrahydrobiopterin. *Pediatrics*, **70**, 376–380.

Koch, R., Azen, C., Friedman, E. G., & Williamson, E. L. (1982). Preliminary report on the effects of diet discontinuation in PKU. *Pediatrics*, **100**, 870–875.

Koch, R., Azen, C., Friedman, E. G., & Williamson, M. L. (1984). Paired comparisons between early-treated PKU children and their matched sibling controls on intelligence and school achievement test results at eight years of age. *Journal of Inherited Metabolic Diseases*, **7**, 86–90.

Koch, R., & Wenz, E. (1987). Phenylketonuria. *Annual Review of Nutrition*, **7**, 117–135.

Kolb, B., & Whishaw, I. (1985). *Fundamentals of human neuropsychology*. New York: W. H. Freeman.

Kowalska, D. M., Bachevalier, J., & Mishkin, M. (1991). The role of the inferior prefrontal convexity in performance of delayed nonmatching-to-sample. *Neuropsychologia*, **29**, 583–600.

Krause, W. L., Helminski, M., McDonald, L., Dembure, P., Salvo, R., Freides, D., & Elsas, L. J. (1985). Biochemical and neuropsychological effects of elevated plasma phenylalanine in patients with treated phenylketonuria, a model for the study of phenylalanine in brain function in man. *Journal of Clinical Investigation*, **75**, 40–48.

Kubota, K., & Niki, H. (1971). Prefrontal cortical unit activity and delayed alternation performance in monkeys. *Journal of Neurophysiology*, **34**, 337–347.

Kupersmith, M. J., Shakin, E., Siegel, I. M., & Lieberman, A. (1982). Visual system abnormalities in patients with Parkinson's disease. *Archives of Neurology*, **39**, 284–286.

Lajtha, A., Sershen, H., & Dunlop, D. (1988). Developmental changes in cerebral amino acids and protein metabolism. In G. Huether (Ed.), *Amino acid availability and brain function in health and disease*. Berlin: Springer.

Lamb, M. R., Robertson, L. C., & Knight, R. T. (1989). Attention and inference in the processing of global and local information: Effects of unilateral temporal parietal junction lesions. *Neuropsychologia*, **27**, 471–483.

Lamb, M. R., Robertson, L. C., & Knight, R. T. (1990). Component mechanisms underlying the processing of hierarchically organized patterns: Interferences from patients with unilateral cortical lesions. *Journal of Experimental Psychology*, **16**, 471–483.

Lang, M. J., Koch, R., Fishler, K., & Baker, R. (1989). Nonphenylketonuric hyperphenylalaninemia. *American Journal of Diseases of Children*, **143**, 1464–1466.

Larsen, J. K., & Divac, I. (1978). Selective ablations within the prefrontal cortex of the rat and performance on delayed alternation. *Physiological Psychology*, **6**, 15–17.

Ledley, F. D., Levy, H. L., & Woo, S. L. (1986). Molecular analysis of the inheritance of phenylketonuria and mild hyperphenylalaninemia in families with both disorders. *New England Journal of Medicine*, **314**, 1276–1280.

Levitt, M., Spector, S., Sjoerdsma, A., & Udenfriend, S. (1965). *Journal of Pharmacological Experimental Theory*, **148**, 1–8.

Levy, H. L., Shih, V. E., Karolkewicz, V., French, W. A., Carr, J. R., Cass, V., Kennedy, J. L., & MacCready, R. A. (1971). Persistent mild hyperphenylalaninemia in the untreated state. *New England Journal of Medicine*, **285**, 424–428.

Levy, H. L., Waisbren, S. E., Lobbregt, D., Allred, E., Schuler, A., Trefz, F. K., Schweitzer, S. M., Sardharwalla, I. B., Walter, J. H., Barwell, B. E., Berlin, C. M., Jr., & Leviton, A. (1994). Maternal mild hyperphenylalaninaemia: An intentional survey of offspring outcome. *Lancet*, **344**, 1589–1594.

Lewis, D. A., Campbell, M. J., Foote, S. L., & Morrison, J. H. (1986). The monoaminergic innervation of primate neocortex. *Human Neurobiology*, **5**, 181–188.

Lewis, D. A., & Morrison, J. H. (1989). The noradrenergic innervation of monkey prefrontal cortex: A dopamine-ß-hydroxylase immunohistochemical study. *Journal of Comparative Neurology*, **282**, 317–330.

L'Hermitte, F. (1983). "Utilization behavior" and its relation to lesions of the frontal lobes. *Brain*, **106**, 237–255.

Lidsky, A. S., Law, M. L., Morse, H. G., Kao, F. T., & Woo, S. L. C. (1985). Regional mapping of the human phenylalanine hydroxylase gene and the PKU locus on chromosome 12. *Proceedings of the National Academy of Science*, **82**, 6221–6225.

Lou, H. C., Lykkelund, C., Gerdes, A. M., Udesen, H., & Bruhn, P. (1987). Increased vigilance and dopamine synthesis by large doses of tyrosine or phenylalanine restriction in phenylketonuria. *Acta Paediatrica*, **76**, 560–565.

Lovenberg, W., Jequier, E., & Sjoerdsma, A. (1968). Tryptophan hydroxylation in mammalian systems. In S. Garratini & P. A. Shore (Eds.), *Advances in pharmacology* (Vol. **6A**). New York: Academic.

Luciana, M., Depue, R. A., Arbisi, P., & Leon, A. (1992). Facilitation of working memory in humans by a D_2 dopamine receptor agonist. *Journal of Cognitive Neuroscience*, **4**, 58–68.

Luria, A. R. (1966). *Higher cortical functions in man* (1st ed.). New York: Basic.

Luria, A. R. (1980). *Higher cortical functions in man* (2d ed.). New York: Basic.

Mangels, J. A. (1997). Strategic processing and memory for temporal order in patients with frontal lobe lesions. *Neuropsychology*, **11**(2), 207–221.

Martin, M. (1979). Local and global processing: The role of sparsity. *Memory and Cognition*, **7**, 476–484.

Mazzocco, M. M. M., Nord, A. M., van Doorninck, W., Greene, C. L., & Kovar, C. G. (1994). Cognitive development among children with early-treated phenylketonuria. *Developmental Neuropsychology*, **10**, 133–151.

Mazzocco, M. M. M., Yannicelli, S., Nord, A. M., van Doorninck, W., Davidson-Mundt, A. J., Greene, C. L., & Pennington, B. F. (1992). Cognition and tyrosine supplementation among school-aged children with phenylketonuria. *American Journal of Diseases of Children*, **146**, 1261–1264.

McAndrews, M. P., & Milner, B. (1991). The frontal cortex and memory for temporal order. *Neuropsychologia*, **9**, 849–859.

McDonald, J. D., Bode, V. C., Dove, W. F., & Shedlovsky, A. (1990). Pah[hph-5]: A mouse mutant deficient in phenylalanine hydroxylase. *Proceedings of the National Academy of Science*, **87**, 1965–1967.

McKean, C. M. (1972). The effects of high phenylalanine concentrations on serotonin and catecholamine metabolism in the human brain. *Brain Research*, **47**, 469–476.

McKee, R. D., & Squire, L. R. (1993). On the development of declarative memory. *Journal of Experimental Psychology: Learning, Memory, and Cognition*, **19**, 397–404.

Medical Research Council. (1993). Phenylketonuria due to phenylalanine hydroxylase deficiency: An unfolding story. *British Medical Journal*, **306**, 115–119.

Medical Research Council Working Party on Phenylketonuria. (1993). Recommendations on the dietary management of phenylketonuria. *Archives of Disease in Childhood*, **68**, 426–427.

Mesulam, M.-M. (1995, May). *Overview of human frontal lobes.* Paper presented at the meeting of the American Academy of Neurology, Seattle.

Meunier, M., Bachevalier, J., Mishkin, M., & Murray, E. A. (1993). Effects on visual recognition of combined and separate ablations of the entorhinal and perirhinal cortex in rhesus monkeys. *Journal of Neuroscience*, **13**, 5418–5432.

Miller, L., Braun, L. D., Pardridge, W. M., & Oldendorf, W. H. (1985). Kinetic constants for blood-brain barrier amino acid transport in conscious rats. *Journal of Neurochemistry*, **45**, 1427–1432.

Milner, B. (1972). Disorders of learning and memory after temporal lobe lesions in man. *Clinical Neurosurgery*, **19**, 421–446.

Milner, B. (1982). Some cognitive effects of frontal lobe lesions in man. *Philosophical Transactions of the Royal Society of London*, **B298**, 211–226.

Milner, B., Corsi, P., & Leonard, G. (1991). Frontal-lobe contribution to recency judgements. *Neuropsychologia*, **29**, 601–618.

Milner, J. D., Irie, K., & Wurtman, R. J. (1986). Effects of phenylalanine on the release of endogenous dopamine from rat striatal slices. *Journal of Neurochemistry*, **47**, 1444–1448.

Mishkin, M. (1978). Memory in monkeys severely impaired by combined but not separate removal of amygdala and hippocampus. *Nature*, **273**, 297–298.

Mishkin, M., Prockop, E. S., & Rosvold, H. E. (1962). One trial object discrimination learning in monkeys with frontal lesions. *Journal of Comparative and Physiological Psychology*, **7**, 357–364.

Murray, E. A., Bachevalier, J., & Mishkin, M. (1989). Effects of rhinal cortical lesions on visual recognition memory in rhesus monkeys. *Society for Neuroscience Abstracts*, **15**, 342.

Navon, D. (1977). Forest before trees: The precedence of global features in visual perception. *Cognitive Psychology*, **9**, 353–383.

Niki, H. (1974). Prefrontal unit activity during delayed alternation in the monkey. *Brain Research*, **68**, 185–204.

Nord, A. M., McCabe, L., & McCabe, E. R. B. (1988). Biochemical and nutritional status of children with hyperphenylalaninemia. *Journal of Inherited Metabolic Disease*, **11**, 431–432.

O'Driscoll, G. A., Alpert, N. M., Matthysse, S. W., Levy, D. L., Rauch, S. L., & Holzman, P. S. (1995). Functional neuroanatomy of antisaccade eye movements investigated with positron emission tomography. *Proceedings of the National Academy of Science*, **92**, 925–929.

O'Flynn, M. E., & Hsia, D. (1968). Some observations on the dietary treatment of phenylketonuria. *Neuropsychologia*, **72**, 260–262.

Oldendorf, W. H. (1973). Stereospecificity of blood brain barrier permeability to amino acids. *American Journal of Physiology*, **224**, 967–969.

Overman, W. H., Bachevalier, J., Turner, M., & Peuster, A. (1992). Object recognition versus object discrimination: Comparison between human infants and monkey infants. *Behavioral Neuroscience*, **106**, 15–29.

Owen, A. M., Morris, R. G., Sahakian, B. J., Polkey, C. E., & Robbins, T. W. (1996). Double dissociations of memory and executive functions in working memory tasks following frontal lobe excision, temporal lobe excisions or amygdala-hippocampectomy in man. *Brain*, **119**, 1597–1615.

Pardo, J. V., Pardo, V. J., Janer, K. W., & Raichle, M. E. (1990). The anterior cingulate cortex mediates processing selection in the Stroop attentional conflict paradigm. *Proceedings of the National Academy of Science*, **87**, 256–259.

Pardridge, W. M. (1977). Regulation of amino acid availability to the brain. In R. J. Wurtman & J. J. Wurtman (Eds.), *Nutrition and the brain*. New York: Raven.

Pardridge, W. M. (1988). Phenylalanine transport at the human blood-brain barrier. In R. J. Wurtman & E. Ritter-Walker (Eds.), *Dietary phenylalanine and brain function*. Boston: Birkhäuser.

Pardridge, W. M., & Oldendorf, W. H. (1977). Transport of metabolic substrates through the blood-brain barrier. *Journal of Neurochemistry*, **28**, 5–12.

Passingham, R. (1995). *The frontal lobes and voluntary action*. Oxford: Oxford University Press.

Passingham, R. E. (1996). Attention to action. *Philosophical Transactions of the Royal Society of London*, **B351**, 1473–1479.

Pennington, B. F., van Doorninck, W., McCabe, L. L., & McCabe, E. R. B. (1985). Neuropsychological deficits in early treated phenylketonuric children. *American Journal of Mental Deficiency*, **89**, 467–474.

Perret, E. (1974). The left frontal lobe of man and the suppression of habitual responses in verbal categorical behaviour. *Neuropsychologia*, **16**, 527–537.

Petrides, M. (1993). Dissociations of human mid-dorsolateral from posterior dorsolateral frontal cortex in memory processing. *Proceedings of the National Academy of Science*, **90**, 873–877.

Petrides, M. (1995). Impairments on nonspatial self-ordered and externally ordered working memory tasks after lesions of the mid-dorsal part of the lateral frontal cortex in the monkey. *Journal of Neuroscience*, **15**, 359–375.

Petrides, M. (1996). Specialized systems for the processing of mnemonic information within the primate frontal cortex. *Philosophical Transactions of the Royal Society of London*, **B351**, 1455–1462.

Petrides, M., Alivisatos, B., Evans, A. C., & Meyer, E. (1993). Dissociation of human middorsolateral frontal cortex in memory processing. *Proceedings of the National Academy of Science*, **90**, 875–877.

Petrides, M., Alivisatos, B., Meyer, E., & Evans, A. C. (1993). Functional activation of the human frontal cortex during performance of verbal working memory tasks. *Proceedings of the National Academy of Science*, **90**, 878–882.

Petrides, M., & Milner, B. (1982). Deficits in subject-ordered tasks after frontal- and temporal-lobe lesions in man. *Neuropsychologia*, **220**, 249–262.

Phelps, E. A., Hyder, F., Blamire, A. M., Rothman, D. L., & Shulman, R. G. (1994). Functional magnetic resonance imaging of frontal lobes during overt fluency. *Society for Neuroscience Abstracts*, **20**, 5.

Piaget, J. (1954). *The construction of reality in the child*. New York: Basic. (Original work published 1937)

Pietz, J., Landwehr, R., Kutscha, A., Schmidt, H., de Sonneville, L. N. J., & Trefz, F. K. (1995). Effect of high-dose tyrosine supplementation on brain function in adults with phenylketonuria. *Journal of Pediatrics*, **127**(6), 936–943.

Raichle, M. E., Fiez, J. A., Videen, T. O., Macleod, A. M. K., Pardo, J. V., Fox, P. T., & Petersen, S. E. (1994). Practice-related changes in human brain functional anatomy. *Cerebral Cortex*, **4**, 8.

Rapoport, S. I. (1976). Sites and functions of the blood-aqueous and blood-vitreous barriers of the eye. In S. I. Rapoport (Ed.), *Blood-brain barrier in physiology and medicine*. New York: Raven.

Reason, J., & Mycielska, K. (1982). *Absent-minded? The psychology of mental lapses and everyday errors*. Englewood Cliffs, NJ: Prentice-Hall.

Regan, D., & Neima, D. (1984). Low-contrast letter charts in early diabetic retinopathy, ocular hypertension, glaucoma, and Parkinson's disease. *British Journal of Ophthalmology*, **68**, 885–889.

Reynolds, R., Burri, R., Mahal, S., & Herschokowitz, N. (1992). Disturbed myelinogenisis and recovery in hyperphenylalaninemia in rats: An immunohistochemical study. *Experimental Neurology*, **115**, 347–367.

Richer, F., Decary, A., Lapierre, M. F., Rouleau, I., & Bouvier, G. (1993). Target detection deficits in frontal lobotomy. *Brain and Cognition*, **21**, 203–211.

Ris, M. D., Williams, S. E., Hunt, M. M., Berry, H. K., & Leslie, N. (1994). Early-treated phenylketonuria: Adult neuropsychologic outcome. *Journal of Pediatrics*, **124**, 388–392.

Robbins, T. W. (1996). Dissociating executive functions of the prefrontal cortex. *Philosophical Transactions of the Royal Society of London*, **B351**, 1463–1472.

Roberts, A. C., de Salvia, M. A., Muir, J. L., Wilkinson, L. S., Everitt, B. J., & Robbins, T. W. (1991). The effects of selective prefrontal dopamine (DA) lesions on cognitive tests of frontal function in primates. *Society for Neuroscience Abstracts*, **17**, 501.

Roberts, S., & Morelos, B. S. (1982). Inhibition of cerebral protein kinase activity and cyclic AMP-dependent ribosomal protein phosphorylation in experimental hyperphenylalaninemia. *Biochemical Journal*, **202**, 343–351.

Robertson, L. C., & Delis, D. (1986). Part-whole processing in unilateral brain-damaged patients: Dysfunction of hierarchical organization. *Neuropsychologia*, **24**, 363–370.

Robertson, L. C., Lamb, M. R., & Knight R. T. (1988). Effects of lesions of temporal-parietal junction on perceptual and attentional processing in humans. *Journal of Neurosciences*, **8**, 3757–3769.

Robertson, L. C., Lamb, M. R., & Knight, R. T. (1991). Normal global-local analysis in patients with dorsolateral frontal lobe lesions. *Neuropsychologia, 29,* 939–967.

Roth, R. H. (1984). CNS dopamine autoreceptors: Distribution, pharmacology, and function. *Annals of the New York Academy of Sciences, 430,* 27–53.

Sahakian, B. J., Sarna, G. S., Kantamaneni, B. D., Jackson, A., Hutson, P. H., & Curzon, G. (1985). Association between learning and cortical catecholamines in non-drug-treated rats. *Psychopharmacology, 86,* 339–343.

Saint-Cyr, J. A., Wan, R. O., Doudet, D., & Aigner, T. G. (1988). Impaired detour reaching in rhesus monkeys after MPTP lesions. *Society for Neuroscience Abstracts, 14,* 389.

Saunders, R. C. (1989). Monkeys demonstrate high level of recognition memory in delayed non-matching to sample with retention intervals of 6 weeks. *Society for Neuroscience Abstracts, 15,* 342.

Sawaguchi, T., & Goldman-Rakic, P. S. (1991). D1 dopamine receptors in prefrontal cortex: Involvement in working memory. *Science, 251,* 947–950.

Schmidt, E., Rupp, A., Burgard, P., Pietz, J., Weglage, J., & de Sonneville, L. N. J. (1994). Sustained attention in adult phenylketonuria: The influence of the concurrent phenylalanine-blood-level. *Journal of Clinical and Experimental Neuropsychology, 16*(5), 681–688.

Schneider, J. S., & Kovelowski, C. J., II. (1990). Chronic exposure to low doses of MPTP: 1. Cognitive deficits in motor asymptomatic monkeys. *Brain Research, 519,* 122–128.

Shedden, J. M., Christoforou, N., Nahmias, C., Hahn, M. C., & Noll, D. C. (1997, March). *Attending to global and local elements of form: fMRI of hemisphere asymmetries in normal subjects.* Paper presented at the meeting of the Cognitive Neuroscience Society, Boston.

Shedlovsky, A., McDonald, J. D., Symula, D., & Dove, W. F. (1993). Mouse models of human phenylketonuria. *Genetics, 134,* 1205–1210.

Shimamura, A. P., Janowsky, J. S., & Squire, L. R. (1990). Memory for the temporal order of events in patients with frontal lobe lesions and amnesic patients. *Neuropsychologia, 28,* 803–813.

Simon, H., Scatton, B., & LeMoal, M. (1980). Dopaminergic A10 neurones are involved in cognitive functions. *Nature, 286,* 150–151.

Skrandies, W., & Gottlob, I. (1986). Alterations of visual contrast sensitivity in Parkinson's disease. *Human Neurobiology, 5,* 255–259.

Smith, I., & Beasley, M. (1989). Intelligence and behaviour in children with early treated phenylketonuria. *European Journal of Clinical Nutrition, 43,* 1–5.

Smith, I., Beasley, M. G., & Adee, A. E. (1991). Effect on intelligence of relaxing the low phenylalanine diet in phenylketonuria. *Archives of Disease in Childhood, 66,* 311–316.

Smith, I., Beasley, M. G., Wolff, O., & Adee, A. (1988). Behavior disturbance in 8-year-old children with early-treated phenylketonuria. *Journal of Pediatrics, 112,* 403–408.

Smith, M. L., Klim, P., Mallozzi, E., & Hanley, W. B. (1996). A test of the frontal-specificity hypothesis in the cognitive performance of adults with phenylketonuria. *Developmental Neuropsychology, 12*(3), 327–341.

Spreen, O., & Benton, A. L. (1969). *Neurosensory center comprehensive examination for aphasia.* Victoria: University of Victoria Neuropsychology Lab.

Squire, L. R., & Shimamura, A. P. (1986). Characterizing amnesic patients for neuro-behavioral study. *Behavioral Neuroscience, 100,* 866–877.

Squire, L. R., Zola-Morgan, S., & Chen, K. S. (1988). Human amnesia and animal models of amnesia: Performance of amnesic patients on tests designed for the monkey. *Behavioral Neuroscience, 102,* 210–221.

Stuss, D. T., & Benson, D. F. (1986). *The frontal lobes.* New York: Raven.

Stuss, D. T., & Benson, D. F. (1987). The frontal lobes and control of cognition and memory. In E. Perecman (Ed.), *The frontal lobes revisited.* New York: IRBN.

Suzuki, W. A., Zola-Morgan, S., Squire, L. R., & Amaral, D. G. (1993). Lesions of the perirhinal and parahippocampal cortices in the monkey produce long-lasting memory impairment in the visual and tactual modalities. *Journal of Neuroscience*, **13**, 2430–2451.

Tam, S.-Y., Elsworth, J. D., Bradberry, C. W., & Roth, R. H. (1990). Mesocortical dopamine neurons: High basal firing frequency predicts tyrosine dependence of dopamine synthesis. *Journal of Neural Transmission*, **81**, 97–110.

Taylor, J. R., Roth, R. H., Sladek, J. R., Jr., & Redmond, D. E., Jr. (1990). Cognitive and motor deficits in the performance of the object retrieval detour task in monkeys (*Cercopithecus aethiops sabaeus*) treated with MPTP: Long-term performance and effect of transparency of the barrier. *Behavioral Neuroscience*, **104**, 564–576.

Thierry, A. M., Tassin, J. P., Blanc, A., Stinus, L., Scatton, B., & Glowinski, J. (1977). Discovery of the mesocortical dopaminergic system: Some pharmacological and functional characteristics. *Advanced Biomedical Psychopharmacology*, **16**, 5–12.

Tornquist, P., & Alm, A. (1986). Carrier-mediated transport of amino acids through the blood-retinal and blood-brain barriers. *Graefe's Archive for Clinical and Experimental Ophthalmology*, **224**, 21–25.

Tourian, A. Y., & Sidbury, J. B. (1978). Phenylketonuria. In J. D. Stanbury, J. B. Wyngaarden, & D. Fredrickson (Eds.), *The metabolic basis of inherited disease*. New York: McGraw-Hill.

van der Schot, L. W., Doesburg, W. H., & Sengers, R. C. (1994, May). *The phenylalanine response curve in relation to growth and mental development in the first years of life.* Paper presented at the International Symposium on the Occasion of the Sixtieth Anniversary of Følling's Discovery of Phenylketonuria, Elsinore, Denmark.

Warrington, E. K., James, M., & Kinsbourne, M. (1966). Drawing disability in relation to laterality of cerebral lesion. *Brain*, **89**, 53–82.

Weglage, J., Pietsch, M., Fünders, B., Koch, H. G., & Ullrich, K. (1995). Neurological findings in early treated phenylketonuria. *Acta Paediatrica*, **84**, 411–415.

Weglage, J., Schmidt, E., Fünders, B., Pietsch, M., & Ullrich, K. (1996). Sustained attention in untreated non-PKU-hyperphenylalaninemia. *Journal of Clinical and Experimental Neuropsychology*, **18**, 343–348.

Welsh, M. C., Pennington, B. F., Ozonoff, S., Rouse, B., & McCabe, E. R. B. (1990). Neuropsychology of early-treated phenylketonuria: Specific executive function deficits. *Child Development*, **61**, 1697–1713.

Wikmark, R. G. E., Divac, I., & Weiss, R. (1973). Delayed alternation in rats with lesions in the frontal lobes: Implications for a comparative neuropsychology of the frontal system. *Brain, Behavior and Evolution*, **8**, 329–339.

Williamson, M. L., Koch, R., Azen, C., & Chang, C. (1981). Correlates of intelligence test results in treated phenylketonuric children. *Pediatrics*, **68**, 161–167.

Woo, S. L. C., Lidsky, A. S., Güttler, F., Chandra, T., & Robson, K. J. H. (1983). Cloned human phenylalanine hydroxylase gene allows prenatal diagnosis and carrier detection of classical phenylketonuria. *Nature*, **306**, 151–155.

Wurtman, R. J., Lorin, F., Mostafapour, S., & Fernstrom, J. D. (1974). Brain catechol synthesis: Control by brain tyrosine concentration. *Science*, **185**, 183–184.

Zelazo, P. D., Frye, D., & Rapus, T. (1996). An age-related dissociation between knowing rules and using them. *Cognitive Development*, **11**, 37–63.

Zinchenko, V. P., Chzhi-Tsin, V., & Tarakanov, V. V. (1963). The formation and development of perceptual activity. *Soviet Psychology*, **2**, 3–12.

Zola-Morgan, S., Squire, L. R., & Amaral, D. G. (1989). Lesions of the perirhinal and parahippocampal cortex that spare the amygdala and hippocampal formation produce severe memory impairment. *Journal of Neuroscience*, **9**, 4355–4370.

ACKNOWLEDGMENTS

We gratefully acknowledge the support of the National Institute for Mental Health (NIMH R01 research grant MH41842), the March of Dimes (Social and Behavioral Sciences research grants 12-253 and 12-0554), and the University of Pennsylvania (Young Faculty Award of the Natural Science Association).

This work would not have been possible without the help of many people. PKU clinics in Philadelphia and southern New Jersey helped us locate participants, monitored plasma phenylalanine and tyrosine levels, and assisted in a myriad of ways. We would like to express our sincere gratitude to Dr. Warren D. Grover and Linda Tonwes at St. Christopher's Hospital for Children in Philadelphia and Dr. Barbara Evans and Beth Fredericks at Cooper Hospital, University Medical Center, Camden, New Jersey.

We would especially like to thank the many people who helped us stay in touch with the families over the four years of this study, helped us contact schools and families to obtain the normative data, helped with the data collection, helped code the data from the videotape, and helped enter the data into the computer database: Wendy Hurwitz, EunYoung Lee, Carolyn Towle, Lisa Robinson, Nicole Wusinich, Alissa Marshak, Kelly Lengel, Lisa Notes, Yoonie Hong, Cherie Gerstadt, Irene Markman, Amy Carroll, Colleen Taylor, Nancy Levy, Andrea Ribier, Cigdem Tanrikut, Angela Leonhard, Jennifer MacDonald, Mindy Nguyen, and Michelle Damon.

We would also like to thank Dr. Idit Trope for conducting the IQ testing for our study, Weimin Li for conducting the seemingly endless SAS analyses of our data, and Jane Gharibian for help with the final preparation of the manuscript. Most of all we would like to thank the parents and children who participated in this study and allowed us into their lives month after month, year after year.

Adele Diamond (Ph.D. 1983, Harvard University) is the director of the Center for Developmental Cognitive Neuroscience and a senior scientist in the Divisions of Behavioral and Biomedical Sciences at the Eunice Kennedy Shriver Center, Waltham, Massachusetts. Her interests are in the development and neural basis of higher cognitive functions, focusing on the functions of prefrontal cortex and on cognitive and perceptuomotor development during infancy and early childhood.

Meredith B. Prevor (M.A. 1997, New York University) is a first-year medical student at New York University Medical School. She is interested in pediatric medicine and child psychology and worked in the cognitive development laboratories of Adele Diamond and Susan Carey before entering medical school.

Glenda Callender (B.A. 1994, University of Pennsylvania) is a second-year student at Harvard Medical School. Her interests are in surgery and infectious diseases. Before entering medical school, she worked in the cognitive development laboratory of Adele Diamond and the cognitive neurology laboratory of Mark D'Esposito.

Donald P. Druin (B.A. 1991, University of Colorado), a Ph.D. candidate at the Temple University School of Medicine specializing in molecular genetics, is a senior research associate at the Eunice Kennedy Shriver Center. As a graduate student, he developed the monoclonal antibody assay to detect a new DNA adduct and tested the efficacy of the antibody in vitro. His current work involves genetically altered mice, which serve as a model for PKU. His studies are both biochemical and behavioral.

STATEMENT OF EDITORIAL POLICY

The *Monographs* series is intended as an outlet for major reports of developmental research that generate authoritative new findings and use these to foster a fresh and/or better-integrated perspective on some conceptually significant issue or controversy. Submissions from programmatic research projects are particularly welcome; these may consist of individually or group-authored reports of findings from some single large-scale investigation or of a sequence of experiments centering on some particular question. Multiauthored sets of independent studies that center on the same underlying question can also be appropriate; a critical requirement in such instances is that the various authors address common issues and that the contribution arising from the set as a whole be both unique and substantial. In essence, irrespective of how it may be framed, any work that contributes significant data and/or extends developmental thinking will be taken under editorial consideration.

Submissions should contain a minimum of 80 manuscript pages (including tables and references); the upper limit of 150–175 pages is much more flexible (please submit four copies; a copy of every submission and associated correspondence is deposited eventually in the archives of the SRCD). Neither membership in the Society for Research in Child Development nor affiliation with the academic discipline of psychology are relevant; the significance of the work in extending developmental theory and in contributing new empirical information is by far the most crucial consideration. Because the aim of the series is not only to advance knowledge on specialized topics but also to enhance cross-fertilization among disciplines or subfields, it is important that the links between the specific issues under study and larger questions relating to developmental processes emerge as clearly to the general reader as to specialists on the given topic.

Potential authors who may be unsure whether the manuscript they are planning would make an appropriate submission are invited to draft an outline of what they propose and send it to the Editor for assessment. This mechanism, as well as a more detailed description of all editorial policies, evaluation processes, and format requirements, is given in the "Guidelines for the Preparation of *Monographs* Submissions," which can be obtained by writing to the Editor, Rachel K. Clifton, Department of Psychology, University of Massachusetts, Amherst MA 01003.